# THE AudioPro **Home Recording** Course

## Volume 3

*a comprehensive*

*multimedia*

*recording text*

*by Bill Gibson*

6400 Hollis Street • Emeryville, CA 94608

Library of Congress Catalog Card Number: 98-067693
ISBN# 0-87288-715-4

Production staff:
Mike Lawson: Publisher; Bill Gibson: Design/Illustrator/Layout;
Editor: Sally Engelfried; Cover Design: Linda Gough;
Cover Photography: Susana Millman of Coverage Photography, San Francisco, CA

6400 Hollis Street
Emeryville, CA 94608
510-653-3307

**Also from MixBooks:**

*The Studio Business Book*
*The Songwriters Guide to Collaboration*
*How to Run a Recording Session*
*500 Songwriting Ideas*
*Critical Listening and Auditory Perception*
*Keyfax - Omnibus Edition*
*The AudioPro Home Recording Course Vol. I and II*
*Professional Microphone Techniques*
*Modular Digital Multitracks - The Power User's Guide*
*Live Sound Reinforcement*
*Music Publishing - The Real Road to Music Business Success*
*I Hate the Man who Runs this Bar - the survival guide for real musicians*
*How to Make Money Scoring Soundtracks and Jingles*
*The Art of Mixing*
*Hal Blaine and the Wrecking Crew*
*The Home Studio Guide to Microphones*
*The Mix Reference Disc*
*Concert Sound*
*Sound for Picture*
*Music Producers*

**Also from EMBooks:**

*Making the Ultimate Demo*
*Anatomy of a Home Studio*
*Making Music with your Computer*
*Tech Terms - A Practical Dictionary for Audio and Music Production*
*The Independent Working Musician*

**Also from the publishers of Mix and Electronic Musician:**

*The Recording Industry Sourcebook*
*Mix Master Directory*
*Personal Studio Buyer's Guide*
*Digital Piano Buyer's Guide*

Special thanks to Bob Weir for the use of his home studio in
the cover photograph and to studio technician, Mike
McGinn—the sharp dressed man behind the board.

All vocals performed by Jamie Dieveney. Special thanks to
Jamie for sharing his incredible musical gift, vocal talent,
and friendship.

## A very special thanks to:
## Alesis
Jeff Klopmeyer: The use of the QS8 with Q Cards, ADAT XT20, Q20 Master Effects, and DM5 Drum Module made a huge difference in the quality of these audio examples. The company who had the vision, wisdom, and guts to provide the ADAT format deserves our thanks, respect, and support. Thank You.

## Antares
Marco Alpert: Thanks for the use of Auto-Tune, the JVP Voice Processor plug-in, and the MDT Multiband Dynamics Plug-in. Your products show forward thinking and sensitivity to what we, the users, want and need.

## Acoustic Sciences Corp. (ASC)
Thanks to all the guys who've built and designed such innovative and effective products. Tube Traps and Studio Traps have been a regular part of my recording world since Bruce Swedien turned me on to them in 1993. For acoustic shaping at home and in the studio, I know of no better tool. Don't leave home without 'em.

## Gibson Guitars
Robbie Johns: The use of the Les Paul Standard and the Acoustic CL40 provided the basis for a large portion of the enclosed audio examples. The Les Paul is the standard. I've owned several and played many with no disappointments. The CL40 Artist Series acoustic blows me away. I've never heard a more tonally balanced acoustic. A chord sounds like one smooooooth event on this instrument—no disco smile! I love it.

## Line 6
Doug Provisor and Tim Godwin: Your company amazes me. The AX212, Flextone, and POD sound so good. Your 24-bit models of amp setups I've played through for years are like a trip down memory lane. They're accurate, they sound great, and they feel good. Makes me want to practice again.

## Mackie.
Greg Perry, Bobb Haskitt, and Bub Tudor: Thanks for making the D8B happen. This is one incredible product. Its flexibility, ergonomics, sound quality, ease of use, and just overall feel are wonderful. The effects, EQ, dynamics, automation, and routing have performed flawlessly. A company that's revolutionized everything it's touched has my highest respect. Thanks for making our audio lives better.

## Mark of the Unicorn
Jim Cooper: Thanks for supplying Digital Performer, Freestyle, and the 2408 Hard Disk Recording System. I've been an avid MOTU fan since version 1 of Performer. Your products are very powerful, intuitive and they always look cool. Your multicable interfaces have revolutionized MIDI for many of us, and the 2408 is one of the most powerful tools to come around in a long time, at any price. Much applause.

## Monster Cable
Greg Pederson and Tom Menwrath: Your cables provide the benchmark for what good sound is! They make these audio examples honest, true, and accurate. Thanks for helping educate our readers. In an industry that largely ignored the sonic impact of cabling for years, Monster Cable exploded on the scene with mind blowing cable concepts. I've experienced it time and time again in the recording world: Cable make a huge difference! And you guys are at the top.

## Opcode
Dino Cattane and Johnny Gillham: Many thanks for Studio Vision Pro, Vision DSP, and the Fusion Effects Library. Vision was the first quality sequencer I used, many years ago. Studio Vision Pro has features today that lead the industry. The way you've implemented many features is not only visionary, but it makes us all wonder why nobody ever did it that way before. Thanks to Opcode for setting many of the standards others aim for in the MIDI and digital audio worlds.

## Heartfelt Appreciation to Mike Kay at Ted Brown Music in Tacoma, WA.
Thanks for filling in the gaps when I needed some extra gear for the examples in this book. Your constant desire to do music the right way speaks highly of your character and talent. The service you provide and the knowledge you lend are a shining example of why the local music store is so important to our industry.
For bailing me out on more than one occasion, Thank You.

# Table of Contents

# Chapter 3

## *MIDI Sequencing*

# Chapter 4

## *Digital Recording*

# Chapter 5

## *Digital Multitracks*

# Chapter 6

## *Digital Effects*

# Chapter 7

## *Random Access Editing*

# Chapter 8

## *Synchronizing*

# Chapter 9

## *Digital Mixing*

# Chapter 10

## *Master Preparation*

# Chapter 11

## *The Best of Both Worlds*

# Audio Examples

## CD-1

---

### Chapter 2

---

**CD-1: Track 1**
Audio Example 2-1 Daisy Chain Delay

**CD-1: Track 2**
Audio Example 2-2 Drum Groove: Original, then 100 percent Quantize

**CD-1: Track 3**
Audio Example 2-3 Drum Groove 80 percent Quantize

**CD-1: Track 4**
Audio Example 2-4 Drum Groove 50 percent Quantize

**CD-1: Track 5**
Audio Example 2-5 Reference Groove

**CD-1: Track 6**
Audio Example 2-6 50 percent Sensitivity

**CD-1: Track 7**
Audio Example 2-7 Negative 50 percent Sensitivity

**CD-1: Track 8**
Audio Example 2-8 Absolute then Partial Quantize

**CD-1: Track 9**
Audio Example 2-9 100 percent Quantized Reference Groove

**CD-1: Track 10**
Audio Example 2-10 50 percent Randomize

**CD-1: Track 11**
Audio Example 2-11 10 percent Randomize

**CD-1: Track 12**
Audio Example 2-12 Original Performance Without Sequencer

**CD-1: Track 13**
Audio Example 2-13 Real-time Sequence of 2-12 at 24 Pulses per Quarter Note (ppq)

**CD-1: Track 14**
Audio Example 2-14 Original Performance Without Sequencer

**CD-1: Track 15**
Audio Example 2-15 Real-time Sequence of 2-14 at 480 ppq

**CD-1: Track 16**
Audio Example 2-16 Original Performance Without Sequencer

**CD-1: Track 17**
Audio Example 2-17 Real-time Sequence of 2-16 at 960 ppq

**CD-1: Track 18**
Audio Example 2-18 Unrealistic Step Recording

**CD-1: Track 19**
Audio Example 2-19 Reference Groove

**CD-1: Track 20**
Audio Example 2-20 Snare Drum Shifted Forward

**CD-1: Track 21**
Audio Example 2-21 Reference Groove 95 percent Quantized

**CD-1: Track 22**
Audio Example 2-22 Example 2-21 with Tracks Shifted

---

### Chapter 3

---

**CD-1: Track 23**
Audio Example 3-1 Several Drum Grooves

**CD-1: Track 24**
Audio Example 3-2 100 percent Quantize

## Chapter 7

# Chapter 8

**CD-2: Track 58**
Audio Example 8-1
Panned Clicks Simulating MTC Error Factor at 0, 8.333, 16.666., and 33.333ms Delay

**CD-2: Track 59**
Audio Example 8-2 Original Drum Part

**CD-2: Track 60**
Audio Example 8-3 Drum Part Delayed by 33 1/3 ms

**CD-2: Track 61**
Audio Example 8-4 Drum Part Moved Ahead by 33 1/3 ms

# Chapter 9

**CD-2: Track 62**
Audio Example 9-1 Scrolling Through Snapshots

**CD-2: Track 63**
Audio Example 9-2 Original Drum Track

**CD-2: Track 64**
Audio Example 9-3 Drum Track Through Digital Compressor 4:1 Ratio, -8dB

**CD-2: Track 65**
Audio Example 9-4 Drum Track Through Tube Analog Compressor 4:1 Ratio, -8dB

**CD-2: Track 66**
Audio Example 9-5 Drum Track Through Digital Compressor 12:1 Ratio, -12dB

**CD-2: Track 67**
Audio Example 9-6 Drum Track Through Tube Analog Compressor 12:1 Ratio, -12dB

**CD-2: Track 68**
Audio Example 9-7 Original Guitar Track

**CD-2: Track 69**
Audio Example 9-8 Level and EQ Change to Repair Track

**CD-2: Track 70**
Audio Example 9-9 Poorly Blended Vocals

**CD-2: Track 71**
Audio Example 9-10 Blended Backing Vocals

**CD-2: Track 72**
Audio Example 9-11 Backing Vocals with Sloppy Articulation

**CD-2: Track 73**
Audio Example 9-12 Backing Vocals with Repaired Articulation

**CD-2: Track 74**
Audio Example 9-13 Contrasting Snapshots

**CD-2: Track 75**
Audio Example 9-14 Contrasting Mix Textures

# Chapter 10

**CD-2: Track 76**
Audio Example 10-1 The AM Version

**CD-2: Track 77**
Audio Example 10-2 The Album Version

**CD-2: Track 78**
Audio Example 10-3 The Dance Mix

**CD-2: Track 79**
Audio Example 10-4 Normal Mix

**CD-2: Track 80**
Audio Example 10-5 3dB louder

**CD-2: Track 81**
Audio Example 10-6 6dB louder

**CD-2: Track 82**
Audio Example 10-7 Comparison of First Through Sixth Generation DAT

# Chapter 11

**CD-2: Track 83**
Audio Example 11-1 Voice Recorded With and Without Studio Traps

**CD-2: Track 84**
Audio Example 11-2 Acoustic Guitar With and Without Studio Traps

**CD-2: Track 85**
Audio Example 11-3 Distant Voice and Guitar With and Without Studio Traps

# Preface

The AudioPro Home Recording Course, Volumes I and II progress through the fundamentals of audio recording in a clear and easy to understand manner. In Volume III we move into the next millennium. Our topics include the theory, practice, and techniques of digital recording, as well as the finer points of MIDI, editing, mastering, automation, modular digital multitracks, digital effects, synchronization, and the musical considerations that guide their use.

Audio technology is increasing at an incredible pace. If we're going to keep up, we each need to stay in tune with the industry. This book is written with continuing education in mind. If we're all to stay in touch with current reality in today's technical extravaganza, we need immediate sources of information. Manufacturers are definitely knowledgeable about their own segment of the marketplace, but they're often difficult to contact—it's their business to dole out product, not information. The Internet comes to the rescue, bringing current information and access to almost everything and everybody. If you're not Internet-savvy, you need to be. Most technical information can be obtained from the Web within minutes, even on a cold search. As manufacturers come out with more software-upgraded hardware, along with software-based plug-ins, the Internet becomes our primary source of updates and other information regarding product standard.

In the course of preparing this book, I wanted to demonstrate the use of technology produced by manufacturers proven to understand the needs of musicians, producers, technicians, engineers, and any combination thereof. I have to say that all were happy to assist with whatever we needed to get the audio examples prepared properly—many thanks for everyone's help. I made a special point to only request assistance from a select group of manufacturers. These companies all have a history of not only providing quality tools for audio production, but also of listening to their users and responding to their needs. At the same time, they've demonstrated vision and innovation, each impacting the recording process in a major way.

We have an amazing ride ahead of us. Technology is on the loose. We'll be amazed at what we can accomplish in 5 years, and at how inexpensively we'll be able to accomplish it. Remain diligent in your quest for knowledge. The one constant among those who succeed is a relentless, persistent, and resilient spirit. It's there for each of us if we preserver.

# 1 The Third Millennium

## Moving Ahead

Change is happening at a phenomenal rate. The progress of technology is on a wildly accelerating, runaway path. Your survival in the third millennium—at least in the technical world—is going to be determined by your ability to adapt to change.

Things are not the way they were ten years ago, or five years ago, or even one year ago. For that matter, the changes that have taken place in the last couple of months will have a dramatic effect on the way we all relate to data storage in the technical world. The good news is: we're in for some exciting, stimulating, and incredibly thought provoking fun and games. The bad news is: if you're going to stay in the game, you must be willing to spend your valuable time and finances on education, upgrades to your computers, and data storage devices. Each of us will be required to continually reevaluate the way we work with music, data, video, and archival for historical purposes.

We can no longer refer to recording in the same way we have since the middle of the twentieth century. Tape recorders are less and less common in the home recording world. They've become an item reserved largely for the upper echelon, professional recording facility, where they're available solely for their sonic quality, which lends warmth and appeal that's tough to duplicate digitally. Most recording is—and will continue to be—performed in the digital domain. We are seeing, almost monthly, new developments in the digital recording world, and we ain't seen nothing yet!

## History

Since the middle of the twentieth century, recording and technology in general have been on an amazing path of acceleration. We have been through wire recorders, 78s, and cylinder recorders. Magnetic tape recorders saved the day, as they allowed for a smooth editing process on a reusable medium.

The first two active reel-to-reel recorders were smuggled into the states by some American soldiers stationed in Germany. A German scientist had discovered bias—the missing ingredient in a formula for accurate audio recording on magnetic tape. These recorders ended up being taken to Los Angeles and used to record, among other things, the Bing Crosby radio show. The first American-made reel-to-reel machines were made by Ampex, largely from parts used on the first American space capsules. The history of our industry is very interesting. Moreover, it's recent enough that these original recorders and tapes are still accessible, and they show up periodically at industry trade shows.

Fifteen years ago, I went to the Audio Engineering Society International Convention in New York City. The CD was a new product at the time, but the most impressive tidbit of cranial data I came home with was talk of recording mediums of the future. One technical paper talked of a recording process that encoded and decoded concentric rings in the molecular structure of glass. The system involved no transport; it simply used a data scanner that processed information to and from a glass cube. It seemed pretty amazing at the time, but today the concept, although impressive, is certainly not mystical.

## Preparation for What's to Come

We're going to a place we've never been, and we're probably going to get there in a way that will blow us away. Cool, huh?! One's ability to learn how to use new gear will be the point of delineation between the men and the boys, the women and the girls, the pups and the dawgs.

During the '70s and much of the '80s, there was a period of time when I really got know the gear I was working on. I was chief engineer at a facility south of Seattle, and I did a lot of projects on the same gear. Day after day, I figured out how to exploit the idiosyncrasies of nearly every piece of gear in the studio. I taught engineering classes on the gear, so I constantly had to think of answers to questions about it. I knew right where to go to complete almost any task. My life today is incredibly different from that scenario!

Things are changing so fast now that I hardly do a project on which I'm not using a few pieces of equipment or software that are new to me or didn't exist on the previous project. Granted, I like to push the boundaries and jump into a pile of new toys. However, I haven't met many people who aren't also ready to use these amazing new tools because of the mind-bog-

gling creative possibilities they bring to the table.

## The Internet

Commercial development of the Internet has changed the pace of technology. Just a few years ago, if you had a glitch in a new piece of software, you needed to call tech support. Then you'd need to wait at least day, if not a week, to receive the update, the patch, or the makeshift software fix. If you were mentally locked into a piece of music, that time would not only be frustrating but probably damaging to the final product through lost creative flow or emotional dejection—artistic flow is often very fragile.

In today's world it's assumed, when you contact tech support, that you have Internet access. Software fixes can be downloaded within minutes and you can be back up and running in no time. With the competitive nature of the audio/video/multimedia industry, it seems like everyone is releasing their newest product as soon as it seems even remotely usable! There's often a minimum amount of testing, so the end user finishes the testing process. On the upside, we get new technology—and we get it fast. On the downside, many software and hardware packages require a bit of a tweak within weeks of the time they become commercially available.

Therefore, access to the Internet is a must from now on. If a user calls tech support with a question and there's a fix required, it's assumed that the user has access to the Web. The tech support specialists don't even ask anymore—they just give out the Web address where the user can find the update, and that's the end of it.

If you want to see what a new piece of software can do, simply download the demo from the manufacturer's Web site. Almost all manufacturers have a Web address complete with product data, specifications, and demo programs. The demos are typically fully functional. Most of them will either stop working after a predetermined time period, or they won't let you save your work. This way, they're protected from software theft, but you get to experience a little hands-on time with their product.

If you're interested in a particular manufacturer's product and have access to the Internet, you can search for their name through an Internet search engine, or you can guess their address. Almost all commercial Internet addresses start with "http://www." Most manufacturers follow that with their company name followed immediately by ".com" (pronounced "dot com"). For example, the MixBooks Web address is http://www.mixbooks.com; the Opcode Web address is http://www.opcode.com; the Gibson Guitars Web address is http://www.gibson.com—I'm sure you get the picture. Every once in a while, a company with a longer than average name will use the company initials for their Web address—the Mark of the Unicorn address is http://www.motu.com. If you haven't already done so, I highly recommend checking these and other Web sites out. We're in the information age. The Internet is the key to unlocking tons of information.

## My Turning Point

I offer the following account of a project that marked the turning point for the way I thought about the recording process. I present it as an instructional lesson concerning the development of the creative process in the third millennium. Each of the points covered in this account relate to subject matter we all need to understand, overcome, conquer, live with, and apply

practically to the course of our real-world audio activity.

This project was primarily about vocals. We wanted to highlight some amazing harmonies along with incredible solo vocal textures and techniques. All this was set in a commercial pop structure aimed at the mass market and offered in comparison to the world market. We decided to use the best of each recording medium.

We hired an excellent rhythm section to perform the basic tracks and unanimously preferred the sound offered by analog 24-track. So we scheduled the basic tracking session in a very nice facility, recording to Studer 820, 24-track analog recorders using 2-inch tape. We used a great set of microphones on the drums—vintage Neumann and Sony mics, combined with an array of newer AKG, B&K, and Shure models. Throughout the tracking, we used combinations of vintage and new equipment. It's amazing how many of the mics and processors from the '50s and '60s can't be beat for specific applications.

Our approach to vocal recording was totally different from that of the instruments. We wanted the flexibility and pristine clarity offered by digitally recording all the vocals to a computer-based sequencing/digital recording package. We knew we wanted the ability to shift vocals in time; to cut, copy, and paste; and to pitch shift in a way that didn't change vocal character. Every vocal track was recorded digitally into the computer using classic mics through handpicked mic preamps and equalizers. The recording console was only used as a monitor controller.

The vocals could have been recorded at my home studio, but we opted for a commercial facility, based on isolation, availability, and rate. We didn't need a huge room at a high daily rate.

We did, however, need a facility with isolation between the control room and the studio, great microphones, great preamps, and some portable acoustic deflector/absorbers. We recorded an amazing amount of vocal tracks for not an awful lot of money. Several days in the studio gave us ample takes from which to select. We spent time in an effort to get as close to perfection as possible.

My computer was set to record up to 16 mono tracks and 8 stereo tracks for each song. We recorded a lot of tracks. Sometimes we started all over on a section and, rather than trashing the previously recorded takes, I'd clear out a space to stash the tracks in case we needed them later. This area—affectionately referred to as "the basement"—included a set of inactive tracks that were usually hidden from view. Being able to have instant access to the basement tracks saved my bacon a number of times. In all the projects I've been a part of, it was not possible to just stash audio somewhere in case it was needed later before the inclusion of the computer in the recording process.

In addition to the basement, we had the ability to perform and keep multiple takes. All of the 16 mono and 8 stereo tracks could capture and instantly recall as many takes as the hard drive would allow for. In other words, we could record practically as many takes as we could ever use on each track. Each lead vocal track had about 20 takes, which we later listened through to find the best performance of each. Sometimes we'd use nothing but a portion of a word from one take, a phrase from another, a word from another …the possibilities were seemingly limitless. This process, called *comping*, is not new; it's been used since multitrack recording came into being. However, there

are far more tracks available when using a computer-based multitrack than when using a tape-based system with a fixed number of tracks. Prior to the hard disk recording era, there were never enough tracks to keep doing more and more lead vocal tracks, let alone to save several options for the second, third, or fourth harmony part.

We wanted to streamline the mixdown process, efficiently focusing on mix details. Once mixdown began, we didn't have the desire or time to fight machine communication problems or to spend time repairing vocals, and we didn't want to go over budget. To facilitate this end, we spent many hours adjusting, tuning, trimming, crossfading, blending, and comping vocal tracks. This process was completed at home, completely separate from the outside studio's rate clock. We were able to walk into mixdown with vocal tracks that were complete, ready for mixdown, and often premixed and blended. The fact that we were able to adequately prepare in a less expensive environment made the actual mixdown a joy—once we got over some technical difficulties.

Here's where everything became tedious, stressful, and downright scary. From the start, we knew the path we wanted to take. We wanted to dump all data to a 48-track digital reel-to-reel tape-based machine. Therefore, all the tracks from the analog 24-track tape and all the tracks from the computer had to be combined, in perfect sync, to one machine. From day one, my concern was the verification of a perfect, sample-accurate sync all the way through the recording chain. In theory, this seemed completely realistic and, if everything communicated the way it was supposed to, there shouldn't have been a problem.

The gear we were using at the time was

new and somewhat pushing the boundaries on the then-current technology. I bought the right box for the job: a multiformat sync router-controller. This box was designed to simultaneously read, translate, and generate SMPTE (LTC), Video sync (VITC), two forms of word clock, S/P DIF, DA-88, ADAT, Sony 9-pin, and 2 system-specific controllers. It could read and generate all forms of time code, complete with pull-up, pull-down compensation for cross communicating between the film and video world.

I don't always read manuals very thoroughly, but in this case I did. By the time I started this series of sessions, I was prepared. Just to confirm my thoughts and methodology, I called tech support for the sync box a few days before the basic tracking sessions began. When I told them my approach, they confirmed that I was going about the task properly, but I was given this additional reply (paraphrased), "You know, this is a pretty new box and we don't have all the gear you're talking about using. If you get this to work, would you please let us know the setup you used, so we can spread the word?" So, I went into a series of sessions with major-label involvement, tracking in the coolest room in Seattle, mixing at an amazing facility in Nashville, and that's the kind of emotional support I got! In addition, it was from the manufacturer of the hub of my synchronization system. Do you think I should have been concerned? I don't usually get stumped on these kinds of things, at least not forever, so I was still ready to jump in all the way.

From the first day in the tracking sessions, I became familiar with the "blank stare." When my computer wouldn't sync to house sync and de-stripolated SMPTE, I was perplexed. All the settings seemed to be correct. When I summoned

assistance from the house engineer and the studio manager I got the blank stare. They had no clue as to what my problem might be. I struggled through the sessions, while the rhythm section, singers, label folks, and techs waited to be able to lay down the magic.

At this point, I'm going to make a long and technically involved story much shorter. If I continue, I'll start venting—and that's not my point in this explanation. Everything worked out okay in the end. We went through substantial struggles with technology that was still maturing. I was frustrated, irritated, confused, and humbled. Yet, through it all, I gained an amazing amount of knowledge—knowledge that I would have missed had it not been for these trials.

The truth is, gear will always be changing so fast that we, as end users, shouldn't expect much help in the heat of a session. Once a piece of gear has been around for a while, that's another story, but we need to take responsibility to know what we're doing. Education is paramount. Practice is essential. Patience is required. Perseverance is a prerequisite to success, and relentless pursuit of your musical and technical goals pays off. In addition, for those who achieve greatness, a God-given gift in technical understanding and persistence is inherent.

If you keep up with technology, you'll always be confronted with new challenges. These days, it's not likely that others will take the responsibility to keep up with the gear you need to use—there's too much change ahead. Each of us needs to understand and master as many of the tools around us as possible—nobody else will. The only way I've found to avoid the blank stare is to not need to ask blank stare questions.

The fact is, support technicians are almost always proficient users and, over time, become effective educators. Call or e-mail them when you have a problem. It's usually the demand that we, who operate the gear, place on the manufacturers that forces them to release their product—often prematurely. Therefore, features sometimes don't quite work the way they're supposed to, or they cause your computer to crash. Software and hardware designers do an incredible job of feeding us tools that facilitate the creative process. We owe them thanks, appreciation, patience, and understanding—and usually about a hundred dollars for the latest upgrade.

These days I take it upon myself to research each piece of gear that I'll be using in any way remotely associated with synchronization. I get copies of the equipment manuals from the studio or check them out on-line. I get documentation from the studio tech on how the house sync is resolved to the time code generator and the type of machine synchronizers involved and how they're resolved to house sync, etc.

How does this all apply to the home studio? The bulk of the project I previously described was done at home. That's becoming the way of the recording world—I doubt that will change. With good planning and the use of the best of all worlds, each of us can produce a world class product, largely in the comfort of our own homes. Almost daily, gear is getting better and less expensive. We can do things at home today that couldn't be accomplished ten years ago in any studio in the world, for any price!

Persistence is a necessary attribute in today's audio world. Don't give up, even when the going is very rough. There is usually a way to make the system work. Sometimes it takes some mental gymnastics and a willingness to go outside the lines to find a solution, but the payoff is in a job well done and great music. Keep after a problem. You can get it! If you have time, get some help from the manufacturer, call tech support, call a friend, call the salesman, then put all the pieces together to form the scenario most likely to succeed. Think the problem through, step by step. Be deliberate and calculating. Music and electronics are very logical. If you can break a task into small bits, chances are that each little bit will be logical and easy to understand. Although you might lose a little sleep while you mull over the possibilities to successful completion, once you get the old brain cells ticking, they wake up and start looking at life differently. During my escapades in the sessions above, I figured out a complete theory explaining the coexistence of simultaneous realities. It's really a pretty clever scheme and I think it might contain the answers to the secrets of the universe! But I haven't had it checked out by a qualified genius yet.

# 2 MIDI Theory

This chapter covers the fundamentals of the MIDI process. We won't cover every parameter here, but we will cover the features and parameters that must be understood in order to address and successfully operate most of the newer MIDI-based devices. Hardware-based sequencers, software-based sequencers, digital audio workstations, drum sequencers, signal processors, mixers, and notation software packages all use MIDI as a central control and communication language. Most of the information in this chapter applies to the practical use of these key tools used in the audio, video, and multimedia industries.

Though MIDI is somewhat old news for a third millennium book, it still pertains directly to the operation of many current and forthcoming mixers and processors. Not only do many digital audio software packages use MIDI parameters to control mixdown, but many hardware mixers use MIDI to automate and control all audio parameters—sequenced and digitally recorded.

With an understanding of the information in this chapter, you should be able to easily and willingly tackle any MIDI equipment you'll encounter. There are no mysteries to MIDI. The system is logical and powerful.

## Intro to MIDI

The first MIDI sequencer I ever had was a Yamaha TX-7. It did next to nothing compared to the tools we have available today, and it did it in such a cumbersome way that it was hard to get motivated to use it. Then I was introduced to my first Macintosh 512 with rev. 1.0 of Performer, the hottest sequencing package from Mark of the Unicorn. Now we were talking! MIDI sequencing that was easy to use, made sense, and was designed to be used by musicians. Heaven! Sequencing packages today are amazing, and the manufacturers are very competitive. Even if one company develops an edge, the rest follow quickly behind with nearly identical features. Fine sequencing software is also available from Opcode, Digidesign, and many others. These sequencing tools revolutionized the way we can all work. We've worked through the initial obsession of trying to produce complete MIDI projects, and we can now go ahead and combine real instruments and musicians with MIDI instruments and digital audio. And it's only going to get better. I really think the twenty-first century will see amazing applications for holography, virtual reality, and multisensory recording and playback. Wherever our minds can wander, technology will follow.

# MIDI Basic Training

## The Language

MIDI has been the fundamental Musical Instrument Digital Interface since the early '80s. It behooves us to understand the communication principles involved in MIDI data transfer, even as newer and more improved formats evolve.

MIDI is nothing more than a common language used by synthesizers, sound modules, and any other MIDI-implemented instrument to communicate either with each other or with a hardware- or software-based MIDI sequencer. A MIDI interface is simply an interpreter to assist in communications between the MIDI instrument and a computer.

The communication language is based on a hexadecimal (16-digit) binary code. In other words, each parameter and function of a MIDI device is represented by a unique arrangement of 16 1s and 0s. Middle C on the synthesizer keyboard is assigned a unique and specific binary number. Anytime that note is played, its unique binary code is transmitted from the MIDI

## Illustration 2-1
### MIDI Communication

Anytime a note is played or a controller is used, its unique binary code is transmitted from the MIDI OUT port. That code is then received by another synth through the MIDI IN port. When the synth recognizes the unique binary code for whatever MIDI parameter has been transmitted, it, too, responds to the command. This process takes about three milliseconds.

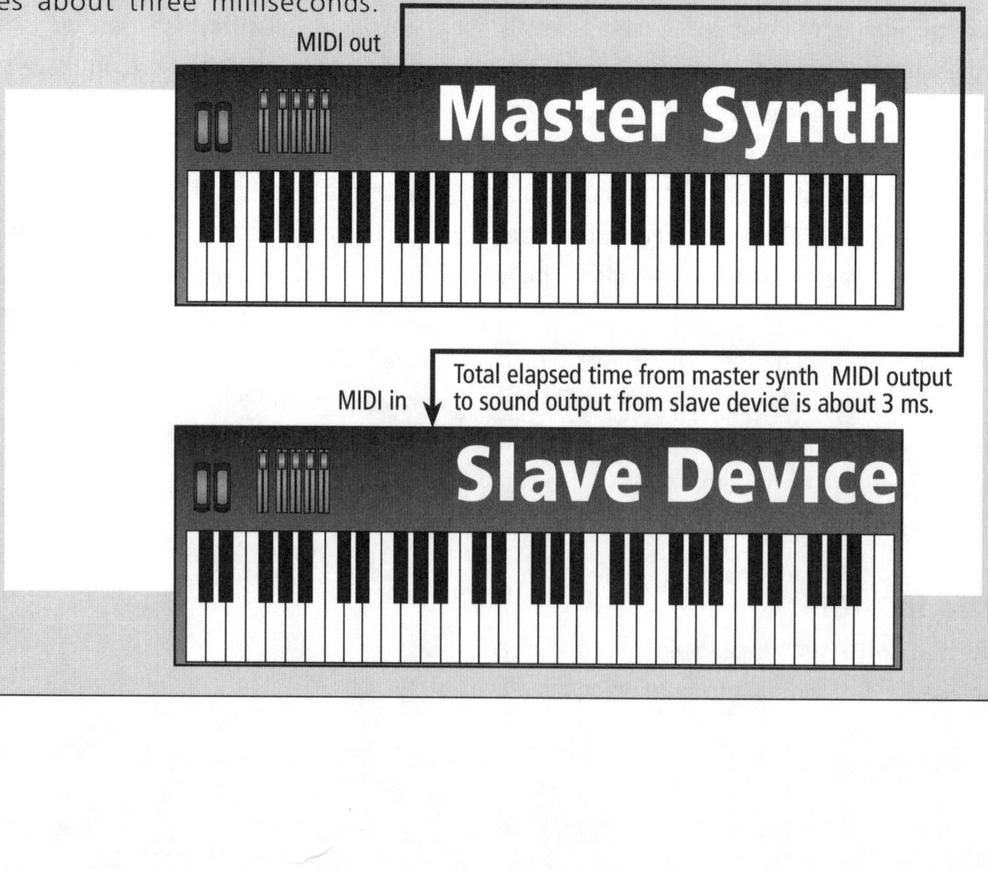

MIDI out

**Master Synth**

MIDI in — Total elapsed time from master synth MIDI output to sound output from slave device is about 3 ms.

**Slave Device**

## Illustration 2-2
### MIDI Ports

There are typically three MIDI port on the back of a MIDI device: MIDI IN, MIDI OUT, and MIDI THRU. A 5-pin DIN connector and jack are used to interconnect MIDI devices.

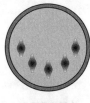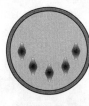

MIDI IN       MIDI OUT       MIDI THRU

OUT port. That code is then received by another synth through the MIDI IN port. When the synth recognizes the unique binary code for middle C it, too, plays middle C. This process takes about three milliseconds (Illustration 2-1).

This simple concept is applied to each MIDI parameter, forming a powerful and musically efficient means of communication in the electronic music genre. The list of MIDI controllable parameters is extensive, ranging from note value to portamento value to poly/mono/omni mode selection.

### MIDI IN, OUT, and THRU

There are typically three MIDI port on the back of a MIDI device: MIDI IN, MIDI OUT, and MIDI THRU (Illustration 2-2).

To connect MIDI equipment together, connect the MIDI OUT of the controlling device to the MIDI IN of the device being controlled. Once this connection has been successfully completed, the pathway is clear for communication (Illustration 2-3).

### MIDI Cables

MIDI cables use a standard 5-pin DIN connector. The cable is similar to a mic cable in that it utilizes a twisted pair of conductors, surrounded by a shield. Even though the connector has five pins, only three are in use for the standard MIDI format. Pins 1 and 3 (the outer two pins) are not connected in the classic MIDI cable—they're left for future development and manufacturer-specific design. Pin 2 is connected to the shield for ground, and pins 4 and 5 are used to conduct the MIDI data (Illustration 2-4).

It's even possible to make adapter cables with the 5-pin DIN connector on one end and a standard XLR connector on the other. Since both standards only use three pins, there's no loss when converting to XLR. Simply connect pin 2 of the DIN connector to pin 1 of the XLR, then connect the DIN pins 4 and 5 to the XLR pins 2 and 3. Adapters like this can enable a MIDI signal to pass through an already existing microphone patch panel—a very handy feature when trying to run the sound module (in the control room) from the keyboard (in the studio). Avoid any MIDI cable run longer than 50 feet.

## Illustration 2-3
### MIDI Connection

To connect MIDI equipment together, connect the MIDI OUT of the controlling device (Master) to the MIDI IN of the device being controlled (Slave). Once this connection has been successfully completed, the pathway is clear for communication. Remember, MIDI cable carry controlling data only. They don't carry audio signals.

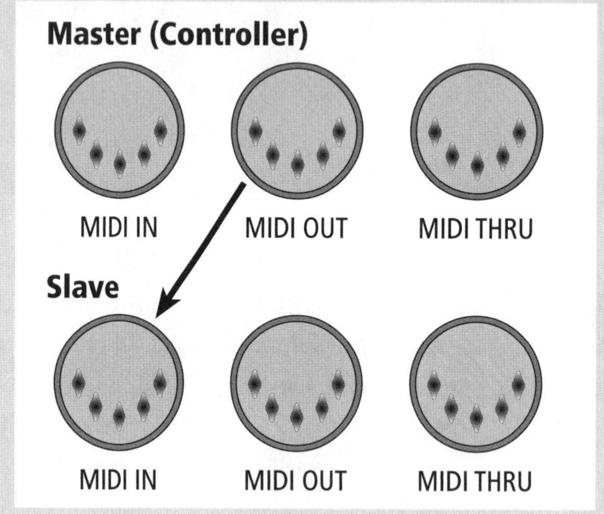

**Master (Controller)**

MIDI IN      MIDI OUT      MIDI THRU

**Slave**

MIDI IN      MIDI OUT      MIDI THRU

## Daisy Chain

If you'd like to control two separate MIDI devices with one MIDI controller, connect MIDI OUT of the controlling device to MIDI IN of the first device being controlled, then connect MIDI THRU of that device to MIDI IN of the second device being controlled. This procedure is called "daisy chaining." It isn't the best way to connect several MIDI devices together, but it is an acceptable setup if you don't connect more than a few MIDI devices to the chain.

Remember, each additional device adds approximately a three-millisecond delay to the chain. So, if you use three keyboards (one controller and two sound modules) the first module would be delayed three milliseconds and the second would be delayed six milliseconds. If you

keep the instruments that need to rhythmically lock together (like drums and bass) at the very front of the daisy chain and instruments with

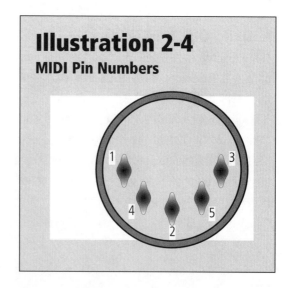

## Illustration 2-4
### MIDI Pin Numbers

slower attacks (like strings) at the rear of the chain, all should be well.

If you're using a computer-based sequencer, chances are the sequencer program will let you shift tracks in time. Try shifting each track in the daisy chain forward in multiples of three milliseconds, depending on which link each part is in the chain (Illustration 2-5).

Listen to Audio Example 2-1 to hear the effect of daisy chaining. By the time the seventh slave device has received its MIDI data there's a noticeable delay. Using these percussive sounds, it's clear that there's an adverse rhythmic consequence when daisy-chaining.

*Audio Example 2-1 Daisy Chain Delay*
*CD-1: Track 1*

# Illustration 2-5
## Daisy Chaining

Remember, each additional device adds approximately a three-millisecond delay to the chain. So, if you use three keyboards (one controller and two sound modules) the first module would be delayed three milliseconds and the second would be delayed six milliseconds. If you keep the instruments that need to rhythmically lock together (like drums and bass) at the very front of the daisy chain and instruments with slower attacks (like strings) at the rear of the chain, all should be well.

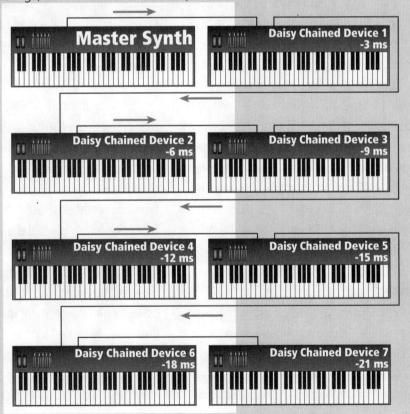

## Channels

The MIDI communication language provides an option that is not only convenient, but also essential when using multiple MIDI sound sources. MIDI channels help the sound modules or synths determine which data to receive. You can send the piano, bass, drums, etc., all at once, in the same MIDI data stream. If you select MIDI channel 1 for the piano send, channel 2 for the bass, and channel 3 for the drums, you can send them, even through a daisy chain, to three separate sound modules. Simply set the piano module to receive only MIDI channel 1, the bass module to receive only MIDI channel 2, and the drum module to receive only channel 3. The modules will sift through all the MIDI data and receive only that which is tagged as belonging to its channel.

There are 16 standard MIDI channels written into the MIDI language specification; therefore, in theory, you could daisy chain up to 16 sound modules, instructing each module to receive a unique MIDI channel. In other words, you could send 16 separate musical parts—one to each module. This approach is often unacceptable because, by the time the signal reaches the end of the daisy chain, the signal has been delayed by about 45 milliseconds; that's a substantial delay.

The multicable MIDI interface is the answer to this delay problem.

## MIDI Interface

Even though MIDI is a computer language, it doesn't naturally fit into the operating system of most computers. A MIDI interface is the actual hardware that transforms the MIDI language into a format that can be sent and received from a computer. Most workstations contain their own internal MIDI interface that interprets data for the built-in processor. Some computers are equipped with an internal MIDI interface, but typically the most flexible and expandable approach involves an external interface.

Some interfaces are very simple, containing one or two MIDI inputs and one or two MIDI outputs. For a small system, utilizing only a few synths or sound modules, this type of interface works very well.

With the advent of multichannel sound modules and MIDI controlled mixers and processors, the MIDI language by itself runs out of gas, quickly. It's just not practical to daisy chain everything together, and many MIDI instruments can send and receive 16 MIDI channels at once.

Instruments capable of receiving more than one MIDI channel at the same time are called multitimbral. A common setup includes several multitimbral sound modules along with MIDI controlled effects processors, a MIDI controlled mixer, and probably MIDI machine control running the multitrack (Illustration 2-6).

The multicable MIDI interface addresses this problem very sufficiently. Its basic operating principle is the same as the simple interface, although it processes all 16 MIDI channels though multiple cables. Most interfaces of this type offer eight separate cables that contain information for all 16 MIDI channels. This increases the power of MIDI dramatically. Not only does it multiply the available channels by the number of separate cables, but it sends all the data in perfect sync. Daisy chaining, and its time delay problems, becomes a non-issue. You could use eight multitimbral sound modules with this type of interface and gain access to 128 MIDI channels! (That's eight cables multiplied by 16 MIDI channels.)

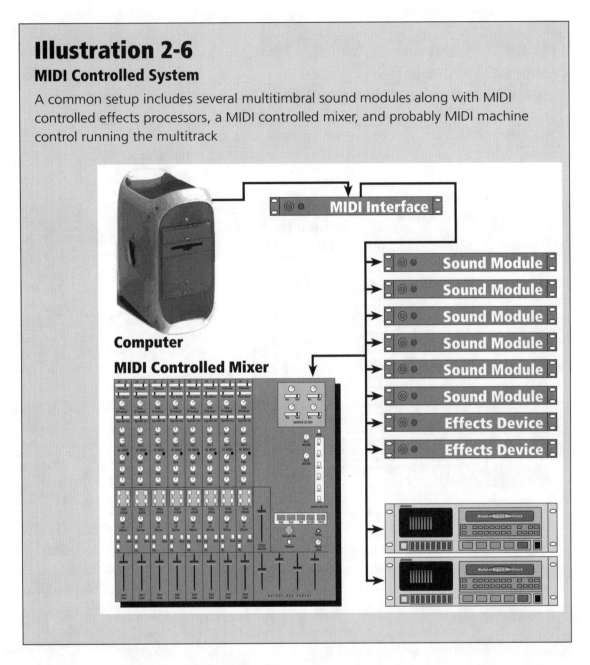

# Illustration 2-6
## MIDI Controlled System
A common setup includes several multitimbral sound modules along with MIDI controlled effects processors, a MIDI controlled mixer, and probably MIDI machine control running the multitrack

MIDI Interface

Computer

Sound Module
Sound Module
Sound Module
Sound Module
Sound Module
Sound Module
Effects Device
Effects Device

MIDI Controlled Mixer

To add to the power offered by this kind of setup, the interfaces can usually be chained together. Four of these interfaces together would let you access 512 MIDI channels, although one would have to create quite a huge MIDI setup to need 512 MIDI channels (Illustration 2-7)..

# MIDI Parameters

### What Do MIDI Parameters Affect?
The MIDI language has been developed to control almost any part of the performance imagin-

# Illustration 2-7
## Multicable MIDI Interface

The multicable MIDI interface sends all 16 MIDI channels simultaneously out of eight MIDI ports. Using this type of interface, the user can access up to eight multitimbral devices with absolutely no timing discrepancies among them. Devices can still be daisy chained from any of the out MIDI outputs, but that's not typically necessary.

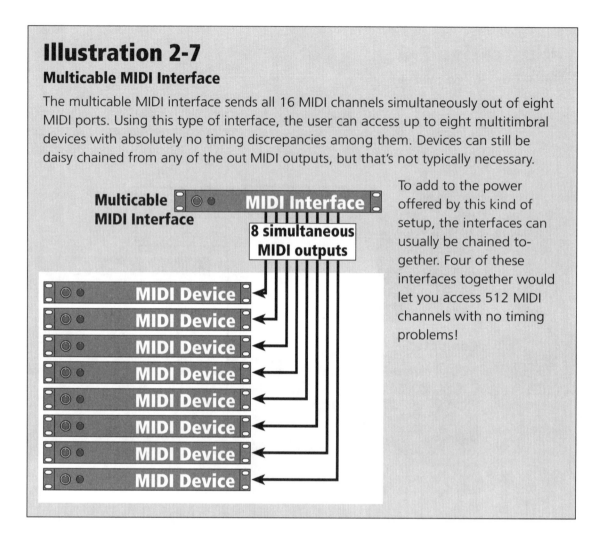

To add to the power offered by this kind of setup, the interfaces can usually be chained together. Four of these interfaces together would let you access 512 MIDI channels with no timing problems!

able. When a key is struck, a MIDI interpretation is rendered for the note name as well as when it was struck; how fast it was struck; when it was released; what happened with the key pressure while it was sustained; whether and how a pedal, mod wheel, or pitch control was used; the volume, pan, effects, and balance settings. There's also protocol for customizing the language for updates as well as instrument-specific instructions and commands.

The MIDI language only offers 128 steps of resolution (0–127). Therefore, if you use MIDI volume controller number 7 for a volume fade out, you don't really get an infinitely smooth fade

as you would with an analog fader. What you do get is a stair-step transition through 128 MIDI values. It's not likely that you'll hear each individual step, but sometimes the MIDI parameter adjustment is audible. We refer to this audible stair-step as the zipper effect.

## Controllers

Many of the MIDI parameters deal with musical expression as it would be conveyed during a live performance. MIDI instruments utilize continuous and switched controllers to control things like pitch bend, modulation, volume, and sustain. There are a total of 128 controllable parameters in MIDI spec. Controllers 0–63 are used as continuous controllers. Controllers 64–95 are used as switches. Controllers 96–121 are undefined, and 122–127 are reserved for channel mode messages (Illustration 2-8).

Two or more performance wheels located to the left of the master keyboard typically vary these controller values. The performance wheels can usually be assigned to control any of the continuous controllers as well as some of the switched parameters. Aside from the perfor-

mance wheels, foot pedals can also access the controllable parameters, which are also assignable to various MIDI control functions.

# Channel Modes

### Omni Mode

A sound module set to Omni MIDI mode hears and responds to all MIDI signals on all chan-

## Illustration 2-8
### MIDI Controllers

There are a total of 128 controllable parameters in MIDI spec. Controllers 0–63 are used as continuous controllers. Controllers 64–95 are used as switches. Controllers 96–121 are undefined, and 122–127 are reserved for channel mode messages

| | | | | | |
|---|---|---|---|---|---|
| 0 | Bank Select | 65 | Portamento | 92 | Tremolo Depth (Effect 2) |
| 1 | Modulation Wheel | 66 | Sostenuto | 93 | Chorus Depth (Effect 3) |
| 2 | Breath Controller | 67 | Soft Pedal | 94 | Celeste Depth (Effect 4) |
| 3 | Undefined | 68 | Legato Footswitch | 95 | Phaser Depth (Effect 5) |
| 4 | Foot Controller | 69 | Hold 2 | 96 | Data Increment |
| 5 | Portamento Time | 70 | Sound Variation/Exciter | 97 | Data Decrement |
| 6 | Data Entry | 71 | Harmonic | 98 | Nonregistered Parameter |
| 7 | Main Volume | | Content/Compressor | | Number LSB |
| 8 | Balance | 72 | Release Time/Distortion | 99 | Nonregistered Parameter |
| 9 | Undefined | 73 | Attack Time/Equalizer | | Number MSB |
| 10 | Pan | 74 | Brightness/Expander- | 100 | Registered Parameter |
| 11 | Expression | | Gate | | Number LSB |
| 12 | Effect Control 1 | 75 | Undefined/Reverb | 101 | Registered Parameter |
| 13 | Effect Control 2 | 76 | Undefined/Delay | | Number MSB |
| 14 | Undefined | 77 | Undefined/Pitch | 102 – 119 | |
| 15 | Undefined | | Transpose | | Undefined |
| 16 –19 | | 78 | Undefined/Flange-Chorus | 120 | All Sound Off |
| | General Purpose 1 – 4 | 79 | Undefined/Special Effects | 121 | Reset All Controllers |
| 20 – 31 | | 80 – 83 | | 122 | Local Control |
| | Undefined | | General Purpose 5 – 8 | 123 | All Notes Off |
| 32 – 63 | | 84 | Portamento Control | 124 | Omni Mode Off |
| | LSB Value for | 85 – 90 | | 125 | Omni Mode On |
| | Controllers 0 – 31 | | Undefined | 126 | Mono Mode On |
| 64 | Damper/Sustain Pedal | 91 | Effects Depth (Effect 1) | 127 | Poly Mode On |

nels. This is not a common usage mode for song production, but it's a good mode for verifying connection between MIDI devices.

## Multi Mode

Multi mode (multitimbral mode) is the most common MIDI working mode. Sound modules and synths set to multi mode discriminate between channel-specific signals. MIDI channel 1 only responds to information sent on channel 1; MIDI channel 2 only responds to information sent on channel 2; and so forth. This mode lets you develop the most individual parts from the available MIDI tools.

## Mono Mode

Mono mode sets the synth to respond to just one note at a time. The original synths from Moog and Arp only had mono mode with no MIDI. They were simply single-voice oscillators with a set of filters to carve away at the sound. This subtractive form of synthesis had its own character and personality. To create a vintage musical line with a vintage synth feel, set up a fairly edgy sound in mono mode.

Mono mode is also applicable when you're driving a sound module with a guitar synthesizer, or anytime you're trying to emulate an instrument that only emits one note at a time, like a flute, clarinet, trumpet, saxophone, etc.

## Polyphony versus Multitimbrality

Polyphony is simply the synth's ability to output more than one note at a time. Most modern synthesizers offer at least 32-voice polyphony; many offer 64-voice polyphony or more.

Whereas a polyphonic synth is capable of playing many notes at once, a multitimbral synth is capable of playing more than one MIDI channel at a time. Most modern synths and sound modules have 16-part multitimbrality—they can output sounds from all 16 MIDI channels at once.

Polyphonic voices are typically allocated to multitimbral MIDI channels on an as needed basis. If your sound module has 32-voice polyphony, you could theoretically use seven voices on a piano harmony part, along with eight drum and percussion tracks, a 6-voice string pad, a 4-voice guitar part, a 1-voice bass guitar track, a 1-voice melody track, and a 5-part brass section track before you ran out of voices—and that's only if all the parts were playing at once. Voice allocation uses whatever voices are available at any given moment. Your arrangement might only use 16 voices at the peak of its activity, so this type of arrangement would probably be pretty safe to perform on a 32-voice multitimbral sound module. Keep in mind, if any of the sounds you're using are layered, the number of voices used multiplies by the number of layers.

# MIDI Time Code

MIDI Time Code is the MIDI equivalent to SMPTE Time Code. MIDI language converts the hours, minutes, seconds, frames, and subframes from SMPTE into MIDI commands. MIDI Time Code (MTC) lets MIDI devices communicate via a time specific reference in much the same way a machine synchronizer communicates through SMPTE to match the time address of two mechanical drive systems.

# System Messages

### System Exclusive (Sys Ex)

Each manufacturer develops a communication language that's specific to its own gear. They customize their commands and develop product-specific languages for patch dumps, preset selections, editing parameters, and other special commands. All of these forms of data can be stored in a musical sequence, greatly increasing its power and flexibility. It also allows the accurate recall of sounds and adjustments that are so musically important; it's never fun to rebuild the sounds in a mix. System exclusive messages provide a means to restore the magic at a later date, with minimal discomfort.

System exclusive data consists of three parts: the header, the body, and the "end of message" byte. The header simply identifies the manufacturer specific codes; the body contains the actual data; and the end of message byte, F7, simply signifies the end of the sys ex transmission.

MIDI specification requires that system exclusive messages begin with F0 and end with F7. The body is determined by the equipment needs and the manufacturer's specifications. These messages vary in size but are always recorded as a single event by a MIDI sequencer; therefore, on particularly large sys ex messages

## Illustration 2-9

### System Exclusive Messages

A system exclusive message looks like a single line in most sequencing software packages. In reality, they are typically fairly large hexadecimal files. This data can usually be edited, but be sure to do your homework on the product before you start tweaking a system exclusive message—you could cause more problems than you solve.

**System Exclusive Data**

| | | | | | |
|---|---|---|---|---|---|
| Length: 408 | F0 | F0 | | Ok | Cancel |

```
  0:   FO 00 00 0E  0E 00 00 00    ........
  8:   60 2A 25 0B  67 28 0B 25    `*%.g(.%
 10:   0B 1F 05 18  79 05 2A 41    ....y.*A
 18:   11 23 46 31  1B 06 40 1C    .#F1..@.
 20:   0E 73 36 6C  18 4C 30 6C    .s6l.LOl
 28:   18 40 2C 14  40 67 02 6C    .@,.@g.l
 30:   5B 04 52 17  41 06 00 10    [.R.A...
 38:   4B 29 46 37  60 02 10 4E    K)F7`..N
 40:   31 63 40 02  00 40 31 63    1c@..@1c
 48:   40 02 00 40  31 63 00 64    @..@1c.d
 50:   46 15 00 46  71 78 18 40    F..Fqx.@
 58:   31 4A 31 40  71 36 30 2C    1J1@q60,
 60:   61 0B 30 03  60 4B 47 01    a.0.`KG.
 68:   00 05 0A 0F  14 19 1E 23    .......#
 70:   28 2D 72 00  40 32 6C 00    (-r.@2l.
 78:   00 23 46 0C  63 36 0C 00    .#F.c6..
 80:   39 1C 66 6D  58 31 18 61    9.fmX1.a
 88:   58 31 00 59  28 00 4F 05    X1.Y(.O.
 90:   58 37 09 24  2F 02 0D 00    X7.$/...
 98:   20 16 73 7A  1F 41 05 20     .sz.A.
 A0:   1C 63 46 01  05 00 00 63    .cF....c
 A8:   46 01 05 00  00 63 46 01    F....cF.
 B0:   48 0D 2B 00  0C 63 71 31    H.+..cq1
 B8:   00 63 14 63  00 63 6D 60    .c.c.cm`
 C0:   58 02 17 60  06 40 17 33    X..`.@.3
 C8:   01 00 0A 0A  1E 28 35 55    .....(5U
 D0:   4E 57 5A 64  01 20 60 15    NWZd. `.
 D8:   28 05 46 0C  19 46 6D 18    (.F..Fm.
 E0:   00 72 38 6C  5A 31 63 30    .r8IZ1c0
 E8:   42 31 63 34  7F 51 00 1E    B1c4.Q..
 F0:   0B 30 6F 12  48 5E 04 1A    .0o.H^..
 F8:   00 40 2C 26  19 56 01 0B    .@,&.V..
100:   40 38 46 0D  03 0A 00 00    @8F.....
108:   46 0D 03 0A  00 00 46 0D    F.....F.
110:   03 10 1B 56  00 18 46 63    ...V..Fc
118:   63 00 46 29  46 01 46 1B    c.F)F.F.
120:   40 31 05 2F  00 1C 00 2F    @1./.../
128:   0E 05 00 14  28 3C 50 64    ....(<Pd
130:   78 0C 21 35  49 03 00 41    x.!5I..A
138:   31 03 00 0C  19 32 0C 5B    1....2.[
140:   31 00 64 71  58 35 63 46    1.dqX5cF
148:   61 04 63 46  69 7E 23 01    a.cFi~#.
150:   3C 16 60 5E  25 10 3D 09    <.`^%.=.
```

### System Exclusive Message

```
2|1|062   <408> FO 00 00 0E 0E 00 00 00 60 2A 25
```

(some can be 10–20K), the sequencer might halt playback for a second or so while the data is transmitted. This can cause a problem if you don't strategically position sys ex data transmission within the sequence. It's typically workable to place sys ex transmissions at the beginning of the sequence, separated from the first MIDI note by a measure or so, depending on the amount of information that needs to be transferred. If the setup for a sequence requires a lot of system exclusive data, it's a good idea to place the sys ex data in a separate setup sequence.

A system exclusive message looks like a single line in most sequencing software packages. In reality, they are typically fairly large hexadecimal files. This data can usually be edited, but be sure to do your homework on the product before you start tweaking a system exclusive message—you could cause more problems than you solve (Illustration 2-9).

## Data Dump

A MIDI data dump is merely a MIDI data transmission, either from the MIDI device to a sequencer or from a sequencer back to the device. Some manufacturers have set a product-specific specification that transmits system messages on only one channel; but, as a rule, system exclusive messages typically have no channel assignment. So, if you're daisy chaining synths together, all synths and sound modules connected together to a single MIDI output will receive the entire sys ex dump. This usually isn't a problem if all the modules and synths are made by separate manufacturers because they shouldn't recognize each other's specific data. If you have two or three synths from the same manufacturer connected in a daisy chain to one MIDI out port, they'll all receive the sys ex information—no

matter what MIDI channel they're assigned to! If you don't want them all set exactly the same, this is a big problem. An error in system exclusive transmission could wipe out the programs, layers, presets, and multitimbral combinations in one or more of your sound modules!

The multicable MIDI interface helps this problem because information can sent through only one cable to a single module, with no daisy chaining involved. With this kind of setup, there shouldn't be any problem transmitting sys ex information because the data is only sent to the module on the assigned MIDI port.

If you have a large daisy chain set up, you might need to connect your modules, one at a time, for a system exclusive data dump, reconnecting the daisy chain only when all units' system exclusive transmissions have completed.

## The Handshake

Some MIDI devices require a specific handshake message before they'll play, receive, or dump any data stream. If you experience a problem with transmitting and receiving sys ex messages, consult the manual for the device; if your piece of gear requires a handshake message, that message will most likely be noted in the chapter on system exclusive.

If you're using a computer-based sequencer, you can usually simply enter the handshake message in a system exclusive sequence. Once it's entered and can be transmitted, everything should work well. Keep in mind that the handshake will probably need to be sent to the device before the device will dump to the sequencer. It will also need to be transmitted before the sequencer can dump into the device.

## Data Backup

Since system exclusive data transmissions have the potential to wipe out your synth, sound module, processor, or mixer settings, it is a very good idea to always keep a backup of your important system exclusive data for each MIDI instrument. It's a fairly simple procedure to create a system exclusive archival sequence for each MIDI instrument. Name and date the sequence. If applicable, include a reference to the song title in the sequence name. Do whatever it takes to eliminate the guesswork when you need to restore your MIDI gear to a previous configuration.

If, by chance, you transmit a spurious system exclusive message and one of your MIDI devices locks up or seems to have lost its data, try turning the unit off and then back on again before you break out your backup system sequences. Many devices recall their settings when powered up—or there might be a key combination that restores all default settings on power up.

# Quantizing

## The Basics

Quantizing cleans up inaccuracies in a musical performance. For the purposes of this section, we're considering the quantizing of musical notes, but many sequencers offer the ability to quantize many different MIDI parameters.

In the process of quantizing, each note is viewed by the sequencer in relation to a note-value grid. The user specifies whether the grid references quarter notes, sixteenth notes, eighth note triplets, etc. Each note of the performance is pulled to the closest grid unit. If you play a note just after the third sixteenth note of count three, and your grid is set to sixteenth notes, the sequencer will pull the note exactly to the mathematically correct third sixteenth note of beat three. If you perform a note between two grid units, the sequencer will pull the note onto the closest grid unit; so, if the performance is too sloppy, the sequencer might pull some notes to the wrong beats (Illustration 2-10).

Early model sequencers popularized the concept of quantizing, sometimes called *auto-correct*. The idea that you could play rhythmically sloppy parts, then have a box make your performance rhythmically perfect was a big hit. The only problem is that nobody really plays rhythmically perfect every time, so the sequencer was soon labeled as mechanical sounding, or machinelike. Since everything was quantized to perfection, there was no emotional personalization.

In reality, music at its best contains plenty of rhythmic imperfections. One artist might be famous for a tendency to produce music that is very intense—often playing ahead of the beat, ever so slightly. Another artist might produce a very laid-back type of music, demonstrating a tendency to play behind the beat. Good studio musicians need to control beat placement constantly; they know how to create different emotional intensities simply by how they approach the groove. An excellent drummer can adjust beat placement of individual instruments. It's common to hear a drum groove with all of the drums playing right on the beat with the exception of the snare drum, which might be laid back or pushed to create an entirely different feel.

It didn't take sequencer manufacturers long to recognize and address the "feel" issue.

# Illustration 2-10
## Quantizing

The process of quantizing pulls each note of a performance to the closest background unit. If you've set the sequencer to quantize to the closest eighth note (like the example below) each note will be drawn to the closest eighth note. Notice the inaccuracy of the beat placements in Example 1—hardly any notes fall directly on the beat. Example 2 has been quantized; notice how each note is perfectly placed on the eighth note grid.

Be careful. If you perform a note between two grid units, the sequencer will pull the note onto the closest grid unit; so, if the performance is too sloppy, the sequencer might pull some notes to the wrong beats.

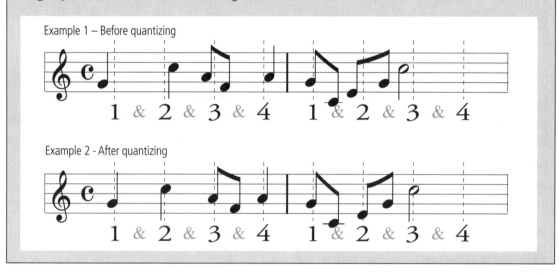

Example 1 – Before quantizing

Example 2 - After quantizing

Modern sequencers let you adjust levels of quantize in minute detail. Almost anything you can imagine being done to a musical note can be performed quickly and easily. Quantizing is referred to in terms of sensitivity and strength; these days, it's rare to perfectly quantize any part of a sequence, unless you're trying to achieve a very mechanical-techno feel.

## Strength

Strength is a quantize parameter that determines the degree of perfection attained. Consider that a perfect quantize conforms the notes perfectly to the user-defined grid. The strength of a perfect quantize is 100 percent because it draws the notes 100 percent of the distance toward the grid—all the way. If you set the strength of the quantize to 50 percent, the notes are only drawn half the way to the closest grid value. At 50 percent strength, a note that is 20 percent away from the grid would be drawn to a distance 10 percent away from the grid.

Imagine a magnet, pulling the MIDI notes toward the grid. At 100 percent strength the magnet pulls the notes all the way to the grid. At 80 percent strength, the magnet only pulls the notes 80 percent of the way toward the grid.

Using the strength option is an excellent way to tighten up a musical performance without sterilizing it. I use the strength command on almost all sequenced parts, even if just a little. On a piano part, adjusting the strength lets you tighten everything in proportion. You can still keep the roll feel of the chords, while at the same time tightening the groove of the song. I'm an okay keyboardist, but with the right amount of MIDI manipulation I can sound pretty good—can anybody relate? (Illustration 2-11)

*Audio Example 2-2*
*Drum Groove: Original,*
*then 100 percent Quantize*
*CD-1: Track 2*

*Audio Example 2-3*
*Drum Groove 80 percent Quantize*
*CD-1: Track 3*

*Audio Example 2-4*
*Drum Groove 50 percent Quantize*
*CD-1: Track 4*

## Sensitivity

The sensitivity control adjusts the area that can be quantized. In a lot of rhythmic feels, the notes that are in between the beats are very style-driven, and they change depending on the emotion of the song. To quantize the notes closest to the grid and leave the notes between the grid alone, you could adjust the sensitivity control

# Illustration 2-11
### Quantize Percentage

Strength is a quantize parameter that determines the degree of perfection attained. Imagine a magnet, pulling the MIDI notes toward the grid. At 100 percent strength the magnet pulls the notes all the way to the grid. At 80 percent strength, the magnetic only pulls the notes 80 percent of the way toward the grid.

Using the strength option is an excellent way to tighten up a musical performance without sterilizing it.

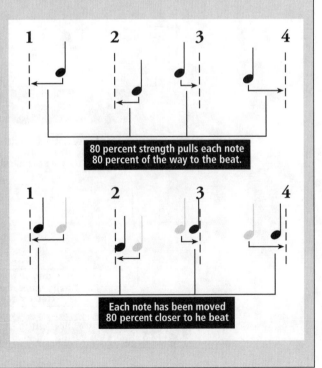

80 percent strength pulls each note 80 percent of the way to the beat.

Each note has been moved 80 percent closer to he beat

on a percentage scale.

At 100 percent sensitivity the area of effect extends continuously between the grid locations. At 50 percent sensitivity, the notes in the middle 50 percent between grid locations would not be quantized, while the notes in the area extending 25 percent on either side of the grid would be quantized either perfectly or in relation to the percentage selected in the strength option (Illustration 2-12).

## Illustration 2-12
### Quantize Sensitivity

At 50 percent sensitivity, the notes in the middle 50 percent between grid locations would not be quantized, while the notes in the area extending 25 percent on either side of the grid would be quantized either perfectly or in relation to the percentage selected in the strength option.

Negative numbers tell the processor to quantize in relation to the center point between grid locations. So, a –50 percent sensitivity leaves the notes that surround the grid (25 percent on either side) alone, while quantizing the notes that surround the center point between grid location (25 percent on either side) according to the grid and strength settings.

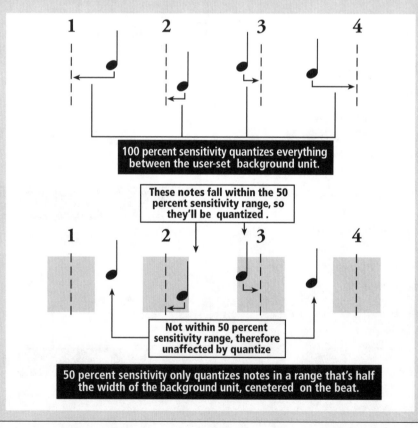

The sensitivity option also allows for quantizing only the notes in between the grid locations. Negative numbers tell the processor to quantize in relation to the center point between grid locations. So, a −50 percent sensitivity leaves the notes that surround the grid (25 percent on either side) alone, while quantizing the notes that surround the center point between grid location (25 percent on either side) according to the grid and strength settings.

**Audio Example 2-5 Reference Groove**
**CD-1: Track 5**

**Audio Example 2-6 50 percent Sensitivity**
**CD-1: Track 6**

**Audio Example 2-7**
**Negative 50 percent Sensitivity**
**CD-1: Track 7**

When these features are used in a musical way, the effect is a very real, precise, and lifelike sequence. The primary problem with 100 percent quantizing lies in the hiding of notes. If all notes are lined up perfectly on the beat, the

# Illustration 2-13
## Absolute versus Partial Quantizing

The primary problem with 100 percent quantizing lies in the hiding of notes. If all notes are lined up perfectly on the beat, the brain doesn't have time to recognize the individual ingredients. Once the parts are spread out in a more realistic way, it's amazing how much more fun the sequence is to listen to.

Notice in Example 1 how the notes lay on top of each other. The instruments are all fighting for visibility. In Example 2 each note is more realistically spread out around the beat and is, therefore, much easier to hear and recognize. This simple concept explains why sequences often sound sterile, lacking personality and impact.

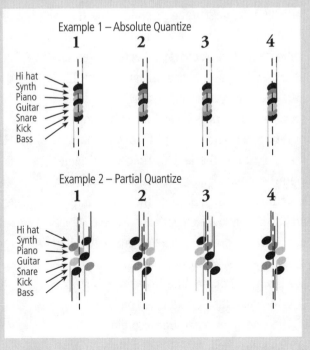

brain doesn't have time to recognize the individual ingredients. Once the parts are spread out in a more realistic way, it's amazing how much more fun the sequence is to listen to (Illustration 2-13).

In Audio Example 2-8, notice how the track comes to life when only partially quantized.

---

*Audio Example 2-8*
*Absolute then Partial Quantize*
*CD-1: Track 8*

---

## How Tight Is Tight Enough?

Once we're in the "let's make it perfect" mode, it's hard to know when to turn back. How perfect is good enough and how loose is loose enough? Good, objective decisions regarding the appropriate feel only come from being fully immersed in the style you're recording. Refer to recordings of live musicians in the style you're recording. Some vintage recordings are downright sloppy at times. Was this because it was stylistically correct, or was it because the players weren't capable of executing their parts? The '50s and '60s were an era of growth in R&B and rock. Folks with passion and vision but not a lot of refinement laid down many of the roots. At the same time, the jazz and big band genres were becoming quite sophisticated; not only were the players totally into their style, but the art had grown to a high performance level. Some of the jazz recordings from that era were full of artistic genius. However, early rock and R&B music was full of life—those recordings mark a peak of inspiration and innovation.

Some of the Steely Dan recordings or Toto's efforts were phenomenal from a musical, artis-

tic, and technical viewpoint. These works represent great musicians performing at an amazingly proficient level. The performances are always right in the pocket; it would be tough to find anything that seems rhythmically or melodically misplaced, yet there is life, energy, and personality. Many current recordings retain those same qualities and, yes, even a sequenced song can sound full of life.

I try to quantize so that the parts feel great; sometimes that means 50 percent, other times 95 percent, and still others 0 percent. Use the tools available to bring out the life of the music. I've seen young producers intentionally leave a very sloppy performance in a sequence in an attempt provide life. In reality, the sloppiness can become a distraction, especially when it's outside the boundaries of tolerance for live performance.

Technology has given us nearly complete control over musical performances. Nowadays, the recordist can be blamed as much for a sloppy performance as the artist. However, even with the nearly complete control available in recording, it's important to understand that recording decisions must be based on musical grounds, not on binary hexadecimal codes.

## Randomize

Randomize is the opposite of quantize. This feature represents the attempt to put some human feel back into a previously quantized sequence. If you're provided a sequence that's been put together on a low-end sequencer that doesn't offer the sophisticated controls mentioned herein, or that's been constructed by someone with a lack of understanding in this area, randomizing could be your key to success.

Randomizing is also referred to in percentages, like sensitivity and strength. 100 percent randomizing results in repositioning of the notes anywhere within the range 50 percent on either side of the grid. In most cases, this degree of randomizing creates rhythmic pandemonium. However, when randomizing to smaller percentages, an otherwise sterile sequence can regain life and impact.

In Audio Example 2-9 through 2-11 the background unit is based on 16th notes. Notice the difference in feel between the perfectly quantized Audio Example 2-9 and the randomized examples (Illustration 2-14).

**Audio Example 2-9**
**100 percent Quantized Reference Groove**
**CD-1: Track 9**

**Audio Example 2-10**
**50 percent Randomize**
**CD-1: Track 10**

**Audio Example 2-11**
**10 percent Randomize**
**CD-1: Track 11**

# Illustration 2-14
## Randomizing

Randomizing is also referred to in percentages, like sensitivity and strength. 100 percent randomizing results in repositioning of the notes anywhere within the range 50 percent on either side of the grid. In most cases, this degree of randomizing creates rhythmic pandemonium. However, when randomizing to smaller percentages, an otherwise sterile sequence can regain life and impact.

Although the effect of randomizing looks much like partial quantizing, on paper, it doesn't usually provide the same kind of rhythmic feel. Partial quantizing retains the rhythmic tendency of each musical part. If one part tends to push the groove, when originally recorded, partial quantizing tightens up the "personality" of the part. Randomizing, on the other hand, simply places notes randomly around the background unit without regard to feel or rhythmic tendencies.

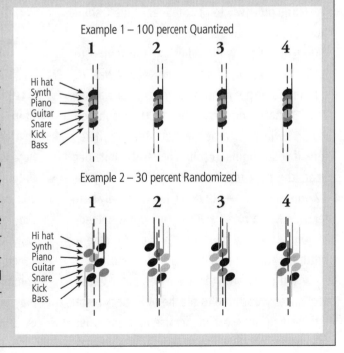

Example 1 – 100 percent Quantized

Hi hat
Synth
Piano
Guitar
Snare
Kick
Bass

Example 2 – 30 percent Randomized

Hi hat
Synth
Piano
Guitar
Snare
Kick
Bass

## Real-Time

Real-time recording in the MIDI world is a totally relative concept. In concept, the MIDI information is recorded without being quantized, but the drawback is the resolution of the MIDI clock. The early MIDI sequencers only had a resolution of 24 or 48 units per quarter note. That resolution is nowhere near fine enough to render a realistic real-time recording. The results were always very choppy and uncomfortable.

---

*Audio Example 2-12*
*Original Performance Without Sequencer*
*CD-1: Track 12*

---

*Audio Example 2-13*
*Real-time Sequence of 2-12 at*
*24 Pulses per Quarter Note (ppq)*
*CD-1: Track 13*

---

The only way to beat the real-time resolution game was to set the sequencer so that it didn't quantize, while adjusting the tempo to its fastest setting. If your song tempo was 70 quarter notes per minute but the tempo was set to 210 quarter notes per minute, the resolution would be increased by a factor of three. Therefore, if your original resolution was 24 units per beat, the new resolution would effectively be 72 units per beat—not good, but definitely better. This was a bit of a cheesy fix, but it helped, as long as the sequence data didn't create a bottleneck at the accelerated tempo setting.

With the growth of the computer-based sequencer, we started to see the MIDI clock resolution increase. Most modern sequencers offer resolutions of 480 or even 960 units per quar-

ter note. These increased resolutions offer a much more realistic sounding real-time recording, though complete capture of the musical interpretation is still debatable.

---

*Audio Example 2-14*
*Original Performance Without Sequencer*
*CD-1: Track 14*

---

*Audio Example 2-15*
*Real-time Sequence of 2-14 at 480 ppq*
*CD-1: Track 15*

---

*Audio Example 2-16*
*Original Performance Without Sequencer*
*CD-1: Track 16*

---

*Audio Example 2-17*
*Real-time Sequence of 2-16 at 960 ppq*
*CD-1: Track 17*

---

## Step Record

Step recording is simply a means of recording a rhythmic part, one note at a time. The grid and note values are determined ahead of time. If you determine the note value to be sixteenth notes, you can play the notes or chords in order, but they don't need to be in rhythm. There is typically a set of computer keyboard commands to speed up the process. When you press the key command for quarter notes, whatever notes you play from then on will have a quarter note value. Once you press the key command for eighth notes, the notes you play will be eighth notes, and so on. You can determine any note or tuplet value.

Step recording is most useful as a tool to compensate for a lack of performance proficiency. Every once in a while a musical part is calling out to be included, but it's a little too difficult to actually play into the sequence, even if you slow the tempo way down. Simply figure out the notes and rhythm, then step record it into the sequence. When you play the sequence back at the correct tempo, you'll probably be amazed at how impressive the part sounds.

The main drawback to step recording is that every note is 100 percent quantized, and they're usually all the same volume, velocity, and expression. Randomizing after the fact, or adjusting some of the note velocities, can help revitalize an otherwise sterile step recorded part.

Be careful that the musical parts you create through step record mode are believable. It's a natural tendency to create lines that are too fast or too harmonically dense. Parts like these might be acceptable as an effect when used sparingly, but they usually distract more than they enhance.

---
***Audio Example 2-18 Unrealistic Step Recording***
***CD-1: Track 18***
---

## Shifting Tracks

Since MIDI values are simply binary codes referenced to a time clock, it's become commonplace to move tracks, notes, and segments. The shift feature is a boon to the process of creating a specific musical feel. If an ingredient needs to feel aggressive and on-edge, shift it forward slightly in relation to the rest of the sequence. If an ingredient needs to feel more relaxed, delay it slightly. It's effective when building a drum and percussion track to shift certain ingredients to lend the appropriate emotional feel and support to the music. The snare track is often shifted forward in time to help the momentum of the drum track.

---
***Audio Example 2-19 Reference Groove***
***CD-1: Track 19***
---

---
***Audio Example 2-20 Snare Drum Shifted Forward***
***CD-1: Track 20***
---

Listen to Audio Examples 2-21 and 2-22. Audio Example 2-21 has been quantized to 95 percent strength, with no tracks shifted. Audio Example 2-22 has some tracks shifted in either direction to help add life. See if you can tell which tracks were moved and which direction they were moved. Notice the difference in emotional feel of each example.

---
***Audio Example 2-21***
***Reference Groove 95 percent Quantized***
***CD-1: Track 21***
---

---
***Audio Example 2-22***
***2-21 with Tracks Shifted***
***CD-1: Track 22***
---

# Velocities, Durations, and Tempos

Velocities, durations, tempos, and many other musical aspects are completely controllable and moldable through MIDI manipulation. Each sequencer handles adjustments of these parameters in its own way, but the concepts are typically identical. Once you begin to understand the basics of these controls, the details fall painlessly into place. You should be able to cross between hardware and software sequencers with a minimal amount of adjustment, primarily because you'll know what to expect—you'll know what to look for.

Many terms common to analog signal processing have been adopted by MIDI program developers. Most programs give you the option to create delays, compression, echoes, arpeggios, choruses, and more. The controls have come to resemble a piece of hardware rather then a box full of numbers.

# Notation Software

### Uses

Most computer-based sequencing packages offer a music notation view of the individual parts.

## Illustration 2-15
### Transposed Score

Transpositions are a snap with a notation package. The chord symbols typically transpose just as easily as notes. This is a great feature for creating parts for a trumpet, sax, or other transposing instrument. The software does all the instrument transpositions automatically.

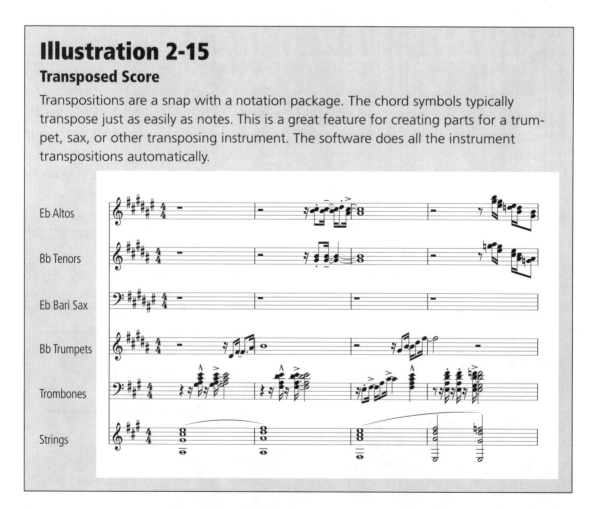

## Illustration 2-16
### Lyric Sheets

Most good notation software packages let the user type lyrics into a lyric sheet, much like a word processor document. Once they're entered, the lyrics can be automatically scrolled under the notes of the leadsheet by the software.

```
▽╳╳▣ ◪╚╳╳╳╳╳╳╳╳╳╳╳  Lyric-1 (Example Song APIII)
.You.a-maze..me.in.the ways.you.go.on.|                    △
.You.tell.me.that.you.want.to be._with.me._|
.then.I.can.see you're.not.a part.of.my.life;...|
.The.way.you're.go-ing.you.might grow.old.a-lone.

You.need.to.buy.,ev-'ry._ Aud-i-o,_Pro .book.that's.in._.the.ser-.
ies_|
Ev-'ry._one_.please.don't._ miss.an-y-_thing,.
'Cause.that Mix-book's.great.and.that Gib-son.knows.his stuff.
                           ▽
```

This is a very convenient and powerful tool for those who think in terms of traditional music notation. However, if you want to print parts for the rhythm section, string section, woodwind section, or the horn section, invest in a high-quality notation software package. These packages are able to produce professional looking musical parts and, once you get the hang of the program, are time savers. Be prepared to invest a fair amount of time into learning the program.

At first, you'll probably feel like you'd be better off using hand manuscript—that is, until you need to transpose the entire arrangement because the key you selected didn't work. Transpositions are a snap with a notation package. The chord symbols typically transpose just as easily as notes. This is a great feature for creating parts for a trumpet, sax, or other transposing instrument. The software does all the instrument transpositions automatically. In addition, it points out any rhythmic and instrument range errors (Illustration 2-15).

Notation can be entered from the computer keyboard or played in through a MIDI device. The ability to play the musical parts from a keyboard is a huge time saver, especially over hand manuscript. Once the parts are in the notation software, they can be played back through MIDI to verify accuracy. As an arranger, it's very valuable to hear your music before you hand the parts to the players!

### Lyrics

Most notation packages let you type lyrics into a lyric sheet, then the computer simply scrolls the lyrics under the notes. The software compensates for ties, rests, and slurs. This is one of the most useful functions when preparing a lead sheet or backing vocal part—and it looks cool, too (Illustrations 2-16 and 2-17).

## Chord Symbols

Chord symbols are a necessity for rhythm section parts and lead sheets. Notation software typically lets you simply play the chord in on a keyboard. The chords are recognized and entered

# Illustration 2-17
### Lead Sheet

The lyrics in this lead sheet were automatically scrolled under the notes. The software recognizes and adjusts for rests, ties, and slurs. In this software package, the chord symbols are harmonically related to the melody and they transpose automatically, along with any key change.

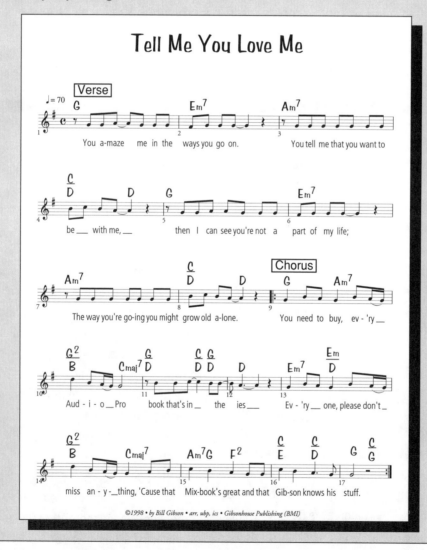

with minimal effort. You can also make up your own chord library so software will recognize your voicings and accurately label the harmonies.

# Mixing with MIDI

## Parameters

Especially with the onset of the combination Digital Audio/MIDI sequencer, all mixing and effects can be performed within the boundaries of your computer. Many home and studio recordists have sold their large recording console in favor of a small, fairly simple mixer. It's common to perform all mixing and effects task on the computer while sending a stereo signal to the mixer for monitoring purposes only. In the final mixdown, you might bypass the mixer altogether, sending a digital signal out of the computer into the digital input of a DAT, CD, DVD, or other digital recording platform.

Not only do you have access to all parameters imaginable through the MIDI but they can also all be automated. By the time the mix is ready to print, all the levels, pans, mutes, equalizations, and fades are happening automatically—all you have to do is just sit back and enjoy the moment.

## Combining MIDI Mix Tools

Amazing power comes from the combination of a digital recording/sequencing package and a digital recording console. If you throw in a modular digital multitrack—or two or three—you're in techno heaven. Prices on this gear have dropped dramatically in the past years. Because of technological advances, recoupment of development costs, and good old-fashioned com-

petition, we can all at least have a shot at owning many of these tools. In many ways, I can do more at my home studio now than I could at any studio in the world not too long ago! The one thing most of us can't replace at home, however, is well-designed space. Professional studios offer recording environments that are full of excitement and inspiration. All you need to do is clap your hands once in a large, impeccably put together studio, and you immediately understand. Synthetic reverberation can't replace the open sound of a recording in an excellent studio.

# General MIDI Specifications

Manufacturers agreed in 1991 to a specific set of MIDI standards called General MIDI (GM). GM standardizes locations and MIDI channels for synths and sound modules, allowing musicians to share sequencing work with some assurance that their sequence can be easily played back.

GM synthesizers support all 16 MIDI channels and offer at least 24-voice polyphony and 16-voice multitimbral output, for a minimum of one voice available for each MIDI channel. Percussion parts are always on MIDI channel 10, using a minimum set of 47 standard drum and percussion sounds, mapped according to the GM standard (Illustration 2-18).

All 128 program sounds are defined as to their type and patch location. Even though sound modules vary substantially in their sound quality and subjective appeal, the General MIDI standard is still very effective in its ability to coordinate an otherwise disjunct and separated segment of the music industry. It's very convenient for publishers and songwriters to distribute MIDI

## Illustration 2-18
### General MIDI Drum Sound Map

| MIDI Note # | GM Drum Sound | MIDI Note # | GM Drum Sound | MIDI Note # | GM Drum Sound |
|---|---|---|---|---|---|
| 35 | Acoustic Bass Drum | 51 | Ride Cymbal | 67 | High Agogo |
| 36 | Bass Drum 1 | 52 | Chinese Cymbal | 68 | Low Agogo |
| 37 | Side Stick | 53 | Ride Bell | 69 | Cabasa |
| 38 | Acoustic Snare | 54 | Tambourine | 70 | Maracas |
| 39 | Hand Clap | 55 | Splash Cymbal | 71 | Short Whistle |
| 40 | Electric Snare | 56 | Cowbell | 72 | Long Whistle |
| 41 | Low Floor Tom | 57 | Crash Cymbal 2 | 73 | Short Guiro |
| 42 | Closed Hi-hat | 58 | Vibraslap | 74 | Long Guiro |
| 43 | High Floor Tom | 59 | Ride Cybmal 2 | 75 | Claves |
| 44 | Pedal Hi-hat | 60 | High Bongo | 76 | High Woodblock |
| 45 | Low Tom | 61 | Low Bongo | 77 | Low Woodblock |
| 46 | Open Hi-hat | 62 | Mute High Conga | 78 | Mute Cuica |
| 47 | Low Mid Tom | 63 | Open High Conga | 79 | Open Cuica |
| 48 | High Mid Tom | 64 | Low Conga | 80 | Mute Trinagle |
| 49 | Crash Cymbal | 65 | High Timbale | 81 | Open Triangle |
| 50 | High Tom | 66 | Low Timbale | | |

files with some assurance that they'll make musical sense on playback. It provides a means to share or sell MIDI tracks that can be edited and customized by the recipient (Illustration 2-19).

General MIDI devices all respond to the same set of controllers, with predetermined and standardized ranges for each. GM devices need to respond, in like manner, to pitch bend, velocity, aftertouch, master tuning, reset all controllers, and all notes off commands.

# Standard MIDI File

## Cross-Platform Compatibility

With so many types of sequencers and software packages available for MIDI sequencing, the MIDI music industry made a mature decision a number of years ago to create a standardized format that could be read by any MIDI sequencer. Sometimes track names or other visual formats are lost in the translation, but, at the very least, all notes and control parameters remain intact whenever a standard MIDI file is saved from one sequencer and then opened in another.

The standard MIDI file is an excellent transition format between your MIDI sequencer and notation software. It's typical to record a sequence in the sequencer software first, in order to determine the arrangement and orchestration, and to later save a copy in standard MIDI file format. The standard MIDI file then opens up splendidly from your music notation software, where the lyrics and print refinements are added to create a professional looking piece of music.

# Illustration 2-19
## General MIDI Voices

| Program Number | GM Voice | Program Number | GM Voice | Program Number | GM Voice |
|---|---|---|---|---|---|
| 1 | Acoustic Grand | 44 | Contrabass | 87 | Lead 7 (Fifths) |
| 2 | Bright Acoustic Piano | 45 | Tremelo Strings | 88 | Lead 8 (Bass + Lead) |
| 3 | Electric Grand Piano | 46 | Pizzicato Strings | 89 | Pad 1 (New Age) |
| 4 | Honky-Tonk Piano | 47 | Orchestral Harp | 90 | Pad 2 (Warm) |
| 5 | Electric Piano 1 | 48 | Timpani | 91 | Pad 3 (Polysynth) |
| 6 | Electric Piano 2 | 49 | String Ensemble 1 | 92 | Pad 4 (Choir) |
| 7 | Harpsichord | 50 | String Ensemble 2 | 93 | Pad 5 (Bowed) |
| 8 | Clavinet | 51 | SynthStrings 1 | 94 | Pad 6 (Metallic) |
| 9 | Celesta | 52 | SynthStrings 2 | 95 | Pad 7 (Halo) |
| 10 | Glockenspiel | 53 | Choir Aahs | 96 | Pad 8 (Sweep) |
| 11 | Music Box | 54 | Voice Oohs | 97 | FX 1 (Rain) |
| 12 | Vibraphone | 55 | Synth Voice | 98 | FX 2 (Soundtrack) |
| 13 | Marimba | 56 | Orchestra Hits | 99 | FX 3 (Crystal) |
| 14 | Xylophone | 57 | Trumpet | 100 | FX 4 (Atmosphere) |
| 15 | Tubular Bells | 58 | Trombone | 101 | FX 5 (Brightness) |
| 16 | Dulcimer | 59 | Tuba | 102 | FX 6 (Goblins) |
| 17 | Drawbar Organ | 60 | Muted Trumpet | 103 | FX 7 (Echoes) |
| 18 | Percussive Organ | 61 | French Horn | 104 | FX 8 (Sci-Fi) |
| 19 | Rock Organ | 62 | Brass Section | 105 | Sitar |
| 20 | Church Organ | 63 | SynthBrass 1 | 106 | Banjo |
| 21 | Reed Organ | 64 | SynthBrass 2 | 107 | Shamisen |
| 22 | Accordian | 65 | Soprano Sax | 108 | Koto |
| 23 | Harmonica | 66 | Alto Sax | 109 | Kalimba |
| 24 | Tango Accordian | 67 | Tenor Sax | 110 | Bagpipe |
| 25 | Acoustic Guitar (Nylon) | 68 | Baritone Sax | 111 | Fiddle |
| 26 | Acoustic Guitar (Steel) | 69 | Oboe | 112 | Shanai |
| 27 | Electric Guitar (Jazz) | 70 | English Horn | 113 | Tinkle Bell |
| 28 | Electric Guitar (Clean) | 71 | Bassoon | 114 | Agogo |
| 29 | Electric Guitar (Muted) | 72 | Clarinet | 115 | Steel Drum |
| 30 | Overdriven Guitar | 73 | Piccolo | 116 | Woodblock |
| 31 | Distortion Guitar | 74 | Flute | 117 | Taiko Drum |
| 32 | Guitar Harmonics | 75 | Recorder | 118 | Melodic Tom |
| 33 | Acoustic Bass | 76 | Pan Flute | 119 | Synth Drum |
| 34 | Electric Bass (Finger) | 77 | Blown Bottle | 120 | Reverse Cymbal |
| 35 | Electric Bass (Pick) | 78 | Shakuhachi | 121 | Guitar Fret Noise |
| 36 | Fretless Bass | 79 | Whistle | 122 | Breath Noise |
| 37 | Slap Bass 1 | 80 | Ocarina | 123 | Seashore |
| 38 | Slap Bass 2 | 81 | Lead 1 (Square) | 124 | Bird Tweet |
| 39 | Synth Bass 1 | 82 | Lead 2 (Sawtooth) | 125 | Telephone Ring |
| 40 | Synth Bass 2 | 83 | Lead 3 (Calliope) | 126 | Helicopter |
| 41 | Violin | 84 | Lead 4 (Chiff) | 127 | Applause |
| 42 | Viola | 85 | Lead 5 (Charang) | 128 | Gunshot |
| 43 | Cello | 86 | Lead 6 (Voice) | | |

There are also very useful applications for beginning your song in the notation package. This approach lets you refine any instrumental arrangements and orchestrations, transferring them through the standard MIDI file to the sequencer once they're perfected. Files that are begun in notation package are typically quantized to 100 percent, so you might need to use the available sequencer functions to randomize, humanize, and generally spruce up the sequence.

# Keyboard and Mix Controllers

## Keyboard Controllers

The hub of any extensive MIDI system is the keyboard controller. The only space-efficient way to set up a MIDI menagerie is to revolve several sound modules around a central keyboard that can access the sound modules in a simple and quick way. The master keyboard controller for a MIDI system might or might not have a sound module built in. Many controllers simply act as a keyboard to send MIDI signals to sound modules. Often, the master keyboard also has sound generators built in, but to be an effective master controller, it should be able to divide into separate regions that can simultaneously drive different MIDI channels and sound modules (Illustration 2-20).

A good master keyboard controller lets you set up presets to instantaneously switch all sound modules to predetermined patches and controller settings.

A separate master controller gives the performer the ability to select an actual keyboard size, design, and action that remains constant no matter what sound module is being driven. Most pianists prefer a natural feeling 88-key weighted action. They just play better in that kind of performance environment, especially when they're playing piano-like musical parts. Some keyboardists prefer a typical plastic non-weighted keyboard when performing organ, strings, brass, or other synthesized electronic sounds; the action is more conducive to the correct stylistic interpretation of these types of musical ingredients.

## Mix Controllers

In the digital recording arena, although all options can be controlled onscreen within the computer or hardware, there's still a place for actually controlling the signal with a physical knob, fader, or button. Several companies offer hardware control surfaces for interfacing with some amazing software packages.

Most mix controllers contain a minimum number of channels (typically eight) but offer a maximum amount of control. Each channel can be assigned to access any number of channels and parameters—the exact number depending on the extent of the digital audio hardware and software. This type of interface offers the ability to actually touch something that feels like a regular console to change a level, pan, aux send, EQ, etc. Along with these tactile mixing and editing capabilities, most controllers provide transport control, moving faders, meters, various windows that read and track the status of any selected parameter, and options for expandability to as many faders and knobs as your needs demand.

Most of these controllers utilize the same MIDI language for parameter control that is used by synthesizers and sound modules. Some manufacturers address the zipper effect (audible stair-stepping through the 128 MIDI parameter levels) by combining two or more MIDI controller numbers for one function. For example, the stereo master fader really should combine at least two MIDI controller parameters in a way that doubles the resolution of the stair steps to 256 discrete levels. Since a fadeout at the end of a song can take ten or more seconds, there is ample opportunity to hear the zipper effect at work. Different manufacturers address this problem in different ways, but most serious audio

## Illustration 2-20
### Keyboard Controller

A good MIDI Controller keyboard can divide into multiple user-selectable zones. Each zone can be sent to its own MIDI channel or device, thereby facilitating easy and quick access to many sounds. Sounds can also be easily layered on controller keyboard.

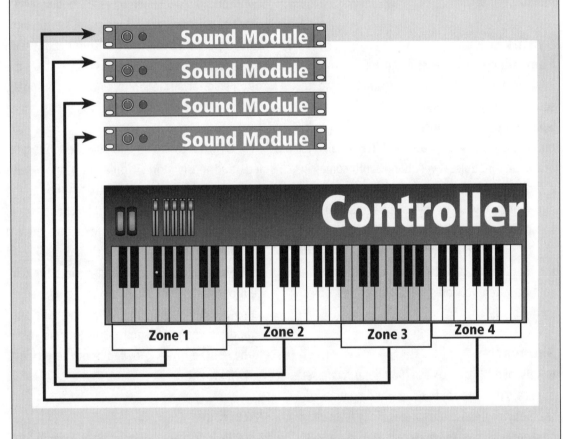

companies design solutions to minimize this effect.

I've worked on small digital mixers with very few faders and one access window, and I've worked on larger surfaces with instant access through faders, buttons, and knobs. Though the digital system allows for a minimal control surface for many channels and parameters, the more efficient systems are set up much like a regular 24-channel mixer. Integration of a computer monitor with the physical mixer provides the best of both worlds: tactile controls and ease of use through the visual onscreen interface.

# MIDI System Design: What Should I Have?

Let's review some MIDI abilities, capabilities, and musical applications while we map out a potential MIDI system.

## Synths

**Controller** – It's necessary to have a master keyboard to access and perform myriad of sounds available in the MIDI world.

**Sound Modules –** Once you've chosen a master controller, it's fun, easy, and inexpensive to add sound modules. Every good synth comes in a rack-mountable version at a significantly reduced price. If you already have a sequencer and a controller, you can often save 50 percent off the keyboard/workstation by simply purchasing the module. It's easier to keep up with current sounds when you only need the scaled down sound module.

## Sequencers

**Hardware Black Boxes –** Some hardware sequencers that are sold as freestanding units offer many professional features. They're usually cheaper than the cost of a computer and a software package (especially if you include the cost of a good multicable MIDI interface), and they require no computer. However, they're more cumbersome, confusing, and time consuming to operate. Black boxes are appealing because they're typically designed from the ground up with accurate sequence timing in mind. They don't share a processor with any other computer function. They're often the most constant, in reference to the groove.

**Computer Software Packages –** If it's at all financially possible, buy a computer and the best software package available. Almost everyone already has the computer, but even if you need to purchase one, this route will probably be much less expensive in the long run. Most users soon feel the frustration of a hardware sequencer (with one or two small access windows and a maze of pages to scroll through). It's often difficult to perform even basic MIDI functions with these hardware-based systems. These boxes are often sold for a fraction of what they originally cost in order to get into a computer-based system.

When it comes time to buy, check out catalogs and music stores. You'll soon find what's hot and what's not. Consider that, although the prices through mail order might be cheaper (and you might be able to dodge taxation), there'll be a time when you need help, and quickly. At those times, you'll certainly appreciate the concept of a local, friendly, knowledgeable, helpful sales person, willing to give you on-the-spot support. If you're talking to a dealer who seems to have little or no knowledge of the product, buy elsewhere.

## Interfaces

**Simple Interface –** If you have a small MIDI setup and you don't expect it to grow much, buy an inexpensive interface.

**Multicable –** If you have several sound modules and see growth in your future, don't waste time or money on anything other than a good multicable interface that reads and writes time code, with provision for further expansion.

## Mixers

**Digital** – Digital mixers have become very affordable and offer tons of features, plus total automation. You can't go too far off base in this arena. But it's always important to test the mixer before you buy. The sound quality on digital mixers is usually good, but some have a grainy kind of a zing-like sound. As with any audio equipment, always listen before you buy. A manufacturer can tout features and sound quality till the cows come home, but we should all make a stand to base our purchasing decisions on sound quality, ease of use, and musicality. We are, after all, dealing with music first and technology second.

**Analog Mixers with MIDI Control** – Most modern analog mixers offer, at the very least, MIDI controlled mutes. There's usually a set of MIDI ports on the console; just plug into your MIDI network, open the manual, and start amazing yourself with the possibilities for creative freedom.

**MIDI Controlled Automation** – There are several MIDI controlled automation systems available. They typically have external hardware that intercepts all mixer outputs, inserting a VCA in each channel that allows for automated fader and mute control. These packages are very powerful aids in the mixing process, but they don't offer the complete control offered by a fully digital mixer.

## Digital Audio Cards

**Combining MIDI Sequencing and Digital Audio** – If you're using a computer-based sequencer, I'd highly recommend upgrading to a combined MIDI/digital audio package. You might or might not need to add an audio card to your computer, depending on your format and needs. The power and flexibility of housing your MIDI sequence and live audio recording in the same box is incredible. You can cut, paste, copy, and undo all audio segments in the same manner as MIDI data, and everything is on one screen. Mixing digital audio and MIDI instruments is all done on the same computer screen. It's the best way to work that I've found so far and, when run in tandem with a digital mixer, it offers phenomenal creative freedom.

## Tactile Control Surfaces for Computer-Based Digital Workstations

If you have everything happening on your computer and you're frustrated by constantly reaching for the mouse and clicking on small pictures of knobs and faders, check out the newest tactile controllers on the block. For not too much cash, you can work on a manual control surface that feels like a mixer but accesses the full power of the digital and MIDI domain. It brings the comfort of an analog mixer into the bliss of digital flexibility.

Be sure the control surface manufacturer offers expansion options. If you like having 8 channels of faders, buttons, and knobs, you might really like having 16, 32, or more.

# 3 MIDI Sequencing

## Building the Band

This chapter gives instruction, suggestions, and insight regarding MIDI sequencing. Equipment is not the main problem most inexperienced recordists face. Modern gear is typically capable of very sophisticated production. Knowing how to optimize the use of modern equipment in a way that creates wonderfully inspired music is the key to musical success and gratification. What I offer here is from my experience with music and equipment. Across the board, I've seen these techniques and tricks make a difference in both sound quality and emotional power of the recording projects I've been involved with.

## Constructing MIDI Drum Parts

### Fundamentals

One of the first things I learned about commercial music was, "A band is only as good as its drummer." The same concept holds true in the MIDI sequencing world. A sequence is only as good as its drum and percussion tracks. If you build a sequence on a foundation made of loose clay, you're in a heap of trouble. If you construct a foundation that's solid granite, finely sculpted and shaped to support the framework in all the right places, you have a chance at greatness.

I'll usually find the stylistically appropriate feel for the song, develop a reference groove, and then, after the arrangement comes together, I'll refine the drum part so it fits with the bass and the other ingredients. Everything needs to work together to create a musical representation that's precise, exciting, and full of emotion.

### The Groove

Once you decide on the perfect rhythmic feel for your music, you've begun to build the road to satisfaction. However, one of the biggest problems for many recordists new to sequencing is the drum track. If you don't have a clue what the drums typically do in the style of music you like to create, you need to do your homework. Most musical styles use a few characteristic drum grooves over and over with some variations for fills and rhythm section interaction. Listen to Audio Example 3-1. Notice the difference in the feel of each drum groove. In most cases, it's obvious, even to the untrained ear, what stylistic family each groove belongs to.

---

*Audio Example 3-1 Several Drum Grooves*
*CD-1: Track 23*

---

Music never has been—and never will be—a stagnant means of expression. Even in music that stays within stylistic borders, there's constant change. Sometimes the change comes in the form of a wild, new, exciting twist that is fresh and alive to all who experience it. Sometimes it comes as a fresh look at a previously used approach. It's up to each of us to jump completely into the music we love, staying in it for the long haul. Even as our likes and dislikes change over the years, there's always a chance that "out of style" will become "back in style" and that we'll become the experts on the latest rage.

There's nothing like an authentic groove, and there's nothing quite as bad as a poor imitation—a groove wanna be. Figure out what it takes to get the perfect groove together for your music. Maybe that means that you should avoid sequencing, that you really should hire a skilled professional to provide the rock-solid foundation your music deserves.

A lot of energy is spent during a serious recording effort finding the right feel. Listen to several different styles of music and describe how they make you feel. Some will probably make you feel on edge, some will make you feel relaxed, some might create a feeling of agitation or irritation, some might make you happy, some might make you sad. Go down the list of emotions and states of mind—you'll probably be able to find music to evoke each one. Our mission here is to find some techniques that'll help provide the appropriate foundation for the emotion inspired by the music you're recording.

Groove is the feel of a musical performance. It consists of such considerations as beat placement, accent placement, accent emphasis, note lengths, chord lengths, rhythmic interactions, emotional passion, and instrumentation.

## Groove Quantize

Quantize isn't always a sterile technique reserved for techno-mania. When properly applied, it helps solidify the framework of the music. Through tasteful applications of quantize strength and sensitivity and through careful beat placement, sequenced drum and percussion parts can be very supportive and downright exciting.

Groove quantize is one feature of modern sequencers that is particularly useful in developing and consistently recreating specific musical feels. This type of quantizing lets you determine the specifications of the quantize grid. If you want beats two and four to push slightly ahead of the beat, you simply access the master grid, setting those beats to whatever position works. In addition, groove quantize includes a customized accent scheme; if you want to accent all the offbeats, simply set the accents in the groove grid. In this way, anytime a track is quantized, even by 100 percent, the beats line up with the customized grid position and accent scheme. Listen to Audio Examples 3-2 through 3-5 for an example of the difference a groove makes.

*Audio Example 3-2 100 percent Quantize*
*CD-1: Track 24*

*Audio Example 3-3 Groove Quantize 1*
*CD-1: Track 25*

*Audio Example 3-4 Groove Quantize 2*
*CD-1: Track 26*

## Drum Set Patterns

If you've been avoiding creating your own drum patterns because you haven't quite been able to understand drum parts, now's the time to jump make the step towards rhythmic freedom. The essentials of drum patterns are simple. The complexities of drum virtuosity are astonishing! Commercial music styles are based on simple drum patterns—patterns and concepts that can be understood and felt by the masses. You don't need to be a virtuoso to understand and create drum patterns that work, and work well.

Most commercial drum patterns are in common time (four beats per measure) and, for the large majority, include a snare drum on beats two and four. The kick drum might play on beats one and three, on all four beats, or often on any combination of eighth or sixteenth notes. What the kick drum does is largely dependent on the bass guitar part. The two instruments must work together to form a solid foundation. The right hand is typically providing the background unit for the groove—either straight eighth notes, sixteenth notes, or quarter notes. The left foot is usually playing on beats two and four, along with the snare. Listen to Audio Example 3-6 through 3-10 to hear examples of different drum patterns (Illustration 3-1).

The previous patterns don't represent all styles, by any means, but they offer the basis for much of what happens in most mainstream commercial styles. In country music and some rock styles, these patterns could cover the essence of 95 percent of the drum parts on a given album. As the musical style becomes more rhythmically complex and aggressive, the drum patterns, likewise, become more rhythmically complex and aggressive.

Listen to the following audio examples. Notice how the drum patterns relate to the previous set. You might feel they're more interesting, or you might think they're kind of busy and confusing—personal taste and musical preference dictate the opinion. Style and emotional requirements indicate their musical relevance (Illustration 3-2).

# Illustration 3-1
## Common Drum Patterns

Most commercial drum patterns are in common time (four beats per measure) and, for the large majority, include a snare drum on beats two and four. The kick drum might play on beats one and three, on all four beats, or often on any combination of eighth or sixteenth notes. What the kick drum does is largely dependent on the bass guitar part.

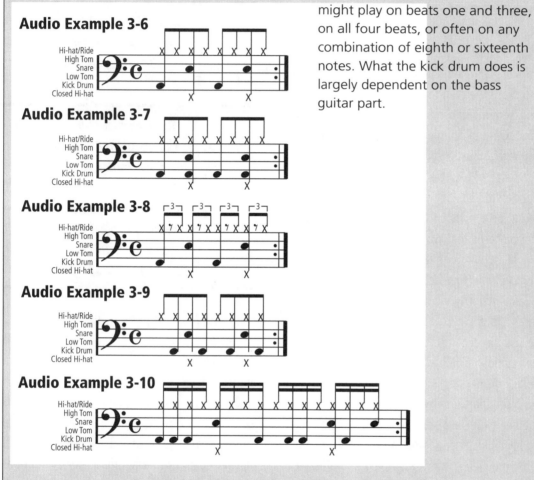

**Audio Example 3-6**

Hi-hat/Ride
High Tom
Snare
Low Tom
Kick Drum
Closed Hi-hat

**Audio Example 3-7**

Hi-hat/Ride
High Tom
Snare
Low Tom
Kick Drum
Closed Hi-hat

**Audio Example 3-8**

Hi-hat/Ride
High Tom
Snare
Low Tom
Kick Drum
Closed Hi-hat

**Audio Example 3-9**

Hi-hat/Ride
High Tom
Snare
Low Tom
Kick Drum
Closed Hi-hat

**Audio Example 3-10**

Hi-hat/Ride
High Tom
Snare
Low Tom
Kick Drum
Closed Hi-hat

*Audio Example 3-11*
*CD-1: Track 33*

*Audio Example 3-13*
*CD-1: Track 35*

*Audio Example 3-12*
*CD-1: Track 34*

*Audio Example 3-14*
*CD-1: Track 36*

*Audio Example 3-15*
*CD-1: Track 37*

A pattern that's more complex is, by no means, better or worse than a pattern that's simple. Young drummers are always trying to play the most complicated stuff. More seasoned

# Illustration 3-2
## More Complex Drum Patterns

Notice how the drum patterns relate to the previous set. You might feel they're more interesting, or you might think they're kind of busy and confusing—personal taste and musical preference dictate the opinion. Style and emotional requirements indicate their musical relevance.

### Audio Example 3-11
### Audio Example 3-12
### Audio Example 3-13
### Audio Example 3-14
### Audio Example 3-15

drummers have learned that drums are all about maintaining a rock-solid foundation; therefore, an experience player usually selects a fairly simple and clean pattern to support the musical vision. A great drummer has the depth and technique to maintain an undeniable groove, even through musically tasteful and well placed fills and embellishments.

Swing and Latin patterns are typically more complex, though most grooves maintain a pulse that revolves around a common time kick, snare, kick, snare pattern. The following audio examples illustrate the relationship of the more complicated patterns to the more basic patterns.

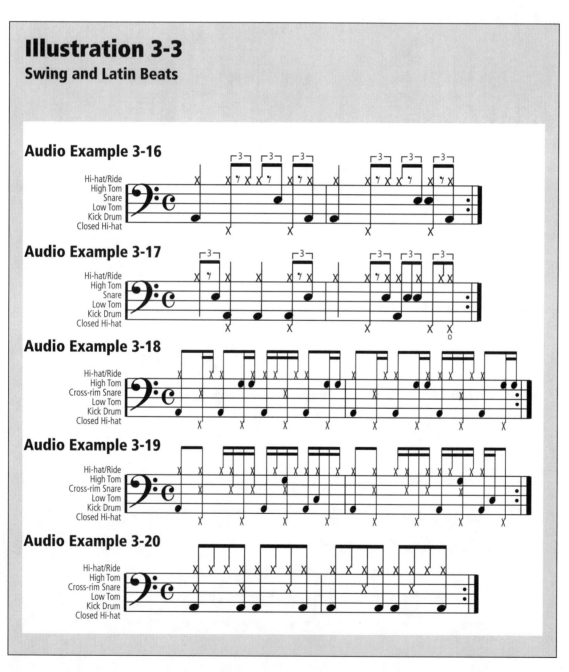

## Illustration 3-3
### Swing and Latin Beats

**Audio Example 3-16**

**Audio Example 3-17**

**Audio Example 3-18**

**Audio Example 3-19**

**Audio Example 3-20**

Illustration 3-3 contains notation for the examples.

---

*Audio Example 3-16 Swing Beat 1*
*CD-1: Track 38*

---

---

*Audio Example 3-17 Swing Beat 2*
*CD-1: Track 39*

---

---

*Audio Example 3-18 Latin Beat 1*
*CD-1: Track 40*

---

---

*Audio Example 3-19 Latin Beat 2*
*CD-1: Track 41*

---

---

*Audio Example 3-20 Latin Beat 3*
*CD-1: Track 42*

---

Practice creating the drum patterns in the previous audio examples, then take them to the next level. Change the kick and snare drum a little, vary the right-hand pattern. Or try something a little different. Always think creatively. These example drum patterns should provide a basis for confidence and experimentation.

## Accents

Drum parts are often full of dynamic changes and great passionate outbursts. Don't overlook the power of dynamics and rhythmic accents in your drum creations. It's typically the accents that really define the emotional impact of music. With drum sequences, you can either play the accents in, when you originally program the parts, or you can simply turn an instrument up in volume for a period of time. Experiment with placement of accents within your drum grooves.

Listen to the following audio examples. Notice that, even though each example contains

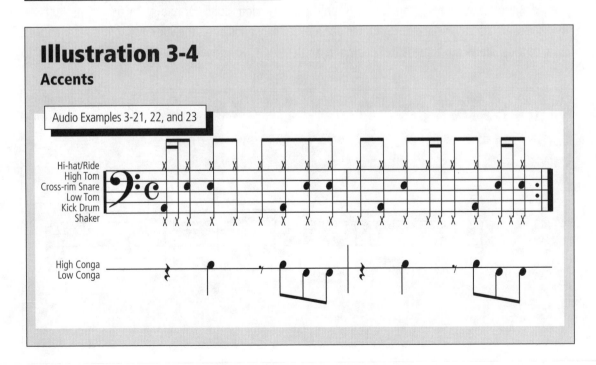

## Illustration 3-4
**Accents**

Audio Examples 3-21, 22, and 23

Hi-hat/Ride
High Tom
Cross-rim Snare
Low Tom
Kick Drum
Shaker

High Conga
Low Conga

the identical rhythm, the feels are markedly different (Illustration 3-4).

---

*Audio Example 3-21 Accents 1*
*CD-1: Track 43*

---

*Audio Example 3-22 Accents 2*
*CD-1: Track 44*

---

*Audio Example 3-23 Accents 3*
*CD-1: Track 45*

---

## Fills

Listen to some of your favorite music in the style you're recording to experience the appropriate types of drum fills. Analyze the fills; try to duplicate the rhythmic feel of each. Drum fills typically include toms but often include snare or even kick drum. The "king of tom fills" is simply four sixteenth notes on each of four toms, for a total of four beats (a full measure) ending in a crash. Young drummers feel like they've arrived when they get the roll around the toms down (Illustration 3-5).

---

*Audio Example 3-24 The King of Tom Fills*
*CD-1: Track 46*

---

Unfortunately, a simple sixteenth-note pattern around the toms usually sounds rigid and mundane in a sequencer. It's possible to creatively add accents to a measure of sixteenth notes to spice things up, but it never sounds as cool sequenced as it does when a real drummer plays it on real drums. Part of the problem with sampled drums sounds resides in the consistent attack sound. A real drum, played with drumsticks, varies greatly from attack to attack because of the variations in speed, attack area, and other human inconsistencies. Some software manufactures allow for variable samples depending on attack velocity and other assignable random considerations. An option like this really adds an authentic edge to drum sequences.

In most cases, it's best to keep fills as

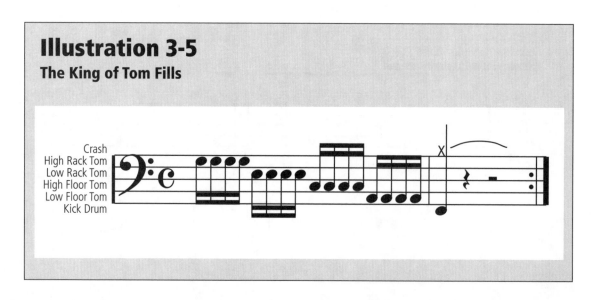

## Illustration 3-5
### The King of Tom Fills

simple as possible. A simple "da dum dum crash" might be the perfect drum fill, whereas a "buddley buddley buddley boom wackiticky brrrrrrrr snap" will probably get in the way and sound silly. With the ability to record fills at a slow tempo—to be played back at a fast tempo—it's easy to get carried away and create a drum fill that could never be performed by a live drummer. A drum fill should always support the flow from one musical section to the next. Flashy fills, for the sake of flash alone, have no place in good music. Flashy fills that build and support the emotional feel of the song are awesome. An unrealistic fill combined with a constant attack makes for a distraction, rather than an emotion filled support.

Drum fills are typically placed at the end of a musical section, leading into the next section. However, they don't need to lead into each section. Sometimes the drums serve the music better by simply playing through a section change with no fill. Other times, a simple crash at the beginning of a section is all that's needed. Taste and discipline should guide your decisions about fills. It's always better to understate fills than it is to stick in too many.

Listen to the following examples of simple fills that work well in the context of sequencing (Illustration 3-6).

*Audio Example 3-25 Groove Into Fill 1*
*CD-1: Track 47*

*Audio Example 3-26 Groove Into Fill 2*
*CD-1: Track 48*

*Audio Example 3-27 Groove Into Fill 3*
*CD-1: Track 49*

*Audio Example 3-28 Groove Into Fill 4*
*CD-1: Track 50*

## Believability

If you'd really like to create drum patterns that sound like a real drummer played them—and those are the best kind—keep in mind that drummers are people, too. They usually don't have more than two arms and two legs. Therefore, they can't play the cymbals while they rip off a huge tom fill; they can't usually play fast sixteenths on the ride cymbal and hi-hat while at the same time performing an intricately syncopated snare-kick combination with tom fills included. Envision a drummer playing the drum parts you devise. If you can visualize a drummer playing the part, your patterns will probably sound authentic.

If you have an excellent sense of time, or if you're a fine drummer, try inputting the drums in real-time. Avoid quantizing just to see how the patterns feel. Sometimes this approach works well, but you really must be able to play the parts right in the pocket, and that's not always easy to do. I've had some success at real-time drum programming, especially after the rest of the ingredients have been entered and finalized, but I usually find that even a slight degree of quantizing cleans everything up very well.

## Construction

Construction and performance of a drum part is much more natural—the beats flow in a much

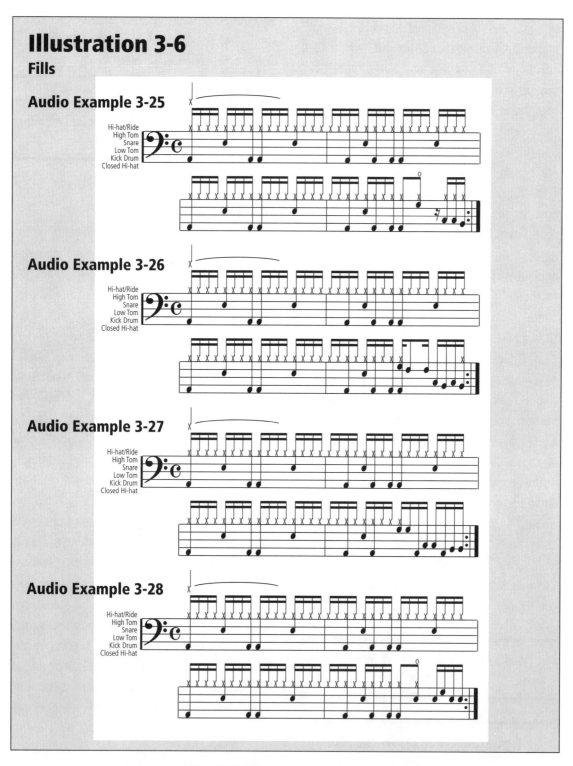

**Illustration 3-6**
**Fills**

more musical way—when the rest of the arrangement has been put together. I typically use a reference groove (a one- or two-bar pattern

that indicates the correct feel) to build the sequence around. Then, once everything is in place, I'll go back through the entire song, playing the kick and snare together first; I find these two ingredients fundamental in the way they interact with the rest of the arrangement. Once I'm satisfied with the kick-snare combination, I add the hi-hat, ride cymbal, and crash cymbal parts—in one pass if possible. I like to add the tom fills last so I can tell where they're really needed.

# Percussion Patterns

## Frosting

Percussion instruments really add the frosting to the groove cake. A simple shaker can propel a drum pattern. The constant action of an eighth or sixteenth note shaker part provides momentum that might not otherwise exist. Experiment with shifting percussion parts forward and back in time relation to the rest of the pattern—use the smallest increment available. Notice the changes in the feel of the following patterns as I move the shaker ahead of and behind the rest of the groove.

*Audio Example 3-29 Groove and Shaker*
*CD-1: Track 51*

*Audio Example 3-30 Shaker Ahead of the Groove*
*CD-1: Track 52*

*Audio Example 3-31 Shaker Behind the Groove*
*CD-1: Track 53*

Try the same techniques on tambourine, clavés, cowbells, hand claps, triangle, or any other percussion instrument.

The following audio examples demonstrate some popular uses for some common percussion instruments. Listen to several recordings that include percussion; see if you hear any of these parts.

*Audio Example 3-32 Tambourine*
*CD-1: Track 54*

*Audio Example 3-33 Cowbell*
*CD-1: Track 55*

*Audio Example 3-34 Conga*
*CD-1: Track 56*

## Many Instruments

There are many percussion instruments. There are hundreds of commercially manufactured percussion instruments readily available. Any number of multiculturally inspired drums can be found along with all sorts of metal clanging, thunking, popping, boinging, tinkling, and crashing instruments. Any instrument that is struck is a percussion instrument, including the piano family—since the hammers strike the strings. If you ever hire a professional percussionist for a session, you'll soon find the studio littered with stuff.

Percussionists are notorious for turning everything into a musical instrument. Keys, beads, pop cans, coffee cups, automobile brake drums, circular saw blades, chunks of metal and wood are all common percussion instruments. It's incredible how a tasteful percussionist can add unique character that's full of life to a recording.

## Simple Parts That Work Together

Be sure to keep percussion parts simple. It's best to create a couple very simple percussion parts that work together well. Throughout your drum set and percussion programming adventure, you'll find the greatest success in creating simple, musical parts that support the flow and emotion of the music. Experiment with the points I've highlighted in this chapter. The art of drum programming demands practice, as well as a thorough understanding of style, musical taste, and creativity. When those ingredients are combined in proper proportion, your music has the chance it deserves to be heard.

# Forming the Bass Line

The bass and the drum parts should work so tightly together that, together, they could almost be considered one part. The bass guitar and kick drum often play the identical rhythm; if they don't, they must at least complement one another. Listen to the following audio examples. Pay particular attention to the way the bass guitar and kick drum support each other.

*Audio Example 3-35 Kick and Bass 1*
*CD-1: Track 57*

*Audio Example 3-36 Kick and Bass 2*
*CD-1: Track 58*

*Audio Example 3-37 Kick and Bass 3*
*CD-1: Track 59*

*Audio Example 3-38 Kick and Bass 4*
*CD-1: Track 60*

## Patterns

The most common chord tones used in bass line construction are the root and fifth of the associated scale. When a bass guitar line flows through passing tones, it's important to use the proper scales. Since this part is so foundational to a song, it almost always sounds best to keep the bass line simple, rhythmically and melodically. To add flow to a bass line, especially leading into a phrase, it's pretty common to go through the sixth and seventh notes of the scale. It's also common to walk up the scale to the next chord.

These techniques are common to most styles; what changes most is the bass sound. The playing approach is so different from style to style, that the resulting sound, feel, and emotion vary dramatically. When sequencing a bass part, always take into consideration the playing techniques used by most bass players active in the particular musical style.

## The Groove

As with drums and percussion, the bass needs to lock into the stylistically correct groove. If you have quantized the drums to a customized groove, it's important that the bass be quantized to the same groove. Audio Example 3-39 demonstrates the bass and drums in and out of the same groove.

**Audio Example 3-39 In and Out of the Groove**
**CD-1: Track 61**

## Reality/Believability

As soon as synthesized bass lines became a usable option, music programmers started to push the bass range envelope. A standard four-string bass guitar has a finite range—from E1 (41.2Hz) to about D4 (293.66Hz). A synthesizer is not bound by those limitations, so, especially in the low end, bass notes started to edge their way to the basement. Low D, C, and even B soon worked their way into contemporary sound.

When synth bass first came into being, we were still bound by the limitation of vinyl records and an evolving cassette technology, so it was held that recordings were more universally acceptable if the bass parts stayed within the bounds of the standard four-string. As CDs and other digital formats became the standard, and with the advent of much improved consumer audio, those low notes became more and more fun to listen to—so, they became more and more common. Life for the bass player was about to change. Most active bassists now carry a five-string bass with a string added to the low end, extending the range down to low B0 (30.87Hz).

## Feel

Depending on the musical style, it might be appropriate to shift the bass guitar forward or back in time, relative to the drums. In certain jazz applications, the bass is right on the front edge of the beat, helping drive the momentum. Other styles require the bass to land precisely on the beat with the drums, or even behind the beat for a more laid back feel. Different personality characteristics absolutely transfer to musical interpretation and feel. A hyper person tends to play ahead of the beat and creates a unique tension in the music. A laid back personality relaxes a groove. The highly skilled and experienced professional can adjust the temperament of a performance to fit the desired effect for the musical application. Since we have the sequencer at our disposal, we only need the knowledge of the effect created by variance in performance and feel. We can direct the computer to adjust the placement of each beat for the perfect blend of aggressive and passive emotion. Cool, huh?

# Guitar Parts

## Believability

It's sometimes difficult for pianists to create an authentic sounding guitar part. The guitar has certain pitch and voicing limitations dictated by the physical design of the instrument. The range of the guitar is from E2 (82.41Hz) to as high as E6 (1318.51Hz). The strings stack up from the lowest E (the sixth string) in fourths, except for a major third interval between the second and third string

Part of the guitar sound comes from the characteristic voicings, which are comfortably played on the guitar, though they might be difficult to play on a keyboard. To create authentic sounding guitar parts, you must use authentic chord voicings. The other idiomatic trait that makes the guitar unique is the strum. Chords are not played all at once. They're either strummed up or down. Good players adjust their pick speed to create differing comp feels but, even at the fastest pick speed, chords are slightly arpeggiated. Some software packages include an option to simulate the guitarist's strum, but the same feel can be accomplished through a stylistically correct keyboard performance.

## The Groove

Guitar relates to the groove completely on a stylistic basis. Imagine the personality of the music, and you'll find the guitar groove. Funky guitar comps are often right on top of the beat; they lock tightly in with the drums and bass, almost becoming a part of the percussion section. A lot of fast country music is driven by the guitarist's aggressive and flamboyant energy. Picture a grunge rock group and, though the music is almost always guitar-driven, the guitar parts are often rhythmically laid back. There are exceptions to all these points, but the key issue is that styles differ in their rhythmic emphasis.

## Patterns

There are countless guitar strum patterns, but if you're really trying to create authentic sounding guitar parts, always keep in mind that the guitarist strums up and down for fast notes. Often, the downbeats are all down strokes and the upbeats are all up strokes. Even if a measure contains all upbeats, the guitarist would probably play all up strokes, simply to stay in the flow of the groove.

Guitarists also use slides, bends, and grace notes in a completely different way than a keyboard. A synth pitch bend is not the same as a guitar note bend or slide. Whereas, a keyboardist bends the entire keyboard through a continuously variable pitch range, a guitarist often bends one note while holding another steady. A guitarist's grace notes and hammer-ons typically contain discrete steps through a chromatic or

diatonic tone set—especially when played within a chord comp. Therefore, to accurately reproduce a fingered slide the keyboardist must adjust the synth pitch bend to chromatically notch through a pitch range. In addition, many of the chord comps need to lead in with a grace note, or a set of grace notes, that could actually be played by a guitarist.

# Grand and Electric Piano Parts

## The Groove

Piano adds a distinct fullness to an arrangement. Sometimes the piano adds such a fullness that it distracts from the rest of the arrangement. In a commercial style, it's rare to hear the piano just going for it. The piano parts are typically finely crafted to lend support at the right times and to release space and openness when it's needed for the other instruments. Like the guitar, piano is style driven. Given an old time rock 'n' roll song, the piano is probably off and running, leading the whole band. Given a contemporary pop ballad, the piano might be laid back beyond belief. Most of the time, an up-tempo piano comp blends in with the percussion and bass guitar to form a solid rhythmic and harmonic support for the rest of the instruments.

## Patterns

Most singer/songwriters who play and write on the piano fill out the sound so much on the piano that there's no room for any other instruments in the orchestration. They get used to playing constant eighth or sixteenth note patterns and arpeggios. These kinds of parts usually need to be set aside to make room for the rest of the instrumentation. Sometimes, in a pop commercial ballad, the piano is the primary source of rhythm and harmony, but in the regular world of popular styles, piano parts are very simple and supportive until the perfect musical moment; then, they add sparkle in a way that no other instrument really can.

Listen to the following audio examples. Notice how the piano gets in the way in Audio Example 3-40 and how it supports the emotion in the Audio Example 3-41.

*Audio Example 3-40 Piano In the Way*
*CD-1: Track 62*

*Audio Example 3-41 Piano Supporting the Song*
*CD-1: Track 63*

## Grand Pianos vs. Rhodes Pianos

The choice between grand pianos and Rhodes sounds is subject to application and taste. Typically, grand pianos are used on aggressive rock or country songs and on big pop ballads. Rhodes piano sounds are more commonly used as a mellow support on mid-tempo middle-of-the-road songs and on mellow ballads. Their sound qualities support these applications, but they both add their own unique personality to whatever music they're included in. Experiment. The choice is yours, and it will be the right choice if it's based on emotion and passion for your song.

Some pieces of music don't call for piano at all. The more experienced you become at producing, orchestrating, and arranging, the more selective you'll become in your orchestration choices.

## Believability

The sequencer provides the opportunity to build piano parts that could only be performed by a 15- or 20-fingered pianist. Really, across the board, in any instrumental part you sequence, it's best to keep the ingredients simple and potentially playable in a live setting. Building parts that are too complicated to play quickly distracts far more than it supports.

Piano requires great care in quantizing. Since pianists tend to roll chords—instead of just pounding the notes all at once—and since the melodic support is typically very expressive, quantizing in any degree has the potential to destroy the performance. If the piano performance comes from an accomplished pianist, try to avoid quantizing. Quantize only to solidify the musical groove, and only quantize in the measures that really need it. Always copy the MIDI piano part to another track before you start to quantize; leave the original untouched. If you keep the original performance intact, you can always go back to it later if you realize the track had more life before you started to fix it.

## Feel

Especially when the piano is the main instrument, its feel is amazingly crucial to a song's development and stylistic impact. Shifting the piano in time makes a huge difference on the feel of the song. The touch of the performer and the use of accents, phrasing, and nuance are what comprise the piano's powerful musical influence. Piano is one of the easiest instruments to ruin through the sequencing process. A simple, emotion-filled performance usually serves the musical needs of a song best.

# The Frosting

Once the basic rhythm section tracks are together and working for the needs of the song, it's time to consider ways to increase the impact through effective orchestrating and arranging. If the rhythm section parts have all been crafted to work together in a musically supportive way, the need for additional parts, like strings, brass, and sound effects, might be minimal. Young musicians tend to keep adding ingredients, hoping that more sounds will add up to a cooler sound. In truth, the opposite usually occurs. The more you add, the less important and more hidden everything is. It's very possible to fill a song up with sound, then realize that nothing sounds close, important, or intimate.

Listen to your rhythm tracks and vocals. Set up a good punchy mix, then look for spots that seem empty or lack emotion. Take notes on exactly where you feel the music is texturally needy. Then, before you start adding parts, tinker with the mix at those spots; see if there's already a musical ingredient that would fill each spot wonderfully if it were simply turned up for a few beats or measures. Try to fill in the song with what you have first. If you need to add some fills, pads, or effects, do so with authority and resolve, but be certain each part is necessary.

*Audio Example 3-42 Three Mixes:*
*Bare Bones, Some Stuff, Lots of Stuff*
*CD-1: Track 64*

## Strings and Pads

String sections and synth pads are commonly used in most styles. We've already covered layering and combining sound modules in this course, so I'll assume you can find the perfect sound for your song. Once you have the sound ready to go—the sound that brings out the best in your music—finding the perfect place to use it is the key. The problem with most synth pads is that they sound so huge and massively warm and inviting that once you start playing them, it's hard to stop.

In most cases, the musical flow is better supported if the pad comes in at key points and then disappears until it's really needed again. When a huge pad sound stops, the space needs to be filled by something else. The ingredient is usually already in the mix; it simply needs to be turned up.

Listen to Audio Example 3-43. Notice how empty the orchestration is when the pad goes away. Then listen to Audio Example 3-44. Notice how the acoustic guitar comes up to fill the hole left by the pad.

*Audio Example 3-43 Empty When Pad Leaves*
*CD-1: Track 65*

*Audio Example 3-44*
*Acoustic Guitar Comes In to Fill Hole*
*CD-1: Track 66*

Pad sounds don't always need to be played as chords. Some of the most effective string and pad lines begin as single notes, building to more notes as the arrangement grows. Try waiting until the middle of the second verse or so; then, bring the pad in on a single note line that starts in the lower (cello) register, moving up and controlling the flow into the second chorus. In the chorus, break into a multi-note pad. You might find this technique really highlights and builds the song. Or, it might not work at all—that's the beauty of music.

---

*Audio Example 3-45 Single Line Pad*
*CD-1: Track 67*

---

## Brass

Used in just the right way, brass sounds add sparkle and life to the right musical style. If you'd like to sequence brass parts so they sound like a brass section, you must research arranging techniques. A brass section that sounds great live is always performing excellent arrangements, using powerful and characteristically appropriate voicings. The players are probably very talented, and they are able to lock into the groove in a way that propels the music to a new level. Excellent brass parts are dependent upon inspired articulation, dynamics, phrasing, and emotion. If you're unfamiliar with these stylistic ingredients, it will be difficult for you to create brass parts that work well.

Listen to some hit songs in the style you're recording. Analyze the brass parts for their melodic, rhythmic, and dynamic content. Try to play the brass parts from several well produced songs. This will give you some insight as to what good brass parts are.

Be sure that, once you begin constructing brass parts, you avoid laying the brass over the vocals. It's usually okay to let the brass play some short punches during the verse or chorus, be-

cause these kinds of parts become very percussive and can support the feel. Longer, more melodic, brass parts that include the entire section should be used carefully so as to avoid conflicting with the melodic vocals. Lower trombone and French horn lines—especially unison lines—don't conflict when they're written in a way that supports the melodic flow. When arranged correctly, they act more as string or pad supports than they do as brass highlights.

## Sound Effects

With the onset of samplers and other digital manipulation tools, almost any sound can show up as a musical ingredient. Sounds are amazing in their diversity and flexibility. The tasteful use of sound effects and unique samples can bring new life and momentum to a musical work. But it can also distract from the purpose of the music. Some producers like to put a different sound in each musical hole or break. This was really popular in the '80s and early '90s. Though this technique can continue to give the listener something to draw them back to the tune, music that offers an excellent performance and enticing lyrics can have longevity and a greater impact with which to draw the listener in.

# Combining MIDI and Live Recording

With the development of digital recording software that also sequences MIDI data, home recording has changed radically. I'm really a drummer who has played a lot of guitar and bass, so I've been forced to grow in my keyboard skills to even sequence the most basic synth and piano parts. In the years since MIDI software became available, I've sequenced the piano and rhythm tracks for several albums and other commercial projects. I've been able to get by, but once I was given the tools to record my guitar parts right along with the sequenced tracks, life changed for me. Plus, I could lay down vocals and percussion and anything else I wanted. It was like a musical revival all over again. Even though I had the tools to sync my multitrack to my computer, the control and flexibility offered by the complete digital/MIDI software was amazing.

Music is changing all the time. The exciting thing about the phenomenal growth of technology is the creative freedom it provides. Most musicians feel more relaxed and emotionally free when they're at home than when they're in the studio performing under the pressure of the record light, the producer, or the clock. Sometimes the realization of the hourly rate stifles the creative flow. Only the most seasoned studio musicians come alive in the studio environment—and then somebody else is probably paying for the time anyway. The creative environment in the home studio should release and increase the depth of modern music. We all benefit.

Depending on the musical style, it's common to record real guitar, grand piano, vocals, and solo instruments over a basic MIDI sequence that includes drums, percussion, bass, and synths. Sometimes, simply adding a sax or guitar solo over a well produced sequence brings new life to the whole project. With the ease of integration between MIDI and digital recording, we hear any combination of recording processes all the time. In this era, we can pick and choose the techniques and instruments that work best for the music, easily combining them all at home. We might be limited by access to proficient musicians to play the parts we need, but the recording tools aren't the problem anymore.

## Drum Loops

Samplers and digital recording have opened a new world for drum tracks. Sequenced drum tracks are difficult to construct in a way that has life, emotion, and groove; therefore, it soon became popular to sample a measure or two of an excellent live or previously sequenced drum pattern, looping it for the duration of the song. This technique provides a solid, almost mechanized, foundation, but the song benefits from an inspired drum groove.

The problem with drum loops is not musical; it's legal. Digital technology provides us with such clean recordings of our favorite music that—when we hear a great drum groove that's all by itself for a while—the temptation to sample it, then use it in our own songs, is strong. The legal and moral implications of this technique are suspect. Copyright laws and the principles of right and wrong are often overlooked in the interest of the excitement of the moment. There are many commercially prerecorded drum loops available. CDs are available, produced solely with drum grooves created for sampling purposes. Most sampling manufacturers have many presampled and prelooped drum tracks available for use with their product. The grooves are available without infringing on anyone's rights of ownership and hard work.

No formula works every time. Anything you hear regarding the development of your music should be taken as a suggestion. Music is such a personal and creative art form that, thankfully, there are no absolutes. Always strive to stretch the boundaries of musical styles and conformities. Use assumed truths about music to help build music that has integrity. Much of what you'll hear about musical considerations comes from years of experimentation by musicians— players as passionate as anyone about creativity and individuality. Take advantage of their experience, and then take it a little further.

# Chapter 4 Digital Recording

This chapter is written to take some of the mystery out of digital recording. Understanding certain elements of the digital recording process is important. Digital technology is very logical, and some insight into the process leads to efficient use and confidence. We'll consider small amounts of information at a time that can easily be understood. By the end of this chapter, you should have a functional knowledge of digital recording; you'll certainly know enough to understand and optimize the process for your application.

Without a basic understanding in this area, you'll constantly be confused and bewildered. Considerations must be addressed in digital recording that are simply not issues in analog recording. Digital recording is amazingly flexible and, as it's matured over the years, has become a brilliant recording process, in many ways unrivaled.

## Analog Recording

It's important that we first share an understanding of the analog recording process. What we learn about digital recording can best be understood when we reference the analog principles and characteristics. Analog recorders utilize a series of transducers, each of which changes one form of energy to another in a continuously variable transfer of energy.

- An acoustic sound source creates waves in air, much like waves in water. These waves are continuously varying air pressure.
- The microphone capsule responds to changes in air pressure, riding the air waves like a surfer rides the waves in the ocean; wherever the wave goes, the mic diaphragm goes.
- As the diaphragm moves, a variance in the flow of electrons is induced, either in a magnet, a ribbon, or a continuously varying capacitor. This variation in the flow of electrons from the microphone is amplified and routed to the record head.
- The record head responds to the mic signal by converting the electrical signal into a continuously changing magnetic flow. The magnet is simply acting as an electromagnet, fed by the signal that originated at the mic capsule.
- Changes in magnetic flow are imprinted on the recording tape and stored for playback.
- The playback head is constantly in the state of being magnetized by the tape. The tape induces a continuously varying magnetism in the playback head.
- The varying magnetic flow from the playback head is converted to an electrical signal that is then sent back to the mixer or to the input of the power amp.
- A power amplifier boosts the level of the signal it receives to the strength required to move a speaker cone back and forth. The

movement of the speaker cone should follow the path of the original signal as it was received at the mic capsule in the first place.

• When the speaker cone moves back and forth, it creates continuously varying changes in the air pressure (waves). If everything goes perfectly, the waves created by the movement of the speaker cone are a precise replica of the waves created by the original sound source as it headed for the microphone.

The above is obviously the condensed version of the analog recording process. There's much more involved but, essentially, those are the key factors. Analog recording has a conceptual edge over digital because it captures a continuously variable change in pressure. There are no discrete steps in the variance in energy levels. Amplitude, electrical flow, flux, and air pressure change in smooth, continuous variation. This system reflects the original waveform in the most accurate way; that's why analog recording continues to be the mixdown media of choice for some.

The problem with analog recording is noise. Even at its best, noise in the analog recording process is louder than noise in the digital domain. Noise reduction and high-quality analog tape have definitely helped analog's signal-to-noise ratio. Nevertheless, the capabilities and creative options provided by modern digi-

## Illustration 4-1
### Analog Wave Compared to Digital Wave (Part 1)

Digital recording is different from analog in that it doesn't operate in a continuous way; it breaks a continuously varying waveform into a sequence of individual amplitude assessments called samples. Digital technology attempts to sample the amplitude enough times per second to accurately recreate the analog waveform. The result is a stair-step version of an originally continuous wave

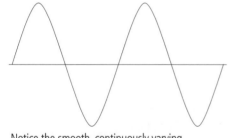

Notice the smooth, continuously varying waveform. This is an analog waveform. To use an analogy to photography, the analog wave form represents reality. The digital waveform, however, represents a grainy picture. The goal in the digital domain is to create a picture with such fine grain that it's not noticed.

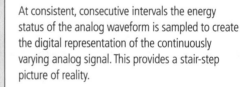

At consistent, consecutive intervals the energy status of the analog waveform is sampled to create the digital representation of the continuously varying analog signal. This provides a stair-step picture of reality.

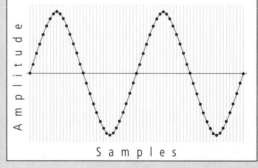

tal equipment are just too awesome to bypass.

Analog multitrack recording is a cumbersome process by today's standards. An analog 24-track recorder typically uses 2-inch tape, with time code striped on track 24. You really should leave a guard band between SMPTE and a recorded track to avoid adverse track interactions due to cross-talk. Audio signal can mess up the time code track, and time code can leak onto the audio track. Therefore, in effect, you're left with a 22-track recorder.

Analog machines do not have the beautiful and wonderful "undo" feature common to digital formats. The only way to repair an unacceptable portion of a lead vocal track is to punch in and out at just the right time. If the vocalist does a good take but convinces the engineer to try the punch again, there may be trouble ahead. Once the punch happens, it can't be reversed, and the vocalist might not be able to perform a comparable take for a long time. Bummer!

Analog master tapes need to be edited with a razor blade. If you want the highest quality audio, you cut the master tapes, and there's no undo. Big bummer!

## Analog vs. Digital

Digital recording is different from analog in that it doesn't operate in a continuous way; it breaks a continuously varying waveform into a sequence of individual amplitude assessments called samples. Digital technology attempts to sample

## Illustration 4-2
### Analog Wave Compared to Digital Wave (Part 2)

Connecting the sample points creates a stair-step version of the analog waveform. The process of changing the analog wave into a digital representation is referred to as analog-to-digital conversion. Conversely, the process of changing the digital picture back into an analog form is called digital-to-analog conversion.

The closer the samples are together, the more accurate the digital version of the waveform. Standard audio compact discs sample at a rate of 44.1 kHz (44,100 times per second). It's suggested that the optimum sample rate might be 192 kHz.

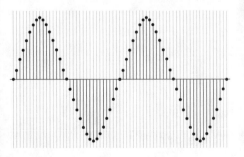

If everything has performed as planned, the digital sample will eventually be converted back into a replica of the original analog wave.

Sampled Waveform

Replica of the Original Waveform

the amplitude enough times per second to accurately recreate the analog waveform. The result is a stair-step version of an originally continuous wave (Illustration 4-1 and 4-2).

Since a digital recorder is typically only referencing digital data stored on a hard drive or other digital storage medium, its actions are usually nondestructive and undoable, with complete provision to perform computer functions like cut, copy, and paste. These feature make for amazing power and manipulative potential. As we jump into the workings of digital recording, we'll see just how capable this system is of providing creative opportunities for building amazing music.

Even with the power offered by digital manipulation of audio data, musical creativity, emotion, passion, and authenticity are essential. No amount of gear can make up for a lack of musical inspiration and talent, but digital tools can help convey the message of a true talent.

They propel the creative process, and, if used properly, won't get in the way and slow things down.

## Physical Properties of Sound

An understanding of the physical properties of sound provides an excellent foundation for the understanding of the digital interpretation of sound. Our ears essentially hear an analog wave; our brain interprets the wave by converting the analog signal to a continuously varying flow of electrons within the brain. As sound arrives at the ears, it has physical properties, governed by and consistent with laws of physics.

In *The AudioPro Home Recording Course, Volume I*, we briefly covered waveform amplitude, frequency, length, harmonics, phase, and speed. I'd like to review and build upon these physical properties of sound, particularly as

## Illustration 4-3
### Amplitude

Amplitude refers to the measure of energy produced by the sound wave in regard to the time axis. A waveform with twice the amplitude creates twice as much energy and has a waveform that's twice as tall. Waveform B has twice the amplitude of waveform A.

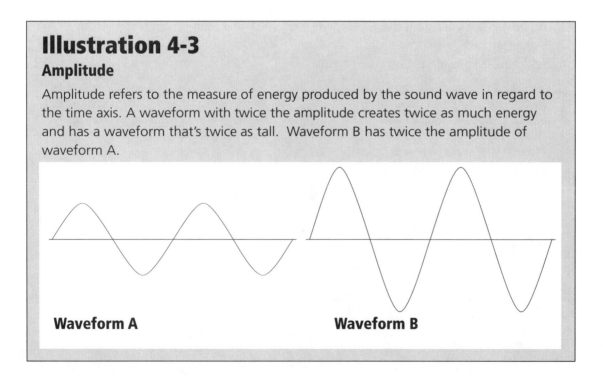

**Waveform A**　　　　　**Waveform B**

they pertain to your forthcoming study of digital recording.

## Amplitude

Amplitude refers to the measure of energy produced by the sound wave in regard to the time axis. A waveform with twice the amplitude creates twice as much energy and has a waveform that's twice as tall. As we delve further into digital recording, we'll see the importance of optimizing the peak amplitude of a sound source.

Amplitude and volume only correlate directly in certain frequency ranges, so, it's not accurate to assume that a sound with twice the energy (amplitude) is always twice as loud (Illustration 4-3).

## Frequency

Frequency refers to the number of times a waveform completes its 360° cycle in one second. The human ear responds to a frequency range of approximately 20Hz to 20kHz. The digital recording process typically filters out frequencies above 20kHz, or so to avoid negative aspects of sampling high-frequency waveforms (Illustration 4-4).

# Illustration 4-4
## Frequency

Frequency refers to the number of times a waveform completes its 360° cycle in one second. The human ear responds to a frequency range of approximately 20Hz to 20kHz. Each consecutive waveform in this Illustration (A, B, C, and D) doubles in frequency.

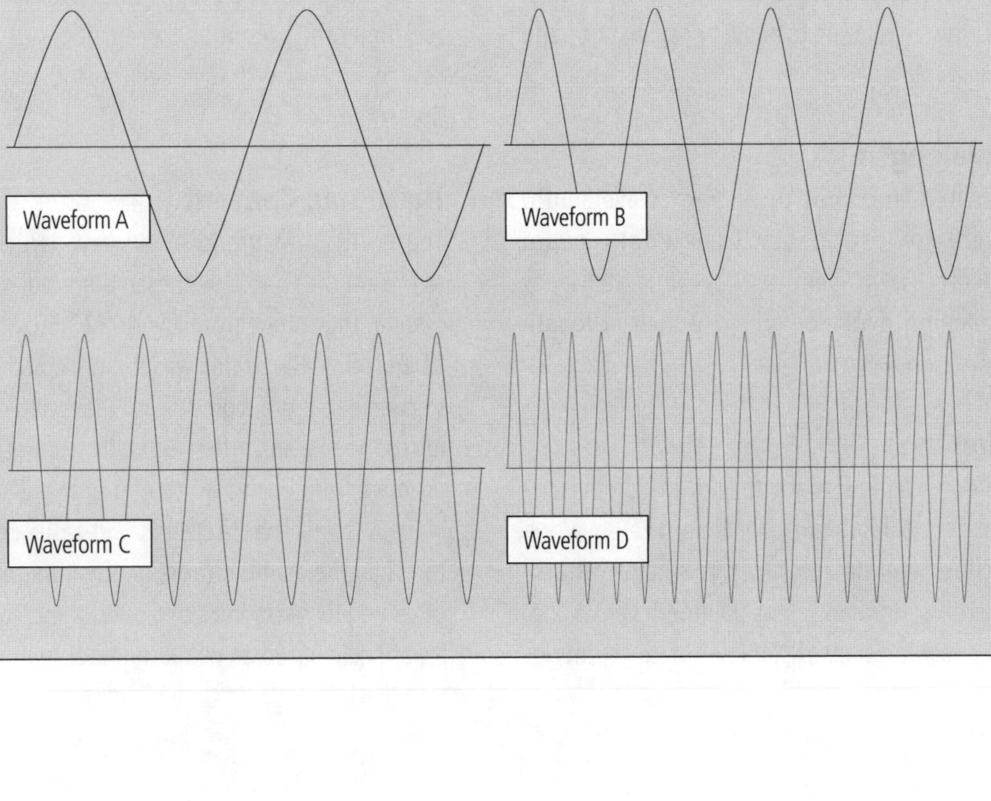

Waveform A

Waveform B

Waveform C

Waveform D

## Illustration 4-5
### Wavelength

Each frequency has a different wavelength. This Illustration is drawn to scale in order to demonstrates the dramatic wavelength difference between the lowest and highest notes on the piano. The piano's lowest note has a frequency of 27.5 Hz and a wavelength of about 41 feet! . Its highest note has a frequency of 4168.01 Hz and a wavelength of only 3.24 inches.

The length of a given frequency is calculated by dividing the speed of sound (1130 feet per second) by the frequency (in Hz). Wavelength $(\lambda)$ =Velocity (feet/sec) ÷ Frequency (Hz)  $\lambda = V/f$

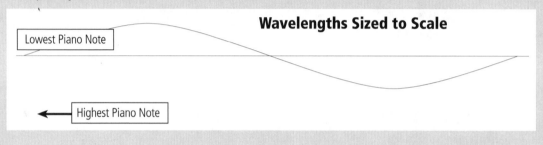

**Wavelengths Sized to Scale**

Lowest Piano Note

Highest Piano Note

## Velocity

Sound travels at the rate of 1130 feet/second at sea level, at about 70° Fahrenheit. This is not a key tidbit for your digital audio study. It's most important in relation to acoustic calculations and predictions.

## Wavelength

Each frequency has a different wavelength. A very low-frequency wavelength could measure 30–40 feet. A very high-frequency wavelength might only be 1/2-inch in length (Illustration 4-5).

## Envelope

Part of a sound's character lies in its development and completion over time. The envelope describes this development. A sound's attack, decay, sustain, and release define its envelope. Any consideration of digital—or any other—recording must include the accuracy of the recording system's dealing with the transient attack and trailing off of the release. A system that can best respond to fast attacks provides the fundamental potential to reproduce a sound source in a way that is accurate, transparent, and clean.

## Harmonic Content

The notes on a grand piano keyboard largely represent the usable pitches in our modern tonal system. They range from low A0 (27.5Hz) to high C8 (4168.01Hz). If this was the only pitch range to consider, there would be no reason to require microphones and other gear to accurately reproduce frequencies up to and above 20kHz.

A sonic character is actually created through the combination of the fundamental pitch and its harmonics and overtones. Harmonics are calculated as whole-number multiples of the fundamental frequency. Therefore, a musical sound with a fundamental frequency of 3kHz, includes several harmonics, along with the fundamental, blended in the unique proportion that creates its own sonic character. The first few harmonics of a 3kHz fundamental pitch are 6kHz, 9kHz, 12kHz, 15kHz, 18kHz, 21kHz, and so on (2 X 3kHz, 3 X 3kHz, 4 X 3kHz, etc.).

The fact that the human ear doesn't typically respond to frequencies above 20kHz does not imply that harmonics and overtones don't exist above 20kHz. They do exist, and they combine with the fundamental in a way that affects the tonal character we hear. Therefore, it's important for our equipment to capture the broadest frequency range possible to guarantee the most accurate and pristine recordings. A heated discussion brews around the discussion of historical archival techniques. Since we know technology advances more and more rapidly over time, it doesn't take much foresight to see that the techniques of today will seem archaic to tomorrow's generation. Therefore, we need to provide the highest quality archives possible for the technology of today so that the data will have relevance tomorrow.

## Phase

Phase involves the relationship of waveforms in time and the interaction between the waves. Two identical waveforms are in phase when they follow exactly the same path throughout the entire 360° wave cycle. Two identical waveforms are out of phase (180°) when the peak of one wave happens at the exact instant that the valley happens on the other.

# Digital Theory

It's important to understand the previous information in order to have a frame of reference to help build an understanding of digital recording. The digital recording concept is actually simple. An energy level reading is taken a specified number of times per second, then recorded on a grid. The individual readings together represent a building-block version of the analog waveform.

Imagine that several times per second an energy reading (called a sample) is taken, measuring the amplitude of an analog sound wave. The first reading measures 9 units of amplitude. The second reading measures three units. The third, fourth, fifth, and sixth readings register 6, 9, 11, and 10 units. These are followed by four more consecutive readings of 11, 9, 6, and 9, then negative values for each of the amplitude measurements. If you were to plot these readings on a graph and draw a line connecting each unit, you'd see the analog waveform represented by this set of discrete amplitude readings. Refer to Illustration 4-6 to see the graphic representation of this scenario.

## What's So Good about Digital Recording?

Both analog and digital recording are ideally transparent—they should represent the real sound faithfully and accurately. Excellent analog recording gear does an amazing job of capturing the depth and warmth of sound. The fact that the information printed on magnetic tape is a true representation of the variations in air pressure, called sound, lends it an indisputable degree of accuracy. However, constant tape hiss

# Illustration 4-6
## Plotting the Digital Wave

Imagine that several times per second an energy reading (called a sample) is taken, measuring the amplitude of an analog sound wave. The first reading measures 9 units of amplitude. The second reading measures three units. The third, fourth, fifth, and sixth readings register 6, 9, 11, and 10 units. These are followed by four more consecutive readings of 11, 9, 6, and 9, then negative values for each of the amplitude measurements.

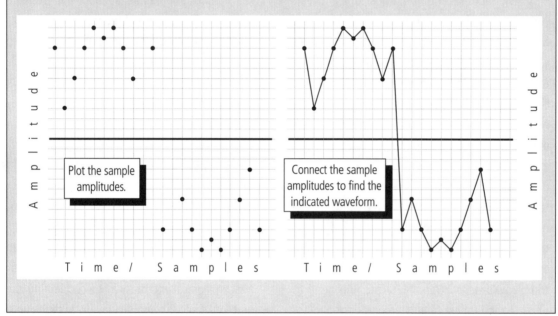

Plot the sample amplitudes.

Connect the sample amplitudes to find the indicated waveform.

is annoying, even at low levels. High-quality equipment minimizes the noise factor of analog tape; as long as the signal level is strong and the orchestration is active, there's little adverse effect from tape noise. But once the sound and orchestration die down, tape noise is distracting and bothersome.

The process of digital recording itself allows for very little noise, unless it comes from the source. The absence of tape hiss is blissful to anyone who struggled through the analog years. A fade to complete silence is taken for granted in the digital era; in the analog days, a fade to silence meant a fade to tape hiss.

Digital recording offers the potential for a system where the copy is as good as the original—an unlikely possibility in the analog domain. Although there's controversy over the accuracy of the digital clone, the possibility is still a theoretical reality. A clone is an exact, number for number, copy of the digital data. Clones are more accurate and dependable when the file stays in the hard disk domain. Copies that go to and from DAT recorders and other such devices are subject to an error correction scheme, therefore running high risk of transferring with several inaccuracies in hard data.

Digital data can be stored on any media

common to computer data storage. A file created on a hard disk recording system can be saved, archived, and played back from several common data storage platforms: magnetic disk, CD, cartridges, or other optical formats. Fast access time is required for playback of digital audio, but the speed requirements are met by most data storage systems.

The cost of storage for digital audio is music less expensive than storage of analog audio. A reel of 2-inch tape—commonly used for 24-track analog recording—might hold 16 minutes of music and cost $175.00. In comparison, an entire album of digital audio can typically be archived on 10 to 15 CDs at a total cost of around $10.00. Data storage is reliable and accurate. In addition, as technology and storage media changes, the data can be easily transferred for future use and long-term archiving.

In the digital domain, the audio becomes data and can be manipulated like any other data. Cut, copy, paste, crossfade, level changes, and undo are common actions. Editing is a dream; the possibilities are boundless.

Digital systems offer an amazing advantage in transport speed. Computer-based systems have no rewind time. Location of musical sections is simple and instantaneous. There is always instant availability of any musical section, track, or instrument. The days of rewinding back and forth through a real of analog tape are fading. Though some still prefer the sound of analog tape and are willing to withstand its pitfalls, working in the disk-based digital domain is far more efficient and hassle free—as long as your computer doesn't crash.

The increase in microprocessor speed in the '90s made this technology affordable and accessible to everyone with a home computer.

Computers are good at taking readings to indicate the status of any energy level at a specific point in time. They're also good at recording that data for future retrieval. In essence, the computer is counting the units of energy (building blocks) at specified time intervals and recording them for a specified duration of time.

## Bits/Bytes/Words

A bit is an individual integer used as part of a group. In my *American Heritage Dictionary*, a bit is defined as:

1. A single character of a language having just two characters, as either of the binary digits 0 or 1.
2. A unit of information equivalent to the choice of either of two equally likely alternatives.
3. A unit of information storage capacity, as of memory—a contraction of B(INARY) and (DIG)IT.

A word is simply a multidigit binary number made up of bits. The number of bits in a word represents the smallest unit of addressable memory in a microprocessor environment (a computer). The number of bits in a word is called its word length.

An 8-bit word is called a byte. The term *byte* comes from the contraction of "by eight," which was derived from the concept of a bit multiplied by eight.

The digit on the left-hand side of the word is called the most significant bit (MSB). The digit on the right-hand side of the word is called the least significant bit (LSB).

## Advantage of Binary Code/PCM

A binary code represents the least possible number of digits for the processing environment, where each representation is compiled of a series of 1s and 0s. Anything that's not 0 is 1. This creates a scenario where there's no question as to the numeric value of a digital code. In digital recording, each value of the sampled waveform is represented by a series of 0s and 1s. Noise on the media is inconsequential, unlike on analog tape. In the digital domain, noise on the actual media or a slight hazing of the data has no real effect on the actual waveform represented. If the D/A converter is sent a 1 in any form, it's registered as a 1. If it's sent a lack of 1, it's registered as a 0.

With only two possible values, methods for encoding and decoding the data flow are simplified. The most common form of digital encoding is Pulse Code Modulation (PCM), where a 1 is represented by the existence of the pulse (pulse on) and 0 is represented by the lack of a pulse (pulse off). With this simple system and a synchronous clock that controls the pulse rate,

## Illustration 4-7
### Pulse Code Modulation

Pulse Code Modulation is a very common means of transmitting digital data. Binary data flow is indicated by a stream of on and off pulses. A pulse indicates the integer one, while the lack of a pulse indicates a zero. This simple means of indicating binary words is common to the digital audio process.

On the sample grid, each of the sample points has a discrete number of possible amplitude steps. These steps are indicated by specific binary numbers which represent the whole numbers used to quantify the closest amplitude step at each sample period.

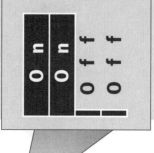

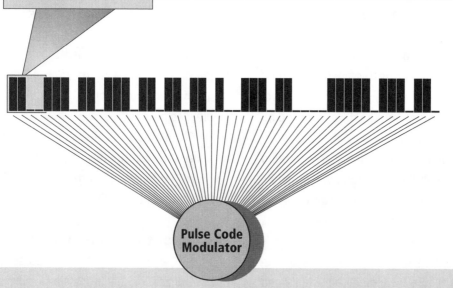

Pulse Code Modulator

it's an elementary matter to read, store, and play back the data. Illustration 4-7 shows the simplicity of the PCM system.

Though noise in the storage media doesn't register as audible noise, it has the potential of confusing the timing values of data being read (played back). Noise is exhibited as slight changes in the waveform pulse definition, relative to time. "On" pulses are stored as a momentary square waves on magnetic tape, or as pits on the surface of an optical media. The ad-

dition of noise doesn't interfere with the processor's recognition of the pulse as a 1, but it might make the processor see the pulse slightly earlier or later than was intended. These discrepancies in timing create a phenomenon known as *jitter*. Jitter is simply an audible timing inconsistency, similar in concept to tape flutter in the analog domain. It's eliminated by locking the playback clock to a stable source so that the pulse grid flows at a solid and controlled rate (44.1kHz for the standard audio CD). All data is

## Illustration 4-8
### Sampling

At each time interval the amplitude is quantified according to the discrete steps available. The number of amplitude steps available is determined by the word size. An 8-bit word allows for 256 discrete steps from amplitude off to peak amplitude. A 16-bit word provides 65,536 amplitude units.

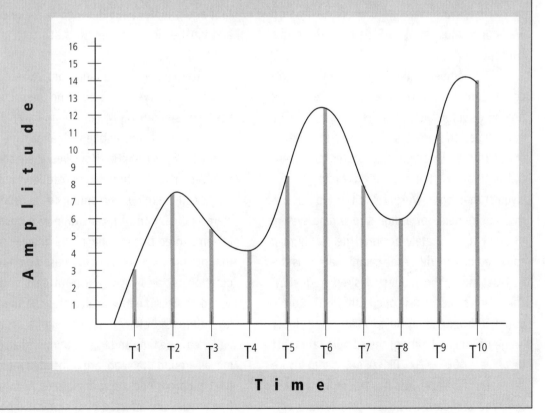

forced to fall neatly into this solidly locked sync grid. Therefore, discrepancies in timing caused by noise on the data storage media are inconsequential. When the flow of data is controlled by an external time reference—time base corrector—the flow of data is said to be phase-locked. It simply joins and follows at the rate of the word clock pulses with no actual time code reference. Since the clock is a stable source, this procedure provides accurate, predictable, and repeatable results.

## Samples

The process of sampling (digital encoding and decoding) breaks the time axis (horizontal) and the voltage axis (vertical) into a specific number of discrete steps. At each step along the time axis, a measurement is taken of voltage (amplitude) status. This process, called sampling, results in a stair-step picture of the analog waveform. Illustration 4-8 demonstrates this concept.

The number of times per second the processor samples the voltage (amplitude) of the analog waveform is called the sample rate. The more times the processor samples the analog status of the waveform, the greater the potential accuracy of the system. According to the Nyquist Theorem—which set out to hypothesize the requirements of a digital recording system in order to accurately portrays the reality of a specified bandwidth—the sample rate must be at least twice the highest desired frequency. Therefore, to accurately and faithfully capture a bandwidth extending up to 20kHz (the upper range of human hearing) the sample rate must be at least 40kHz (2 x 20kHz). In order to insure accuracy and to provide headroom for the system, the standard audio CD sample rate was fixed at 44.1kHz.

Controversy follows the question of whether there is a need for higher sample rates and longer word length. Some feel that a sample rate of 44.1kHz is ample, since filters effectively eliminate any artifacts above 20kHz, and 20kHz is the upper limit of mankind's hearing range. Some feel that a 16-bit word provides more than adequate resolution for accurate audio. However, since all frequencies interact acoustically and work together to create a waveform, it seems believable and practical that capturing a broader frequency range and a more accurate resolution is justifiable. We don't yet realize the impact and result of high-frequency content above 20kHz on the emotional and physical perception of sound. Though the debate continues, many—I think, justifiably—contend that, at the very least, we should be archiving important audio material at the highest sample rate and most exact word length that's technologically feasible.

The concern regarding sample rate isn't simply frequency-related. Since no one, not even the newest born baby, can hear above 25 or 26kHz anyway, the implied ideal sample rate might be 50 to 55kHz. However, there's more involved in our hearing and perception than frequency. Much of our perception comes from our stereo perception of localization and positioning on a three-dimensional plane. The messages that our brain responds to are based on a triangulation process involving both ears and the sound source. The brain calculates the time delay difference between the arrival of a sound at either ear. The time and EQ variations, as a sound moves around the head, are translated into left-right and front-back positioning cues. As the high frequencies are affected by the physical part of the outer ear, called the *pinna*, changes of equalization cue the brain about front-to-back positioning. Perception of left-right positioning is a product of the brain's interpretation of timing differences between the arrival time of a sound at each ear. To complete the system, combined with level changes, the human hearing and localization systems are amazingly complex and efficient.

It's been determined that time delay differences of 15 microseconds between left and right ears are easily discernible by nearly any-

one. That's less than the time difference between two samples at 48kHz (about 20 microseconds). Using a single pulse, one microsecond in length as a source, some listeners can perceive time delay differences of as little as five microseconds between left and right. It is therefore, indicated that, in order to provide a system with exact accuracy concerning imaging and positioning, the individual samples should be less than five microseconds apart. At 96kHz (a popularly preferred sample rate) there is a 10.417-microsecond space between samples. At 192kHz

# Illustration 4-9
## The Ultimate Sample Rate

Sample A represents a 48 kHz sample. The time distance between individual samples, at this rate, is about 20 microseconds (20 millionths of a second). Since many listeners can perceive time delays of as little as 5 microseconds between the left and right channels, it seems obvious that a 48 kHz sample rate is incapable of providing the localization accuracy necessary to guarantee perfectly faithful imaging.

Sample B represents a 192 kHz sample. The samples are just over 5 microseconds apart. The 192 kHz sample offers much greater reliability than other less comprehensive sample rates. Not only does it closely match the perceivable time delay limitation indicated by testing, but also provides much finer resolution for digital storage and reconstruction of the original analog waveform.

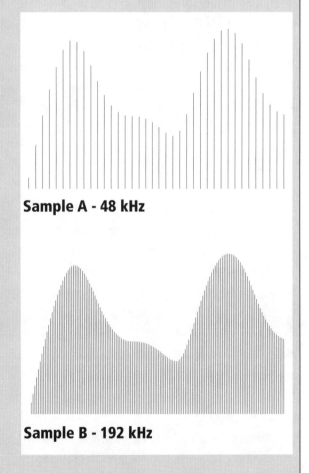

Sample A - 48 kHz

Sample B - 192 kHz

sample rate there is a 5.208-microsecond space between samples. This reasoning suggests that a sample rate of 192kHz is probably a good choice. As processors increase in speed and efficiency and as storage capacity expands high sample rates, long word lengths will become an insignificant concern and we'll be able to focus on the next audio catastrophe. Maybe full integration of tactile virtual audio and video imagery (Illustration 4-9).

## Quantization/Bits

At each sample point, signal strength (amplitude) is calculated. Amplitude, in an analog domain, is continuously variable. In the digital domain, amplitude is measures against a grid of discrete stair steps. The resolution of the stair steps is determined by the binary word length. An 8-bit word offers 256 discrete levels with which to define the momentary amplitude. The more bits in the word, the finer the resolution. A word with more bits can more accurately define the amplitude at each sample point.

At first guess, most of us assume that a 16-bit word offers twice the resolution of an 8-bit word: 512 discrete steps. That is definitely not the case. In reality, each additional bit adds a significant amount of resolution because the increase is calculated exponentially, not through simple addition. If we consider a 1-bit word, there are really only two options: digit on (1) or digit off (0). With this in mind, the number 2 becomes our constant, and the number of bits ($n$) becomes our exponent, expressed as $2^n$— verbally expressed as "2 to the nth power." It simply means two times itself $n$ number of times. The number of discrete steps of resolution available to indicate specific amplitude at any given sample point is easily calculated. If you have an $n$-bit word, where $n$ represents the number of bits, calculate 2 times itself, $n$ number of times. For example, in an 8-bit word, $n = 8$, so the resolution is expressed as $2^8$, or 2 X 2 X 2 X 2 X 2 X 2 X 2 X 2, or 256.

A 1-bit word is mathematically calculated as two to the first power ($2^1$). A 2-bit word offers four steps ($2^2$ or 2 X 2) to calculate amplitude (11, 10, 01, 00). It's easy for us to see all the options when we have small word sizes, but it's also easy to get confused regarding the big picture, so let's continue with our examples. A 3-bit word offers eight steps ($2^3$ or 2 X 2 X 2) of resolution to calculate sample point amplitude: 000, 001, 010, 011, 111, 110, 100, 101. A 4-bit word provides 16 discrete steps ($2^4$ or 2 X 2 X 2 X 2). As the bits increase, the resolution dramatically increases. Notice that each additional bit doubles the resolution; that's the power of the binary system. A change from 16 bits to 18 bits is a full four times greater (400 percent) in resolution; if you calculated incorrectly, you might think there was only a 12.5 percent increase in resolution. The number of steps available to define each sample amplitude in a 16-bit word is calculated as $2^{16}$, which equals 65,536 steps. In comparison, a 24-bit word provides a resolution of 16,777,216 steps per sample point! (Illustration 4-10)

## Aliasing

When a digital recorder attempts to sample a frequency higher than half the sample rate, the sampling process produces inaccurate and randomly inconsistent waveform characteristics. These high frequencies, called *aliasing* frequencies, must be filtered out before they arrive at the A/D converter.

When the audio source bandwidth is prop-

# Illustration 4-10

## Bits and Quantization

This illustration highlights the extreme variation in quantization steps available in differing word length systems. Whereas, a digital audio recording system using an 8-bit word provides 256 steps with which to represent amplitude, a system based on a 24-bit wordlength provides an amazing 16,772,216 steps.

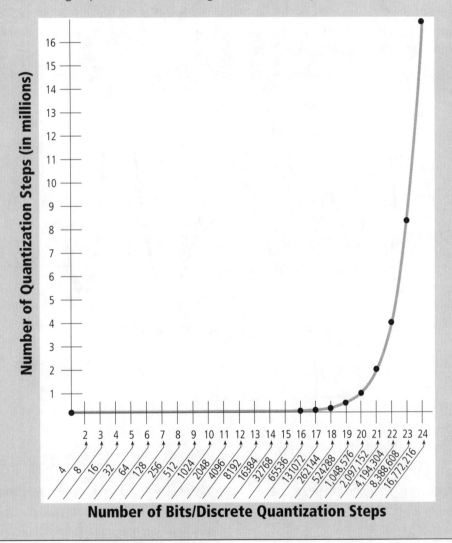

**Number of Quantization Steps (in millions)**

Number of Bits/Discrete Quantization Steps

2 → 4
3 → 8
4 → 16
5 → 32
6 → 64
7 → 128
8 → 256
9 → 512
10 → 1024
11 → 2048
12 → 4096
13 → 8192
14 → 16384
15 → 32768
16 → 65536
17 → 131072
18 → 262144
19 → 524288
20 → 1,048,576
21 → 2,097,152
22 → 4,194,304
23 → 8,388,608
24 → 16,772,216

erly filtered, using a high quality low-pass filter, the sample is accurate and clean. When audio source bandwidth is improperly filtered, the resulting sound is inconsistent with probable random artifacts, sometimes in the lower frequencies. Since low-pass filters cut a bandwidth according to a slope rather than a hard and fast frequency cutoff, sample rates for full bandwidth sound sources are set at about 10 percent higher than twice the highest recorded frequency. This

# Illustration 4-11
## Aliasing

When frequencies are too high, the samples lose accuracy. Since changes in the amplitude of very high frequencies can occur within the spaces between sample points, the resulting digital data representation of the original analog waveform becomes random and ambiguous. It's because of this phenomenon, called aliasing, that sample rates are typically set at twice the user's desired highest frequency. Past this frequency, filters (called anti-aliasing filters) are used to insure that the problem causing high frequencies are eliminated.

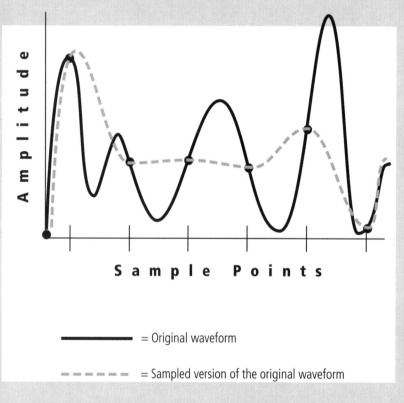

——— = Original waveform

- - - - - = Sampled version of the original waveform

provides processing headroom, assuring the recordist of the best possible sound quality (Illustration 4-11).

## RAM Buffer

Data flow playback rate is important. Since minor distortions, or noise, included in the storage media exhibit the potential to create jitter and other timing anomalies, a system is necessary to stabilize and guarantee accurate and consistent data flow. Digital data, audio in particular, is referenced to a stable, centralized timing clock (word clock) that controls the transmission and conversion of each sample. Samples are played back at a rate controlled by the word clock. In a 16-bit system, the computer progresses through the 16-bit words at the master clock rate. Therefore, data recorded at 48kHz can be played back

## Illustration 4-12
### The Ram Buffer

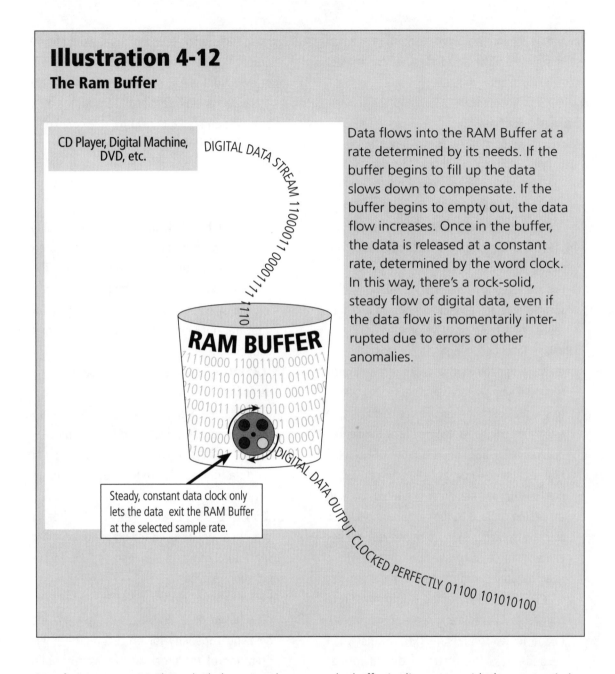

CD Player, Digital Machine, DVD, etc.

DIGITAL DATA STREAM 11000011 0001111 1110

**RAM BUFFER**

11110000 11001100 000011
00010110 01001011 01101
1010101111101110 0001000
1001011 1001010 010101
1010101 01 01001
110000 0 00001
100101 0 01010

DIGITAL DATA OUTPUT CLOCKED PERFECTLY 01100 101010100

Steady, constant data clock only lets the data exit the RAM Buffer at the selected sample rate.

Data flows into the RAM Buffer at a rate determined by its needs. If the buffer begins to fill up the data slows down to compensate. If the buffer begins to empty out, the data flow increases. Once in the buffer, the data is released at a constant rate, determined by the word clock. In this way, there's a rock-solid, steady flow of digital data, even if the data flow is momentarily inter-rupted due to errors or other anomalies.

in reference to a 44.1kHz clock (or any other word clock speed), but its pitch and speed will adjust relative to the playback sample rate.

As an assurance that the playback rate will remain constant and stable, the processor stores up a certain amount of data as a backup—a buffer. This buffer protects the system from pre-maturely running out of data. Data flows from the buffer in direct sync with the master timing clock. The tape speed or disc access is deter-mined by the needs of the RAM buffer. If data is emptying out of the RAM buffer, the tape speeds up to fill it in, or the disk picks up the pace to keep up with the data flow. There is no pitch variation, since the RAM buffer outputs the data at an extremely constant rate, which is determined by the internal word clock, or in external sync source by the word clock of the master device (Illustration 4-12).

## Sample Rates

The number of times a processor samples a waveform is often definable by the user. Nevertheless, standard sample rates apply to specific applications. Most of the following sample rates are common in the digital audio industry.

**44.1kHz** – The standard sample rate for an audio compact disc is 44,100 times per second (also referred to as 44.1kHz, or 44.1k). At this sample rate, it's possible to get an accurate replica of an analog waveform.

**48kHz** – Another common sample rate is 48kHz. It was originally held as more of a semiprofessional sample rate, until recordists began to see that even the small increase in sample rate from 44.1k to 48k made a noticeable difference in the sound quality. Many very high-quality recordings have been mixed to 48kHz sample rate, then mastered through an analog process to the digital compact disc format. In fact, 48kHz sampling quickly became the preferred professional format whenever the project didn't require direct transfer to CD. When developing audio for direct transfer to CD, most engineers prefer to work in the lesser format (44.1kHz) rather than second-guess the effect of digital format conversion.

**32kHz** – The broadcast standard is 32kHz. Most radio broadcasts are operated within the limitations of a 15kHz bandwidth, so a sample rate of 32kHz is a perfect fit. The slower sample rate utilizes about 27.44 percent less storage space, letting radio stations put more programming on each media. Considering

radio's limited bandwidth, there would be no practical benefit to broadcasting at 44.1, 48, or even 96kHz. Any radio show or other program being simultaneously broadcast over airwaves and full bandwidth cable could only optimize their sound quality by transmitting at the full-bandwidth frequency du jour.

**44.056kHz** – This is the original Sony PCM-F1 sample rate.

**22.050 and 11.125kHz** – These lower fidelity sample rates are used primarily in computer-specific documents (Macintosh or PC). The primary purpose of this sample rate is limiting file size for use in programming or for data transmission in low baud rate Internet connections.

**11.125kHz** – This is a low fidelity sample rate used primarily in computer specific documents. Like the 22.5kHz sample rate, the primary purpose in considering this sample rate is limiting file size for use in programming or for data transmission in low baud rate Internet connections.

**22.254 and 11.127kHz** – These low fidelity sample rates are used for playback on older Macintosh computers that don't support 16-bit audio playback.

**96kHz** – Samples performed at 96kHz are typically based on a 24-bit word. They provide amazing capability for precise digital interpretation of the broadest bandwidth audio source. A 16-bit, 44.1kHz sample provides for 2,890,137,600 possible options (grid points) per second to define the analog waveform. On the other hand, consider that a 96kHz, 24-bit waveform supplies a grid of 1,610,612,736,000 possible points per second with which to define the wave. It seems obvious that the 24-bit, 96kHz sample is great way to go—if you have enough room to store all the data.

**192kHz** – Some feel this is the optimum sample rate, primarily because it offers sufficient resolution for precise localization information.

Listen to the following audio examples comparing the sonic character of a few different sample rates. Each example was recorded into its particular format, then rerecorded through the analog outs into a digital editing workstation, so as to capture as much of the personality of each sample rate as possible.

*Audio Example  4-1 44.1 kHz*
*CD-1: Track 68*

*Audio Example  4-2 48 kHz*
*CD-1: Track 69*

*Audio Example  4-3 32 kHz*
*CD-1: Track 70*

*Audio Example  4-4  22.050 kHz*
*CD-1: Track 71*

*Audio Example  4-5 11.025 kHz*
*CD-1: Track 72*

# Dither/Quantization Error

At especially low signal levels, the digital recording system performs very poorly. In a 16-bit sys-tem, a low-level signal, around 10 percent of maximum level, uses just under two bits to record whatever audio signal is present. These low-level signals are common during the fadeout of a commercial song and during classical recordings: symphony, choir, string quarter, etc.

Listen to Audio Example 4-6 through 4-8 for a demonstration of the digital recording system's efficiency at these low levels.

*Audio Example 4-6  8-bit Digital Audio*
*CD-1: Track 73*

*Audio Example 4-7  6-bit Digital Audio*
*CD-1: Track 74*

*Audio Example 4-8  3-bit Digital Audio*
*CD-1: Track 75*

Dither is simply white noise added to the program source at very low levels (typically half the least significant bit). Though it seems ironic to add noise to an otherwise noiseless system, the inaccuracies and waveform distortions of these low-level signals must be addressed.

Dithering provides a means to more accurate recording at low levels. Noise combines with the signal in a way that increases the overall amplitude, therefore realizing greater accuracy through increased bits. In fact, dither enables the encoding of amplitudes smaller than the LSB.

Dither combines with the outgoing digital signal in a way that combines for linearity of audio playback. Although it uses noise as an active part of the process, dithering is worth-

# Illustration 4-13
## Dither

Dither is simply white noise added to the program source at very low levels (typically half the least significant bit). Though it seems ironic to add noise to an otherwise noiseless system, the inaccuracies and waveform distortions of these low-level signals must be addressed.

Success is achieved through the combination of the lowest level bits with specific noise. The noise fuses with low-level digital signal in a way that results in noise blocks rather then stair steps. When these blocks are converted to analog, the result is the average of the level across the time axis. The average closely approximates a smooth waveform. This is far different from what would have been a very inaccurate and grainy sounding facsimile of the original waveform. Dither, though inducing noise, provides a means to more accurate, and pleasing sounding audio at low digital levels.

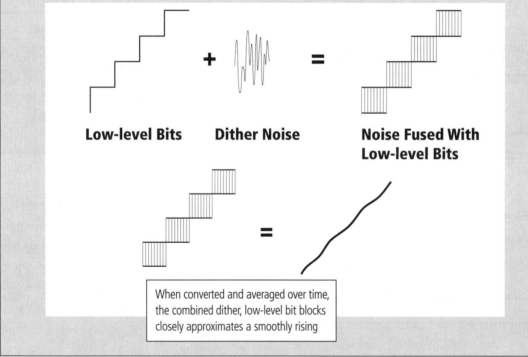

**Low-level Bits**    **Dither Noise**    **Noise Fused With Low-level Bits**

When converted and averaged over time, the combined dither, low-level bit blocks closely approximates a smoothly rising

while, considering the improvement it gives us in accuracy and linearity.

Illustration 4-13 shows a graphic example of the benefit of dither in the conversion process.

Dither is typically selected as a function at the input to the A/D converter or on its output.

The correlation between error and signal can be removed through the addition of dither, prior to the A/D converter. Therefore, the effects of quantization error are randomized. Dither doesn't simply mask the artifacts; it removes them.

Dithering is typically left for the final stage of production. A recordist should rely on the mastering stage of a project to reap the advantages of dithering.

## Noise Shaping

Noise shaping is a part of the dithering process. It helps shift the dither noise into a less audible frequency range to provide the best results with the least audible noise. Digital filters move the dither noise out of the ear's most sensitive frequency range (about 4kHz) and into a less noticeable range. Noise shaping is not a necessary part of the dithering process, but it helps optimize the process through decreased audible noise.

Two types of noise shaping commonly occur in the mastering process:

- **First-Order Noise Shaping** – White noise is optimized for dithering by including a first-order highpass response that rolls off at 6dB/octave below 15kHz.
- **Second-Order Noise Shaping** – White noise is optimized for dithering by including a second-order highpass response that rolls off at 12dB/octave below 20kHz. This scheme also includes a dip in response at 4kHz, where the ear is most sensitive. The actual amount of noise induced by second-order noise shaping is greater the in first-order shaping. However, second-order shaping results in noise that's less audible.

# Converters

Sound originates naturally in an analog manner. The waveform created by any acoustic sound source is analog in that it consists of continuously varying amplitude. The device that calculates the digital equivalent of the analog waveform is called the digital-to-analog (A/D) converter. It samples at the proper rate, and it performs all the functions necessary to insure accurate and dependable transfer of amplitude variations into a continuous binary data flow. The importance of the converter quality is paramount to successful and satisfactory digital recording.

The digital-to-analog (D/A) converter receives the digital data flow at its input and converts the digital information into an analog voltage. Ideally, a signal that starts acoustically and is then converted to digital data will match its analog source once its converted from data back to acoustic analog voltage.

A/D and D/A conversion is very complex. The conversion process must happen synchronous with the storage media, the quantization rate must be stable and controlled, and the converter must be capable of accurately handling the bulk of data involved in high-quality digital audio.

The math involved in this conversion is impressive. The speed with which the data must be processed is overwhelming. The accuracy and clarity of digital recording is amazing. Sampling and quantization are performed by the A/D converter. The D/A converter simply plots the quantized samples back into a continuously varying analog form.

## Oversampling

The purpose of oversampling is to increase the accuracy of the conversion system. The actual process creates a conversion that allows for a gently sloped and less intrusive anti-aliasing filter. Traditional sample recording and playback call for an extreme "brick wall" filter at the Nyquist Frequency (half the sample rate). A less extreme filter causes less phase error and results in a cleaner, smother digital conversion.

The oversampling process is ingenious, requiring a processor capable of high sample rates. Typical oversample systems operate at between 2 and 128 times the regular sample

## Illustration 4-14
### Oversampling

Graph A exhibits the original sample amplitudes of a digital recording that hasn't been oversampled. The analog waveform is indicated accurately but an extreme filter would be necessary to insure against aliasing problems.

Graph B exhibits an eight times oversample of the waveform represented by Graph A. The gray sample amplitudes (S1, S2, S3, etc.) represent the original samples. The black amplitudes , between the gray ones, represent the processor generated and interpolated oversamples. In oversampling the processor creates several zero level samples between the originals. The processor then interpolates (guesses) at what the values of the oversamples should be and adjusts their amplitudes appropriately. Interpolation, in the oversampling process, is fairly accurate, especially when the waveforms are free from data errors or other discrepancies.

Digital audio that has been oversampled is much less prone to aliasing problems. Therefore, anti-aliasing can be designed for a more gentle and natural filtering, while yielding fewer detrimental influences on the final sonic quality.

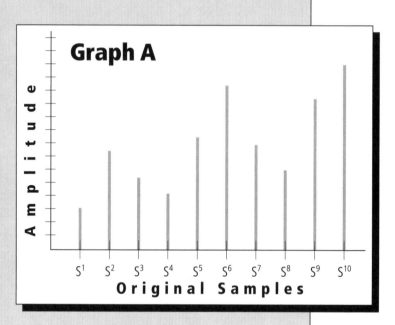

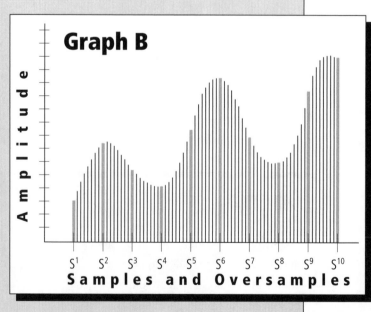

rate. As an example, at eight times oversampling, seven artificial samples are created between the actual samples, all at zero level. Now there are eight samples in the place of the original one, increasing the sample rate by a factor of eight. A 44.1kHz sample rate would, therefore, be increased to 352.8kHz. The seven blank (zero level) samples are interpolated by the processor. In other words, it guesses what their values would be according to the status of the original samples (Illustration 4-14).

Oversampling typically occurs at both ends of the digital data flow. Incoming analog waveforms are oversampled into the A/D converter, providing all the benefits of the oversampling process. For data storage, a circuit called a decimator reverts the high sample rate to the Nyquist rate (44.1kHz in the case of the standard CD). On playback, the digital data is again oversampled by passing through a digital filter called an interpolator. This process allows for the best of both worlds, since the data is efficiently and accurately converted, recorded, and played back. In addition, data storage is at the Nyquist rate rather than the increased rate, providing concise storage and premium audio quality.

## Dynamic Range

The dynamic range of any digital recording system is, roughly, six times the number of bits. The dynamic range of a 16-bit system is about 96dB; the dynamic range of a 24-bit system is about 144dB.

## Format Conversion

Digital format conversion is common and involves converting from one sample rate to another as well as between basic languages (S/P DIF, AES/EBU, TDIF, etc.). The simplest conver-

sions utilize unchanged data with variations in ID codes. Complex format conversions relate sample rates and word length in a mathematical manner. Then it's up to the processor to calculate the comparison.

Format conversions can take quite a while to perform because of the bulk of calculated data. A processor converting a 24-bit 48kHz sample to a 16-bit 32kHz sample must recalculate the sample positions of the new format in relation to the old. Not only does the processor have to calculate the new format data, it also has to interpret the original data and translate it to a form that can then be interpreted. As processor speeds and data transmission rates increase, format conversion will become more accurate and tolerable.

Most conversion software offers different degrees of accuracy in format conversion. In some situations, good sample rate conversion is acceptable: a quick demo, a reference copy, or even an AM radio spot. For music that you've toiled over for countless hours, pouring your complete heart and soul into, go for the best conversion quality. Keep in mind that the better the conversion quality, the longer the process takes. At the highest quality, conversion of a few songs could take several hours. Processing speed is very important here. If you're doing much serious format conversion at all, buy the fastest computer on the planet. The extra money you spend will be more than made up in the amazing savings in time you'll enjoy.

# Errors

It's not practical to expect error-free digital recordings. There's always a chance of imperfections in the media or momentary noise interference with the flow of data. An environment with an ideal signal-to-noise ratio doesn't eliminate the chance of errors. Although it might minimize the chance of errors, it offers no guarantee that they won't happen. Error correction schemes offer a way to overcome error problems, often in a way that restores the data to its original form. However, certain repairs are merely approximations of the original data. These schemes explain the change in audio quality associated with multiple digital copies, especially in the sequential digital recording mediums like DAT.

In the digital domain, two types of data errors occur frequently: bit errors and burst errors. Occasional noise impulses cause bit inaccuracies. These bit errors are more or less audible, depending on where the error occurs within the word. Errors in the least significant bit (LSB) will probably be masked, especially in louder passages. On the other hand, errors in the most significant bit (MSB) can cause a loud and irritating transient click or pop.

Tape dropouts or other media imperfections, like scratches on a disk, can cause errors in digital data flow called burst errors. Burst errors, like bit errors, are potentially devastating to conversion of data to audio, especially considering that they represent larger areas of data confusion.

## Data Protection

Given that errors are certain to occur, a system called *interleaving* is commonly used to minimize the risk of losing large amounts of data. Interleaving data is similar in concept to diversifying investments. If you spread your money between several investments, there's little chance you'll lose it all. Similarly, interleaving

spreads the digital word out over a noncontiguous section of storage media. That way, if a bit or burst error corrupts data, it probably won't corrupt an entire word or group of words. The damage will only affect part of the word, and the likelihood is great that correction schemes will sufficiently repair any losses.

Interleaving happens at both ends of the digital recording process. From A/D, converter data is interleaved as it stores on the media. Just before the data is returned to an analog form, the interleaved data is reconstructed to its original form. This clever scheme provides a system that is completely faithful to the original data, while spreading the risk of damaged or lost data. Illustration 4-15 shows how this useful system works.

## Error Detection

Most error correction schemes utilize a form of a codeword to indicate the existence of an error and to indicate the possible actions necessary for correction. A codeword is made up of additional bits added to each digital word. These bits typically indicate certain traits of the digital word. They're used as a means to verify the integrity of data storage and transfer.

Parity is the most basic form of error detection. The parity system simply adds one bit, called the "parity bit," to each word and attaches a meaning to its status. If there are an even number of 1s in a word, the parity bit status is set to 1. If there's an odd number of 1s in a word, the parity bit is set to 0. Once the parity bits have been set in the record process, they can be checked in the playback process. Parity is checked on each word during conversion to analog. If a bit has been damaged, causing a discrepancy in the relationship between the odd-

# Illustration 4-15
## Interleaving

The interleaving scheme inputs the samples into a grid in numerical order. Once in the grid, they're then sent out in a way that redistributes the sample order. Whereas, the samples enter the grid in rows, they exit the grid in columns. Since sequentially consecutive samples are physically separated during storage, any disk related errors probably won't catastrophically damage audio quality. It is, however, imperative that the samples are put back into their correct order before playback.

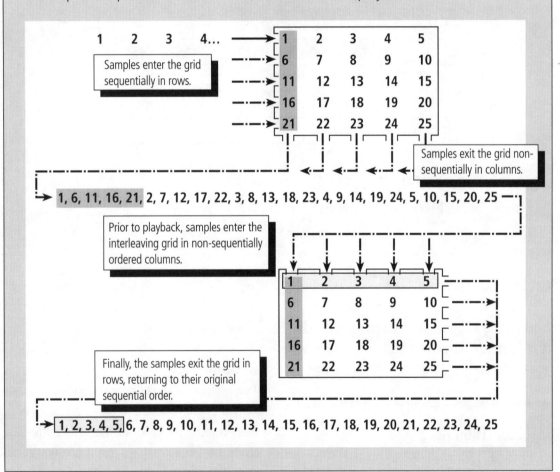

even status of the word and the parity bit, the word is identified to be in error. This is a simple system and introduces an important concept to error detection, though it begins to fail anytime an more than one of the 1 bits have been damaged. In addition, it offers no means of identifying which bit has been damaged (Illustration 4-16).

There are more elaborate codeword systems based on the principal of parity that are more suited to the complex task of faithfully correcting audio data. They extend the concept to

## Illustration 4-16
### Parity

The parity system simply adds one bit, called the "parity bit," to each word. If there are an even number of 1s in a word, the parity bit status is set to 1. If there's an odd number of 1s in a word, the parity bit is set to 0. Whereas, the parity bits are set in the record process, they're checked on each word during playback and conversion to analog. For example, if a word has been tagged for even parity (an even number of 1s) then on playback an odd number of 1s is detected, the word is recognized to be in error. A word recognized in error will be bypassed.

| DATA | Parity Bit | Error Status |
|------|-----------|-------------|
| 1100 0011 0110 0011 | 1 | OK |
| 1100 0011 0110 0011 | 0 | error |
| 0110 0000 1111 0100 | 0 | OK |
| 1010 0100 1000 0001 | 1 | error |
| 0001 0011 0010 0111 | 0 | OK |
| 1100 0011 0110 0011 | 1 | OK |

include additional bits in a complex mathematical relationship to create parity words out of blocks of data. Cyclic Redundancy Check Code (CRCC), Reed-Solomon Codes, Hamming Codes, and Convolutional Codes are examples of these.

# Error Correction

The beauty of the binary system is that data is either correct or incorrect. There's no coloration or subjective influence as there is in the analog domain. If the data is incorrect and it can be identified, there's only one step to correcting it— change the incorrect 1 to a 0, or vice versa. The trick is finding the error, not correcting it.

There are two basic principles behind er-
ror correction: redundancy and concealment. Within these systems, several error correction schemes might be put into action.

## Redundancy

True redundancy involves storing the same data in two or more separate areas on the media, then comparing and reconstructing the data based on those comparisons. If one word contains an error and it can be determined as such, the redundant word or words can be used to verify and restore the data to its original state. The problems with a simple redundancy system lie in the dramatically increased storage capacity and processing speed requirements. Therefore, clever schemes have been developed that add bits to each word to assist in the detection of any questionable data. Though these systems might or might not be successful all the time, they offer partial correction, at the very least. Remaining errors can be handled through concealment or muting.

## Concealment

If data is lost altogether and cannot be reconstructed through a redundancy system, it can be reconstructed through an educated guess on the part of the processor. If a word is missing or corrupt, this scheme simply looks at the word before and after the error, then calculates the average of the two and places it in the gap. This process of mathematical guesswork is called *interpolation*. Though it doesn't guarantee the exact replacement of the lost data, it typically provides a reasonable facsimile that is inaudible in most cases.

## Muting

There is also a protection system in place in case error correction fails. In the case of gross errors, the system simply mutes the particular word or words in question. This is typically an infrequent occurrence and, as such, inaudible in most cases.

# Digital Recording, Transmission, and Digital Playback Formats

There are several different standards for transmission of digital audio signals. Each format is, in theory, capable of accurately transferring a binary bit stream. As long as each 1 and 0 is faithfully communicated in its original form, there should be no degradation at all in the signal from one piece of digital equipment to the next. However, if you find yourself in the middle of a room full of experienced audio gurus, you will definitely walk away wondering if any format will ever provide perfect cloning. The validity to each argument for or against AES/EBU, S/P DIF, S/DIF-2, fiber optics, MADI, or any of the proprietary systems lies in the quantification of errors. Cable quality and length also play a role in the accuracy of the digital transfer.

Audio Examples 4-9 through 4-13 compare an original source to three different digital copying formats and a straight analog to analog transfer. The example was recorded first to DAT at 44.1kHz, then transferred though the specified process. Each example was then transferred digitally into a computer for editing in Digidesign's Pro Tools. The Pro Tools files became the source for digital mastering. The only variable in each chain was the digital transfer process in question. Listen carefully to each example and tally your opinion.

1. Original source (acoustic guitar-oriented)
2. AES/EBU
3. S/P DIF
4. Fiber-optics through the ADAT light-pipe
5. Analog out of DAT A to analog in of DAT B

*Audio Example 4-9 Original Acoustic Guitar*
*CD-1: Track 76*

*Audio Example 4-10 AES/EBU*
*CD-1: Track 77*

*Audio Example 4-11 S/P DIF*
*CD-1: Track 78*

Audio Example 4-12
*Fiber-optics/ADAT Light-pipe*
*CD-1: Track 79*

Audio Example 4-13
*DAT Analog Output to DAT Analog Input*
*CD-1: Track 80*

## AES/EBU

This stereo audio protocol is a professional standard for digital audio transmission between various digital devices. This file transfer format was developed jointly by the Audio Engineering Society (AES) and the European Broadcasting Union (EBU). The 2-channel digital signal is transferred through a single high-quality mic cable using XLR connectors. This low-impedance transfer system allows for cable runs of up to about 100 meters with minimal degradation, offering accurate transmission over longer cable runs than the other formats.

## S/P DIF

The Sony/Philips Digital Interface (S/P DIF) is often available on professional digital equipment, though it's really the standard for digital transmission between consumer devices. The digital transmission process is similar to AES/EBU but is not the same, nor is it cross-compatible. S/P DIF format typically uses RCA phono connectors, allowing accurate transmission over much shorter cables than AES/EBU. S/P DIF protocol provides for digital transmission of start ID and program ID numbers, whereas AES/EBU

does not.

## SDIF-1

One of the pioneer formats in the digital recording industry was the Sony PCM-F1. It used a conventional video tape recorder to store digital audio information, with both channels of the stereo signal multiplexed onto a single video line. The PCM-F1 used the consumer version of Sony's SDIF (Sony Digital Interface Format) protocol. The professional version of the SDIF protocol was used on the Sony PCM-1600 and PCM-1610 converters, typically recording to a 3/4-inch U-Matic professional-format video tape recorder. This combination was the preferred mastering system for years. SDIF and SDIF-1 are the same format. The term SDIF-1 came into use to differentiate the protocol from its successor, SDIF-2.

## SDIF-2

Sony's PCM-1630 mastering system updated the SDIF protocol to use separate cables for left and right channels, along with a word clock channel on a third cable, for syncing accurate digital transfers between SDIF-2 systems. SDIF-2 allows for backward compatibility with SDIF encoded tapes—anything recorded on the older format will play back on the new. This protocol allows for up to 20-bit digital audio. It also includes various control and synchronization bits in each word.

## SMDI

The SCSI Musical Digital Interface is used to transfer digital samples between SCSI equipped samplers and computers. This protocol is up to 300 times faster than a simple MIDI transfer is, and its connections are made with standard SCSI interface cables.

## MADI

The MADI (Multichannel Audio Digital Interface) protocol defines the professional standard for the transmission of multichannel digital audio. This transmission scheme is compatible with many professional digital recorders and mixers, allowing for the transmission of up to 56 tracks of full-bandwidth digital audio.

## DASH

The DASH (Digital Audio Stationary Head) format is used in high-quality digital multitracks. Sony and Studer offer reel-to-reel multitrack recorders in 2-, 24-, and 48-track versions. The multitracks use 1/2-inch tape with provision for either a 44.1 or a 48kHz sample rate. These recorders are very expensive and there are uncommon in home studios.

# Digital Audio File Formats

Most hard disk–based recorders import multiple types of digital file formats. If the recorder cannot directly import the format, there is typically a conversion option capable of changing nearly any digital audio file to the type preferred by the device.

## Sound Designer and Sound Designer II

These are the native file formats used by Digidesign products such as Pro Tools, Session, and Master List CD.

## AIFF–Apple's Audio Interchange File Format

AIFF files are preferred by most Macintosh applications. This file can be used in various soft-ware applications, but they're best suited to use in the Macintosh environment.

## WAV–Windows Audio File Format

The WAV file format is supported by most Windows software applications and many Macintosh applications, though many applications require format conversion to operate optimally.

WAV files are common in the broadcast industry. When sending source material to a computer-driven radio environment, it's common to save 32kHz WAV files to CD in an ISO 9660 format. These files can be transferred directly to the broadcast environment with no format conversion.

Be sure to use the proper suffix. In the audio industry, Macintosh users don't need to consider file naming as an important from-driven procedure. However, anything entering the Windows environment must have the proper suffix or it simply won't work (who thought of this feature anyway?). Always name your WAV file labels with a .WAV extension when they're headed for Windows (e.g., SONG1.WAV).

## QuickTime

QuickTime is commonly used in multimedia applications. Developed by Apple, this audio format is best when in the multimedia authoring environment, using software like Adobe Premiere or Macromedia Director.

## RealAudio

RealAudio is Progressive Network's format for streaming audio over the Internet. This format allows for various sample and bit rates. Since this is an Internet format, audio quality and accuracy might be sacrificed, depending on the specific application. For example, sometimes an

Internet file needs to be quickly downloadable, and audio quality is sacrificed in the interest of file size conservation.

This file format also lets the user determine whether the Internet surfer can download the audio file to their computer or to their portable audio file player. On the other hand, they can also prohibit the RealAudio file downloading altogether.

### SND Resource

The Apple sound resource file type is supported by some Mac software applications, but it's also commonly used by the Macintosh operating for alert sounds and other system-specific audio applications.

# Storage Mediums

Once we enter the digital arena, our music, no matter how artistically inspired or created, becomes data. The simple beauty surrounding this concept lies in the inherent ability to store, restore, copy, paste, encode, and decode this data with, theoretically, no degradation. Once a musical piece is transformed into digital data, there's little significance as to its storage format. As long as the medium is capable of reading and writing quickly enough to avoid a data bottleneck, the data should be stored and retrieved accurately. The primary consideration is the data storage protocol. Does the medium use an error correction scheme, or does it simply transfer the binary file bit by bit?

# Backing Up

Be sure to take the time to regularly back up all data files. If you've had a particularly rough day in the studio, that's a great reason to back up all your files—who wants to relive a bad day?

Storage medium has become so inexpensive that there's no real excuse not to back up. When I'm in the middle of an intense recording time, I back up at the end of each day. Anything that has been changed is backed up. Sometimes, if a file is so huge that it won't easily fit on the backup format I happen to be using, I'll simply copy the entire file to another place on my hard drive. This is a quick process, and I can simply set it to copy and leave.

In the modern world of recording, large drives are inexpensive, and a good DVD drive can save the day. Regular backups can save the day—and the project.

### CD–Compact Disc

The standard compact disc holds 650 megabytes of audio, video, or computer data. This medium revolutionized the public perceptions and expectations regarding the audio world. Sound without scratches, pops, clicks, and hiss was easy to get used to. As a storage medium, they offer an inexpensive option to the high-priced portable hard drive formats.

A CD holds 74 minutes of stereo sound at a sample rate of 44.1kHz with a 16-bit word length.

The CD recording process uses a 4 3/4-inch reflective disk to store data. The data writer creates tiny bumps on the disk surface in correlation to the binary bits. The read head shines an intense beam of light at the disk surface, perceiving each bump through the change in light reflection caused by the bumps themselves. In the absence of a bump, the light is reflected directly to a sensor. The presence of any bump or pit interrupts that reflection, instantly signaling a change in status of digital data. The concept is simple when you know that the presence or absence of a bump on the disk surface merely indicates a variation between 1 and 0. What is mind boggling is the speed at which these changes are recognized

## HD-CD

A high-density compact disk (HD-CD) operates on exactly the same principle as the standard CD—the difference lies in how large and closely grouped the bumps are. An 8x HD-CD has eight times as many bumps in the same amount of space as the standard CD. These bumps are also eight times smaller than the standard CD; therefore, the beam of light required to read the high-density disk must be at least eight times smaller than the standard CD reader.

## CD-R and CD-RW–Recordable and Rewriteable Compact Disc

CD-R disks can only be recorded once, but they can be read any number of times. The early versions of this concept were called WORM drives (Write Once-Read Many). Rewriteable CDs can be reused just like a floppy disk or a regular hard drive. Though the CD-RW disks cost much more than the CD-R disks, they can be cost effective when you know you'll be continually updating data, as is the case with regular data back up.

Like the CD, a CD-R or CD-RW is nonspecific as to the type of data stored on it.

## DAT

The digital audio tape recorder (DAT) was an instant hit in the recording community. It was really the first digital recorder to become universally accepted and used in the recording industry. Before DAT, Sony offered the F-1 processor, which required setup in conjunction with a video tape recorder, but it didn't come on with the same fire as DAT.

DAT tapes are small, storing up to two hours of full-bandwidth stereo audio. The transport mechanism offers fast rewind and fast forward speed, and the machines typically allow for multiple sample rates (32, 44.1, and 48kHz). Keep in mind that the number of minutes available on each tape increases in direct proportion to the decrease in sample rate. Therefore, you can record more minutes of audio on a DAT tape at 32kHz than you can at 44.1kHz.

DAT recorders typically operate using 16-bit linear PCM code, though some DAT recorders also use a 24-bit word capable of very fine resolution.

The DAT recording process that has survived is technically called R-DAT, for Rotating-Head Digital Audio Tape Recorder. This system operates much like a standard video tape recorder. The rotating head helical scan path increases the overall head-to-tape contact speed so that the amount of data required to record high-quality digital audio will fit onto a tape moving at slow speeds (Illustration 4-17).

## MiniDisc

This digital format, like CD, holds up to 74 minutes of full-bandwidth stereo audio. Though it accepts the same 16-bit audio source as a CD, it utilizes a data compression scheme called Adaptive Transform Acoustic Coding (ATRAC).

# Illustration 4-17
## Rotating Head Recorders

Digital Audio Tape recorders (DAT), video tape based recording systems, and most modular digital multitracks utilize a video recorder style transport. Tape is moved, at a relatively slow rate, past a rotating record/playback head. Although the head rotates in the same direction as the tape, it rotates at about 2000 rpm, dramatically increasing the amount of tape to head contact speed and time. It's this process which provides the bandwidth necessary to store high-quality, high-density digital audio.

In addition to digital audio tracks, these systems typically provide one or two analog tracks along with a control track for device synchronization.

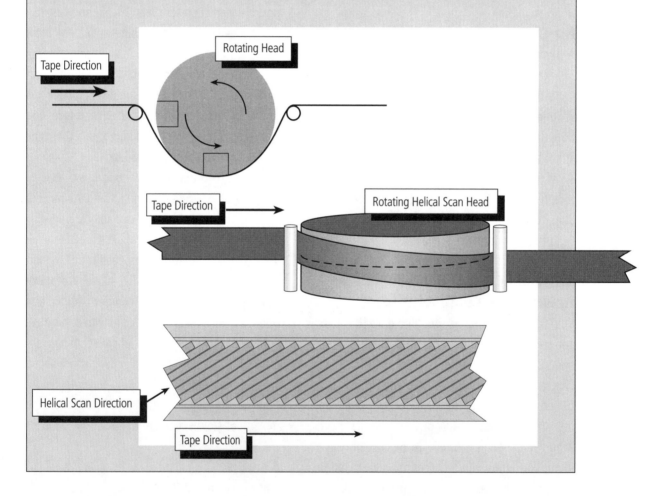

This compression architecture essentially eliminates the inaudible part of each word. It relies on the fact that any resultant artifacts or audio inconsistencies will probably be masked by the remaining sound, and that the compressed material might be below the hearing threshold of the human ear.

The audio data is stored in a RAM buffer

before it is sent through the D/A converter. This RAM buffer holds up to about ten seconds of data (about a megabyte). If the player is interrupted by jostling, bumping, or thumping, the flow of the audio out of the buffer won't be interrupted as long as the disruption has ended before the RAM buffer has emptied. Once the disruption ceases, the data simply fills the buffer back up.

Technically, the MiniDisc is a rewriteable magneto-optical disk that uses a laser to apply focused heat to encode the binary bit stream. The actual heat from the laser randomizes and rewrites over previously recorded data.

The MiniDisc was originally intended to take over the cassette market and has received much industry support and hype from Sony, its founder. The marketplace, however, has been reluctant to let go of the cassette. MiniDiscs are definitely superior in sound quality to cassettes, being nearly up to the sonic brilliance of a CD, but they are much more expensive.

## Hard Drive

The typical hard drive is much like a standard CD in that it writes and reads data from a reflective, spinning disk. Unlike a traditional analog tape recorder, the hard drive doesn't have to write data to the disk in a continuous segment. Depending on the condition, capacity, or fullness of the drive, the data for one song might be written to several noncontiguous (noncontinuous) locations on the drive. Since a hard drive's read/write head moves incredibly fast (faster than the eye can see), data can be accessed randomly from any one point to any other on the disk. When the disk spins fast enough and the read/write moves accurately enough, there's rarely a problem with the continuation

of the flow of digital data.

## DVD

DVD (Digital Video Disc) is an optical storage medium similar to the compact disc and its variations (CD, CD-ROM, CD-Rewriteable). It uses a shorter wavelength that is capable of reading and writing smaller pits on its reflective surface, and it is a two sided medium that uses multiple layers. The laser can focus on one layer and ignore the other, much in the same way the human eye focuses on a close object while blurring out the distant one. The top layer is partially transmissive, so the laser can focus on it or go through it to the bottom layer.

The DVD is the same physical size as a CD (1.2mm thick and 120mm in diameter) and the technologies are similar enough that a DVD player can play back a compact disc.

Whereas the CD holds up to 650MB of data, the DVD holds up to 17GB. A single-sided, single-layer DVD holds about 4.7GB; a double layer DVD holds almost twice that amount (8.5GB); a double-sided, single layer DVD holds 9.4GB; and a double-sided, double-layer DVD can hold up to 17GB. The double-layering method is called Reverse Spiral Dual Layer (RSDL).

Video is stored on the DVD in the Moving Picture Expert Group's MPEG-2 format, while home entertainment audio is stored compressed using Dolby's AC-3 standard, which provides for the 5.1-channel surround sound standard.

Depending on compression schemes, one single-sided, single-layer (4.7GB) DVD has enough room to hold:

- 2 hours and 13 minutes of compressed video at 30 frames per second and 720 X 480 resolution

- Three multichannel audio tracks with 5.1 surround on each track
- Four text tracks for multilanguage subtitles
- Optional flags, placed on specific segments, let the studios encode the disc to play R-rated, PG-13, G-rated, or uncensored versions of the same movie. This system provides parents the flexibility to assign maximum age ratings to their children's access codes.

The DVD specification supports access rates of 60KBps to 1.3MBps. There are five primary forms of the DVD protocol:

- DVD-ROM is a high-capacity storage medium similar to CD-ROM.
- DVD-Video is designed specifically to hold motion picture content.
- DVD-Audio is similar to an audio CD, designed specifically to hold audio.
- DVD-R permits onetime recordability, with multiple read capability. This acts as data storage space, nondiscriminate of format (audio, video, and data).
- DVD-RAM is erasable and rewriteable and, like DVD-R, is nonspecific as to content.

## Divx

Divx is a consumer video format designed by Digital Video Express. It uses the same media as DVD, but it's written according to a different protocol. A DVD disc can be played back on a Divx player but Divx disks can't be played back on a DVD player.

The Divx format was designed as a consumer movie rental format. The disks can only be played back for a specific time period, typically 72 hours, then it needs to be reauthorized through your credit card account with Digital Video Express. Though the disks cost only four or five dollars, each new authorization costs about three dollars, and they can only be played back on the host machine for which they're authorized.

# 5 Digital Multitracks

Alesis started a recording revolution when it introduced the original ADAT. The 8-track digital recorder did so much for the money that it was irresistible to the entire industry. In addition to offering high-quality digital multitrack capability, the ADAT protocol allowed multiple machines to be synchronized together—hence the tag *modular digital multitracks*. In fact, they synchronized together with far greater accuracy than the best analog machines connected to the best machine synchronizers. Up to 16 ADATs could be daisy chained together with near sample accurate sync, for a whopping 128 tracks. With this system, the user was given the freedom to start with one ADAT, adding more modules as need and business supported.

Almost immediately, it seemed that recording facilities of all sizes jumped on the ADAT bandwagon. The excitement created by this device was evident at its introduction at the 1992 Audio Engineering Society show. After schmoozing a pass from the folks at the Alesis booth to stand in line, everyone waited in line for a couple hours just to see it work. The implementation of a system that bridged the gap between home and the full-blown professional facility made it possible for all of us to do some of our work at home and some at a commercial studio. The industry went through a little bit of trauma while everyone positioned themselves for the coming revolution. Big studio owners started to band together to fight the home studio, and home studio owners kept buying equipment that let them do top quality work at home.

Once everything settled down, a good working relationship started to form between the serious pro studios and the serious home studios. It's true that some studios in the middle ground were stretched to maintain commercial viability, but the audio, audio for video, and multimedia markets simultaneously opened up. When studios of the late '80s and early '90's were competing for music and band related projects, they had no idea of the multimedia revolution that was about to begin. The mid- and late '90s brought much more business for studios of all sizes. With the advent of the Internet, multimedia, CD-ROM, online audio, and guerilla video, the project base became diverse and plentiful for those willing to hound out some business.

As gear got less expensive, the quality got higher. Anyone at home could produce a professional product, if they knew how to use their gear. The only problem with this era was that too many people had the tools to do top quality work without first learning how to produce top quality product. As things have settled down, more young recordists have built expertise. In addition, equipment manufacturers have gotten better at providing user-friendly equipment that automatically handles format, technical, and artistic details in a way that increases the quality level throughout the industry.

Now we look at a future in the audio industry that allows the recordist to flourish. Certain functions are best accomplished at home. Other functions can only be done at a large professional facility. The better the recordist gets at producing top-quality audio at home, the more likely they are to rise to the level where a big studio is needed for certain phases of a project. The modular digital multitrack has made an impact on the audio industry indeed.

With the advent of the ADAT, other manufacturers jumped into the arena with their version of this convenient and flexible format. Whereas the ADAT used the SVHS video format, which held about 40 minutes of 8-track audio, the Tascam DA 88 used the Hi 8 video format for storage. Tascam's system aimed toward the film and video industry by providing a system that used Hi 8 video tape that would store up to two hours per tape. Whereas ADAT has dominated the home recording industry, DA 88s have held their own in the film scoring world. Alesis, of course, answered the challenges of both of these with updated models with longer record times and additional professional features—maintaining the ADAT format.

## Comparison of MDMs to Computer-Based Recording Systems

In the long run, both the computer-based hard disk recorder and the MDM hold an important place in the history of recording. The sheer storage capacity of a full-blown MDM system will send the hard disk-based system running in fear. The processor and hard disk capable of storing 128 tracks of full digital audio for 53 minutes (like on an ADAT) or 108 minutes (as with the DA-88/98) would be impressive to say the least.

As of this writing, we haven't gotten there yet.

MDMs excel at simultaneous recordings of many tracks. They also offer a sense of security for those of us comfortable with the concept of data on tape—somehow it's still a little frightening to have your audio data hiding on a hard disk.

Keep in mind that MDMs use a video transport system. The tape your audio lives on follows much the same path that the tape in your VCR follows. How does that make you feel? The reality is that all MDM manufacturers have addressed this issue, and their tape handling systems have gotten faster and much more reliable. However, with two or more MDMs, it's a simple matter to create a backup copy of every track in your production—and I'd recommend it.

I make backups of my backups, no matter what format I'm operating in. In a hard disk system, I make daily archives of my file status to CD or Jaz cartridges. In the scope of a project, the cost of the extra tape or disks used to back up a project is incidental, especially considering the cost of rerecording everything. This concept is not specific to digital systems. It's also common to back up analog multitrack tapes. When I mix and match formats, I'll make a work copy of the analog multitrack (typically, 2-inch tape, 24-track) that provides the reference while recording all the digital tracks (MDM and/or hard disk systems). The better your projects are, the more they need to be protected. Backups are important to the recording process in general.

MDMs also provide an excellent way to archive your hard disk-based recordings. Since a 24-, 48-, or 64-track hard disk recording typically occupies more than 650MB, the CD isn't an appropriate archive medium without a utility designed to split the data between disks. That concept isn't incredibly bothersome, but as soon as you split the data up, there's more risk of part of it corrupting or being ruined. There's comfort in archiving everything in its perfectly crafted sync to a format that remains in sync and is quick at easy to call back up later. Personally, I archive in both formats when presented with this scenario. Archive to MDM and the disk format du jour. With the advent of DVD and other high-capacity storage media, file size is less of an issue, but multiple-format backups are still prudent.

In regard to speed and ease of use, nothing effectively competes with the hard disk system. However, where the hard disk system falls short, the MDM systems excel, and vice versa. The recording era has changed; no longer do we simply buy the popular reel-to-reel analog 8-track, and call it a day. Now, we carefully combine the best of all worlds to help in our creative and musical endeavors.

## Formats

As MDMs and digital technology have evolved, tape transports have gotten more reliable, and converters have gotten much better. 16-bit systems have given way to 20-bit systems (with 24-bit systems in sight), and each new MDM does more than its predecessor. Illustrations 5-1 and 5-2 highlight the comparable features in the two leading MDMs.

## Other MDMs

MDM systems are available from Fostex, Sony, and others. However, operational characteristics and technical specifications tend to mirror the updated status of the Alesis ADAT and Tascam DA series. The audio industry has embraced the ADAT format, and we've all benefited from its

## Illustration 5-1
### ADAT Operational Specifications
- **Tape type** – S-VHS.
- **Sample rate** – Varies from 40.4 to 50.08kHz to provide for pitch change.
- **Tape length** – A 120-minute S-VHS tape provides 40 minutes, 44 seconds of record time on each track. A 160-minute S-VHS tape provides 53 minutes of record time on each track. A 180-minute S-VHS tape provides 62 minutes of record time on each track.
- **Number of tracks** – 8 tracks on each module.
- **Linking machines** – 16 machines can be linked together.
- **Shifting tracks** – Can be shifted in time to compensate for performance and sync inconsistencies.
- **Digital interconnection** – Through proprietary fiber-optic cable, can carry all eight tracks to and/or from: another ADAT, an A1-S/P DIF interface, an A2-AES/EBU interface, Digidesign's Pro Tools Interface, an Alesis Quadrasynth, an Alesis QS8/QSR, and Alesis effects like the Quadraverb II and the Q20.

excellent and insightful design. The original "black-face" ADATs still perform well in many professional applications. The updated models have simply added features, ease of use, durability, and increased digital audio quality.

## Illustration 5-2
### DA-88/98/38 Operational Specifications

- **Transport type** – Hi-8
- **Tape type** – Hi-8 video
- **Tape length** – 108 minutes onto a 120-minute Hi-8
- **Name** – Tascam refers to their MDM system as DTRS (Digital Tape Recording System)
- **Number of tracks** – 8 tracks on each module
- **Linking machines** – 16 machines can be linked together.
- **Digital interconnect** – Accomplished through Tascam's proprietary TDIF-1 (Tascam Digital Interface), which uses a 25-pin D-sub connector to connect to other Tascam MDMs or other Tascam interface accessories.

## Dedicated Digital Recording Systems

Dedicated digital recording systems typically use a proprietary operating system to operate a self-contained digital studio. Audio is usually recorded on an internal hard drive, and all record and playback controls are located on the unit. No other computer is required for operation.

These systems have some advantages:

- They don't tie up a computer. If you use your computer for other musical functions, or if you don't own a computer, this might be a good way to go.
- They often offer a smoother operation, because they're not sharing a processor with other applications and utilities. One of the

disadvantages of the computer-based system is timing. Occasionally, during playback or record, multiple applications place timing demands on the processor. This sometimes results in an awkward rhythmic feel that's inconsistent from one pass to the next.

- Everything in the system is optimized specifically for a digital audio application. This often results in a smooth-running system that doesn't crash often.

These systems also have some disadvantages:

- They're typically not as easily expandable as the computer-based or MDM systems. They contain a certain number of tracks that are simple to synchronize to MTC or SMPTE, although they're not always designed for expandability.
- They can only be used for one function. With a computer-based system, you have the ability to record audio, mix audio, play back audio, do word processing, keep your financial records, write a book, etc.
- They aren't usually as easy to update as a computer-based system. Though they can typically receive software upgrades, hardware is another question. Adding tracks, modules, effects, plug-ins, and other hardware-related functionality is often impossible or cumbersome.

# Samplers

Keyboard-based samplers are essentially dedicated digital recording systems, with some limited record functionality, along with some optimized playback functionality. The original samplers offered very limited sample time. A few seconds were typically available to divide among individual mono samples, which were spread across the keyboard. Modern samplers are limited by disk space. When they're connected to a large, fast hard drive, they can provide hours of full-bandwidth stereo audio.

Excellent samplers are manufactured by Emu, Kurzweil, Ensoniq, and others. These keyboard-based systems add depth and character to any setup. The sample libraries developed for each of these instruments are incredible. In addition, several manufacturers can play back nearly any instrument's sounds. Most systems eventually grow to the point where a good sampler is an essential ingredient.

Many digital effects processors offer varying degrees of sample recording, playback, and manipulation. Companies like Alesis, Lexicon, and TC Electronics offer amazing sampling functionality from their digital effects processors.

Digital samplers provide most of the controls available in the MIDI domain, along with control over most digital audio parameters. Illustration 5-3 lists the basic functions of the sampling keyboard.

# Computer-Based Hard Disk Recording Systems

## History
I am a big fan of computer-based hard disk recording systems. I've been working with them since they became commercially available. The original recorders were very expensive and only affordable to the biggest and most successful commercial recording facilities. These early systems actually worked well, but they didn't have

## Illustration 5-3
**Sampling Keyboard Functions**

Sampling keyboards offer many of the same functions as any other synthesizer, plus some additional features unique to the digital recording arena:

- **Polyphony** – Several samples played across the keyboard
- **Variable sample rates** – 44.1kHz, 48kHz, 32kHz
- **Sample editing** – Truncation, forward and backward looping, bidirectional looping, cut, copy, paste, and undo
- **Layering** – Two or more sounds occurring simultaneously from the same keyboard stroke
- **Reverberation, chorusing, and other effects**
- **Equalization**
- **Pitch adjustment and correction**
- **Gain normalization** – Adjusting the overall track volume so the strongest peak is at full digital level
- **Volume smoothing**
- **Wave sample mixing, merging, and splicing**
- **Data invert, reverse, replicate, add, and scale**

nearly as many bells and whistles as even the most scaled down systems today. However, they were still digital, nonlinear, and totally flexible, even if they were a little quirky to work with. There's still a lot to be said for the sonic character of a good analog system, but the flexibility of the hard disk recorder can't be matched.

# Differences between Hard Disk and Tape-based Recording?

## Linear versus Nonlinear

Tape recorders are a linear, sequential medium. You need to fast forward or rewind the tape in order to hear or record at a specific time point. Whether using a reel-to-reel machine or a modular digital multitrack, the time it takes for the tape to physically wind to the correct spot can be detrimental to the flow of a session.

Hard disk recording is, however, a nonlinear—also called random access—medium. Any point in the time line of your recording is instantly accessible. A keystroke or mouse click immediately locates and plays from any point in your recording. This kind of immediacy becomes an integral part of the recording process. The ability to locate a specified point to perform or repeat a take enables everyone to maintain focus—to get the job done most effectively. Given too much lag time, someone is bound to crack a joke, or get hungry, thirsty, cranky, or just goofy.

## Destructive versus Nondestructive Editing

Whereas a punch-in on a tape-based system obliterates whatever was previously on the tape, hard disk systems allow for completely nondestructive recording and editing. There's no need to erase any take or track, as long as there's enough hard disk space remaining. The nondestructive nature of hard disk-based digital recording systems provides an environment that is much less stressful and much more productive and efficient than that of tape-

based recording.

## Number of Tracks and Takes

Tape has a limited number of tracks. Once the tracks are full, something needs to be erased before something else is recorded. If you are pretty sure you've gotten the hottest guitar solo but the guitarist wants to give it just one more try, you need to quickly evaluate, commit, and destroy what could be the only good take of the day.

In the hard disk arena, takes and tracks aren't necessarily the same thing. Most high-end software packages provide for multiple takes on any given track; each take is kept unless you really want to erase it. The only limitation is hard disk space. I typically record 10 to 20 lead vocal takes that end up fitting together during mixdown, but those 10 to 20 takes only represent options on one track. Try that on a tape-based system! If four vocalists are recorded, each with 10 to 20 takes, along with a full band and several instrumental solo takes, imagine the massive number of tracks that could quickly be used up.

# Things to Look For in the Software You Choose

It's in the best interest of the user to select software from a company that has made proactive strides forward in the industry. Industry leaders tend to survive; trend followers don't. There's nothing more frustrating than buying high-priced software, only to see the manufacturer go out of business a year or so later. Technical support is lost, the possibility of upgraded or improved functionality is gone, and new software must be purchased in order to keep competitive and current.

Check into technical support. The reputation of the tech support staff is easy to discover. Go to the online user group Web site for the manufacturers you're considering. Eavesdrop on the conversation. Pay attention to the tone of the participants. If they're angrily complaining about the lack of technical support or about the incredible difficulty getting through on the telephone lines, be careful. Any popular product inspires a plethora of tech support calls, so be patient, but also be assertive. If the manufacturers are selling massive quantities of their wares, they probably should be able to afford adequate support.

If possible, get a demo version of each software package you're considering. Most companies have demo versions of their wares available on their Web site, or they'll usually be happy to send a demo copy for review. The demo versions are usually disabled in some way, but they provide a good test drive. If you open the software and everything makes sense, that's a good sign. If you open the software and you struggle to get anything to happen, that's a bad sign. Many packages are difficult to use at first. Then, once you learn a few basic procedures, everything falls into place. However, there's positive value in a program that's user-friendly, a program with which you can effortlessly perform basic functions.

## Soundcards

Many software packages work well using the internal audio capabilities offered by some computers. However, the more rigorous the audio demands, the more an audio card of some type should be considered. The soundcard typically offers high-quality analog and digital inputs and outputs. It also offers additional processing power in many cases. Systems like those designed by Mark of the Unicorn and Digidesign lead the industry in features and digital audio power. Other manufacturers offer very competitive packages. The key for each of us is to find the software/hardware package that functionally fits the way we think, with a user interface that looks attractive enough to keep us coming back for more.

# Terms Common to Hard Disk Recording

Some terminology used in hard disk recording is slightly different from the common terminology in the analog domain. These terms often describe a completely new way to work. Sometimes, they use the familiar imagery of terms common to the analog era—possibly with a slightly different application.

**Track** – A track, in a digital-audio software package, is similar to the track in the MIDI software package. Whereas the MIDI track contains MIDI data, the audio track refers to digital audio that's located on the hard drive. Tracks, in both these applications, are different from the traditional use of the term in the multitrack domain. Tracks on an analog reel-to-reel, MDM, or cassette multitrack are finite in number. If the machine is an 8-track, there are eight tracks. Software-based systems allow for relatively unlimited numbers of tracks. Typically, the number of tracks is only limited by the amount of available hard disk space.

**Voice** – Voices are closely related to tracks, but they're limited in their availability. Voices define the possible number of active digital tracks. A system that allows for eight voices can only have eight tracks playing at once. Each track must be assigned to a voice to be heard. Multiple tracks can't play on the same voice at the same time. However, tracks can share a voice if they don't play at the same time (Illustration 5-4).

**Take** – A take is an optional variation of a track. The number of takes is typically limited only by

the amount of available hard disk space. Once the lead vocal track has been recorded, for example, another version of the lead vocal can be recorded without creating a new lead vocal track. By simply selecting a new take, the track can be recorded again as an additional take. Though the concept of takes is similar to simply adding additional tracks, they offer a much more organized approach to digital multitrack recording. Only so much fits on the computer monitor, no matter how large it is. Takes let the user keep

# Illustration 5-4
## Voices

A digital recording system typically offers a limited number of playback voices. The screen below contains an 8-voice system, meaning 8 simultaneous audio tracks can be played back at once—the two lead vocal tracks and all the BGVs can playback at once.

Notice the Lead Vocal 1 track and the Bass Guitar track occupy the same voice and are simultaneously active. In this scenario, only the Lead Vocal 1 track would playback. The Bass guitar wouldn't be heard at all until the lead vocal track became empty. A feature called dynamic allocation distributes multiple audio tracks to playback from a common voice. Typically, the track highest up on the track list is allocated the voice first. The rest must wait for the voice to become available.

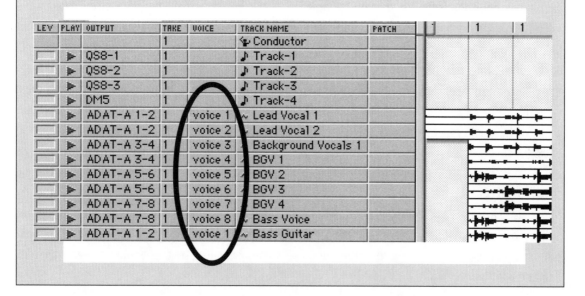

the conceptual number of tracks to a minimum while still providing a system to store options. If you created a new track for each new take, you'd soon find yourself in the middle an organizational nightmare. Using takes helps keep your files easy to manage, follow, and understand (Illustration 5-5).

**Channel** – A channel is a mixer feature. In the

MDM, reel-to-reel, and cassette multitrack domain, tracks always refers to machine capacity and channels refers to mixer capacity. There are no tracks on a mixer and there are no channels on a machine. In the software domain, channels still refer to mixer capacity, whether hardware- or software-based. Each track, within a software system, can have a mixer channel.

# Illustration 5-5
## Takes

Takes provide a means of recording alternate versions of any track without creating an unmanageable mass of tracks. Multiple takes are accessed easily though the takes pop-up list. Simply select the desired take and you're right where you want to be.

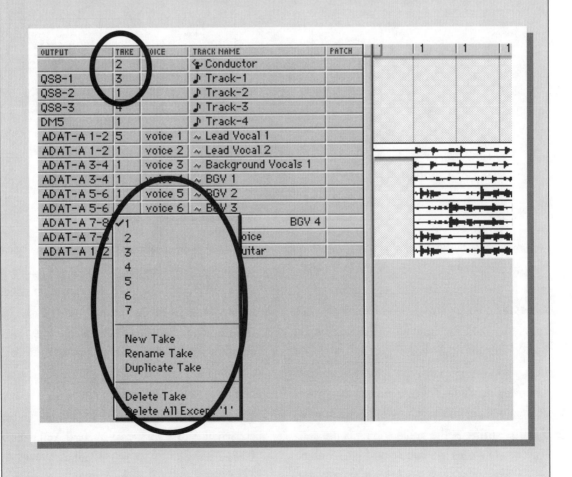

# Illustration 5-6
## Channels

Channels are a mixer feature. Whereas, tracks refer to machine capacity, channels refer to mixer capacity. There are no tracks on a mixer and there are no channels on a machine. In the software domain, channels still refer to mixer capacity, whether hardware- or software-based. Each track, within a software system, can have a mixer channel. However, the audio from the track won't be heard unless there's a voice available for playback.

However, the audio from the track won't be heard unless there's a voice available for playback (Illustration 5-6).

**Crossfade** – The crossfade is commonly used to feather regions together—while one region turns down, the other region turns up. They blend in a way that's inconspicuous and sonically smooth. Crossfades typically provide the answer to an awkward edit scenario (Illustration 5-7).

**Audio Engine** – The audio engine is the software that defines the handling of digital audio within the computer domain. Most manufactur-

ers optimize their products for use with their own audio engine. Many manufacturers cooperate in a way that's beneficial to the consumer. Since most software packages are primarily a user interface created to facilitate manipulation of a combined audio and MIDI environment, manufacturers are less proprietary about the specific engine used to handle audio needs. Some packages provide multiple audio engine selections, chosen directly from the software-driven menus.

**DSP** – DSP stands for digital signal processor. The DSP is responsible the manipulation of digi-

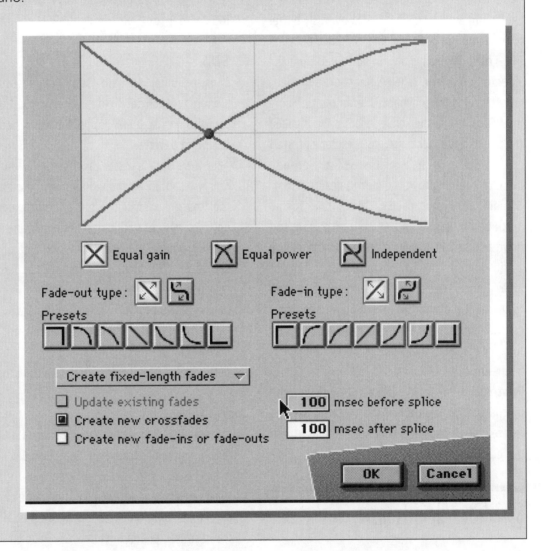

# Illustration 5-7
## Crossfade

The crossfade is commonly used to feather regions together—while one region turns down, the other region turns up. They blend in a way that's inconspicuous and sonically smooth. Crossfades typically provide the answer to an awkward edit scenario.

tal audio data. Effects, equalization, normalization, time compression and expansion, dynamics, etc. are all performed through digital signal processing. In a computer-based system, the DSP functions are handled by the same processor that runs the computer, unless there is a sound card containing additional DSP. The more DSP that's available, the less drain is placed on the system. Digidesign offers a special audio card, called the DSP farm, that contains several DSP chips. A card like this lets the user apply multiple plug-ins and effects in a mixing and playback setting without overtaxing the computer. When there's not enough DSP available, problems start to crop up. Effects either don't work, or they only work part of the time; systems crash; tracks might disappear; settings might disappear; or the entire system might slow way down. It's obviously better to have enough DSP available to do the job right.

**Pre-roll** – Pre-roll is a term borrowed from the video editing field. When a transport automatically rewinds for playback, the amount of time it rewinds before the actual locate point is called the pre-roll. Pre-roll is used to get a running start at the locate point, which is typically an edit point of some type. In the mechanical transport domain, pre-roll is used to allow time for all machines to synchronize together so the edit point can be accurately assessed. In the digital audio domain, the same considerations might be a factor if mechanical transports are locking to the digital platform. If there are no mechanical transports, pre-roll simply provides ramp up time for the brain to accurately understand what it's hearing.

**Post-roll** – Post-roll is the amount of time the mechanical or digital transport plays after the locate point. Post-roll is used to let the user hear the edit/locate point in context.

# Serial Bus/Data Transfer

Serial bus speed and data transfer rates are important factors in the efficiency of any digital audio, digital video, or other digital multimedia system. You can have the fastest computer on the planet, but if your device-to-device communication is performed through an inefficient transfer bus, you'll be in for some heartache. High-quality digital audio and video files are huge. As audio and video have become increasingly interwoven, and with the advent of massive playback mediums like DVD, bus speeds are more critical then ever. The following description of various transfer protocols provides a striking comparison.

## SDS

Sample Dump Standard (SDS) is a protocol designed to facilitate transfer of digital audio samples and sustain loop information between sampling devices.

This data transfer process has been commonly adapted by individual manufacturers to their own systems. Therefore, communication between devices with different brand names isn't usually possible. However, a good computer-based sample editor software package can typically translate sample information for shared use between manufacturer-specific formats.

This protocol is snaillike when it comes to speed, clocking in at around 31,250 bits/second—the MIDI standard serial data transfer rate.

## SCSI

The small computer systems interface (SCSI) offers a marked increase in data transfer speed over the SDS protocol. It is also a more standardized system, so most SCSI-capable devices can cross-communicate. This bidirectional data transfer bus communicates at about 500,000 bits/second, providing a quick and reliable means to transfer audio data between software applications and hardware devices.

Although SCSI provides a stable and efficient means of digital audio transfer, it is incapable of direct digital transfer of high-quality, real-time video and multimedia information. In order to capture video information at a high frame rate when transferring over a SCSI system, a separate video capture card is required.

### Fast and Wide SCSI-2 and –3

Supports 20 megabits/second, 16-bit "wide SCSI" data transfer.

### IDE/ATA

On an IDE (Integrated Drive Electronics) drive, the controller is integrated into the drive mechanism. The terms IDE and ATA are interchangeable.

### Firewire

The Firewire protocol, developed by Apple and applicable to both the Mac and PC formats, was adopted by the Institute of Electrical and Electronics Engineers (IEEE) as IEEE 1394, the industry standard serial data bus. With transfer rates up to 400 megabits/second, it eliminates the need for digital-to-analog and analog-to-digital conversion. This type of speed revolutionizes the capabilities for multimedia production, integration with consumer electronics, and instantaneous access to data sources like the World Wide Web Illustration 5-8 highlight some of the excellent advantages of the Firewire protocol. See Illustration 5-9 for a graphic comparison of data transfer speeds.

# Network and Online Data Transfer Rates

There's an amazingly high degree of integration of music and audio into networks and the Inter-

## Illustration 5-8
**Firewire**

Firewire offers several advantages:

- It is a digital interface that doesn't require conversion to and from analog, therefore insuring the most reliable signal integrity.
- At 400 megabits/second it can transfer data about 800 times faster than SCSI.
- The standard defines 100, 200, and 400 megabits/second devices and can support multiple speeds on a single bus.
- Firewire supports freeform daisy chaining and branching of up to 63 devices to your Mac or PC, using small, thin serial-connecting cables of up to 14 feet in length.
- Each device is hot-pluggable. They don't need to be turned off to connect and disconnect, and your computer doesn't need to be restarted when you make a device change.
- The protocol is auto configuring, with no need for device IDs, jumpers, dip switches, screws, latches, or terminators.
- It supports guaranteed delivery of time critical data, enabling smaller, low-cost buffers.
- It supports two types of data transfer: asynchronous an isochronous.

net. Any recordist must not only be familiar with the options available, but must also strive to optimize these mediums as they apply to recording, data sharing, and communication. Using the correct tools in this area provides opportunity

# Illustration 5-9
## Data Transfer Rates

Data transfer rates vary greatly. The graph below shows the stark contrast between Firewire and any of the other protocols.

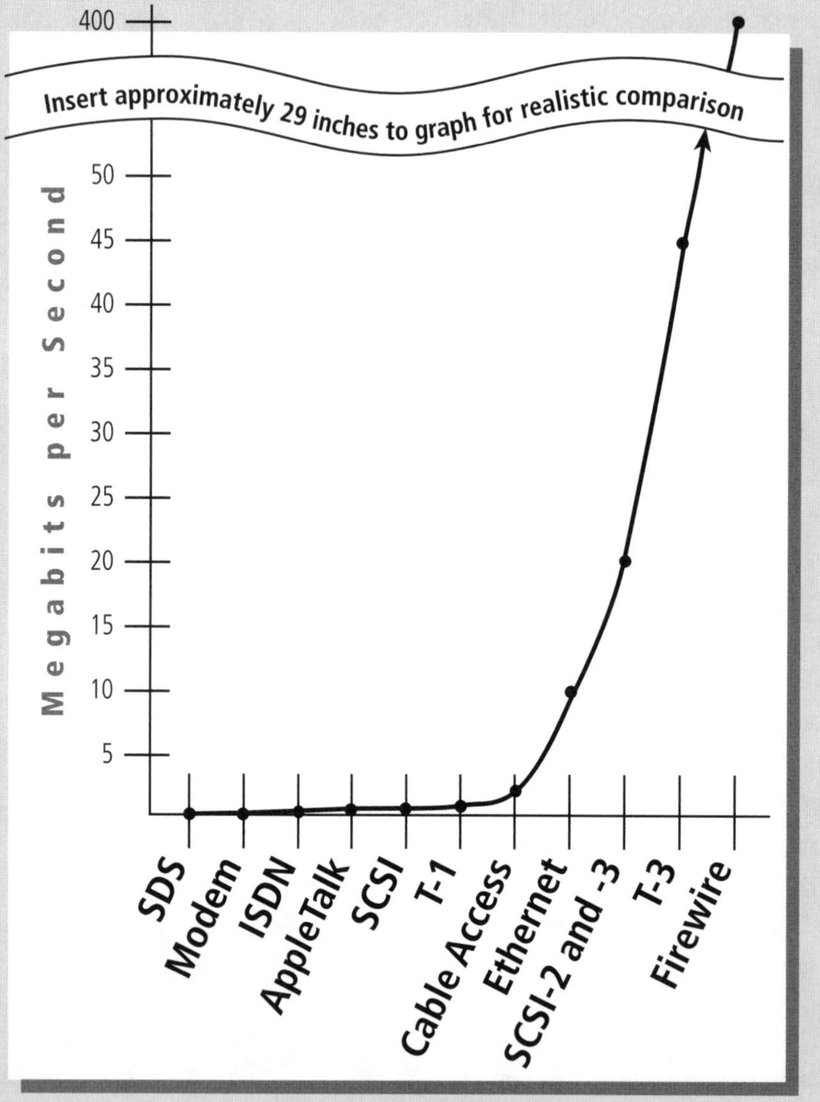

for time saving file transfers and financially beneficial working arrangements. Comparison and evaluation of the functionality and pertinence of each protocol is fundamental to our effectiveness. Optimization of a setup in these regards provides a comfortable, stress-free, and productive working platform.

## AppleTalk

LocalTalk is cabling scheme used to transmit AppleTalk information between Macintosh computers, printers, and other network devices. Its maximum transfer rate is 230,400 bits per second over a twisted pair wire.

## Ethernet

Ethernet is another protocol that uses either twisted pair or a coax type of cabling to run at up to 10 megabits per second.

## Modem

Typically 56,000 bits/second, although the limiting factor is the quality of phone line. Poor quality phone lines can limit the transfer rate to less than 40,000 bits/second.

## Cable

High-speed cable Internet access is about 100 times faster than a 28,800 bits per second phone-line modem. This network uses the same cable television system that runs into most houses. At close to 3,000,000 bits per second, these systems are amazingly quick, include Internet access, and cost about the same as an extra telephone line and a typical Internet service provider.

## ISDN (Integrated Services Digital Network)

Basically, a way to move more data over existing regular telephone lines. ISDN is available to most of the U.S.A., and in most markets it is priced very comparably to standard analog phone circuits. It can provide speeds of roughly 128,000 bits per second over regular telephone lines. In practice, most people will be limited to 56,000 or 64,000 bits per second.

## T-1

A leased-line connection capable of carrying data at 1,544,000 bits per second. At maximum theoretical capacity, a T-1 line could move a megabyte in less than ten seconds. However, that is still not fast enough for full-screen, full-motion video, for which you need at least 10,000,000 bits-per-second. T-1 is the fastest speed commonly used to connect networks to the Internet.

## T-3

A leased-line connection capable of carrying data at 44,736,000 bits per second. This is more than fast enough to do full-screen, full-motion video.

# Disk Management

Disk management is very important in the realm of hard disk audio and video recording. Some programs don't like to recognize drives larger than a couple of gigabytes. Some programs can efficiently use arrays of drives that are several gigabytes each. Formatting, partitioning, defragmenting, and optimizing are all phrases that are unknown in the traditional analog recording world. In the computer-based hard disk arena, however, these terms can be the lifeblood of a successful and lasting career.

Always read up on your specific hardware and software. The manuals will tell you how to deal with all these considerations and probably more.

## Partitioning

Partitioning a disk simply divides it into discrete areas allocated to a particular use or user. Partitioning large hard drives provides an organizational structure for data storage, retrieval, and use. It's common to organize separate partitions for operating system files, applications, data, audio, and video. Determining which portion of the disk holds each specific type of information not only helps the user keep track of files, but it also helps provide a quicker search process for the computer.

Whenever dealing with audio or video files, especially in an edit functionality, it's best to keep all audio and video on separate drives or separate partitions on a large drive. Constant editing causes data to quickly get scattered all over the drive. If there's not enough room to finish writing data at a location on the drive, the computer stores what it can, then stores the rest at a different location. In this way, the drive is continually moving and searching and reading—this slows the entire process down. Regular defragmenting and intelligent partitioning help a system run faster, smoother, and more reliably.

## Formatting

Formatting organizes and prepares the disk for use. During formatting, the drive's controller checks the disks operating parameters, like speed and capacity, then maps the disk into blocks, sectors, and tracks. Bad blocks are marked and placed on a defect list.

A block is the smallest chunk of memory accessed and transferred by the drive. The number of bytes in a block—usually 512 or larger, in multiples of 512—is the same as the block size.

A track on a disk is a concentric circle designated to receive magnetic representations of the digital data to be stored. Each track is a single line of magnetic domains.

A sector is the smallest subdivision of a track. Sectors usually contain 512 bytes of data, but their capacity is set and determined when the disk is formatted.

## Compression

Data compression is a procedure in which data is transformed into a smaller package by the elimination of redundant information. Data compression works well on files containing graphics and text documents, but in general, high quality, full-bandwidth digital audio is best left in an uncompressed state. It's not a good idea to randomly compress audio files using the same type of compression utility commonly used to compress general files. In fact, it can permanently damage audio files. However, when using certain hardware and applications, audio data compression schemes are devised that cater to specific needs and system requirements. These work well, without damaging the audio files, although they don't always maintain the complete integrity of the original audio quality. MiniDisc and Internet audio is typically compressed to aid in the file transfer and storage process. Audio Examples 5-1 though 5-3 demonstrate the difference in audio quality between the original audio, bounced to disk, audio recorded to DAT, and audio recorded to MiniDisc.

*Audio Example 5-1 Bounced to Disk*
*CD-1: Track 81*

*Audio Example 5-2*
*Analog In and Out of DAT*
*CD-1: Track 82*

---

*Audio Example 5-3*
*Analog In and Out of MiniDisc*
*CD-1: Track 83*

---

## Repairing/Defragmenting

Audio and video applications are continually writing and rewriting data; it's the nature of the process. Therefore, it's easy to end up with data stashed all over the disk. A hard disk tries to use all available space. So, if you erase something on an outer track and then record audio or data, the new material will save to the open part of the track first. If there's not enough room there, the rest of the data will save to another part of the drive. If there's still not enough room, it will finish saving to yet another part of the drive. It's easy to see how data could get scattered all over the drive quickly.

This scattering of data is called fragmenting, and it can cause a dramatic reduction of computing speed. When you record a lot of audio and/or video data, it's important to defragment your drives on a regular basis. To defragment is to reorder files on a hard disk platter, so that all the sectors of each file are contiguous. This increased disk organization results in improved access time, eliminating unnecessary read/write head movement.

It's also recommended by most digital-audio software manufacturers that you reinitialize your drives on a regular basis, too. Check with the software and drive manufacturers for your specific tools to find the optimum maintenance schedule for your setup.

It's very important to keep an up-to-date copy of a good hard disk utility package like Symantec's Norton Utilities on hand at all times.

It might save your day when you experience the big crash. It's easy to overlook this process because it seems like everything is just fine, right up to the point where your computer freezes up and you lose the ability to access the drive you've been working on for months. Take it from the voice of experience: it can happen!

## Protection: Practice Safe Computing

Back up your work regularly! I hate the thought of losing a day of work, so I back up very consistently. I've forgotten to save my work before—we all do. Moreover, there's always a chance that something might happen that causes the computer to freeze or crash, obliterating everything since the last save—even this drives the best of us wacky. However, to lose weeks of work on a project that has real artistic value is not only personally humiliating, but also potentially damaging to your professional career.

It seems like a hassle to stop everything to back up your files, but you can usually find a good time or place to designate for this important process. I always archive sessions to CD or another medium at the end of a long day in the studio. Nobody has ever complained—nobody. In fact, I've noticed my system acting a little funny in the middle of a session before and taken a half-hour or so to archive the whole project. Nobody was anything but grateful to feel the peace of mind and comfort knowing that their hard work was being kept as safe as humanly possible.

Backing up to CD is a very cost-effective way to archive your files. At less than a dollar for almost three-quarters of a gigabyte, it's hard to argue with the system's cost-effectiveness.

They are a bit slow though. When you're in a real time crunch and you have a lot of hard disk space available, simply save a copy of your project to a different drive, or at least to another place on the same drive. Be sure to label it as a backup. I like to include the date and often the time in the file name so it's next to impossible to get mixed up with the original file.

When backing up a file like a Pro Tools session, Digital Performer, Studio Vision Pro, etc., always save it in a form that copies all audio files to the new location. A simple Save As… command typically maintains the reference to the original audio files. The new file is nothing more than another edit decision list, referencing old audio files. If you experience a crash with the original file, the original audio might be corrupt, therefore rendering your backup as useless as the original. That's no fun. I've been there, too.

## Keep Current

All software manufacturers who care about their longevity in the industry upgrade frequently. Some upgrades are free, and some cost money. Usually, the upgrades with the cool new stuff cost somewhere between $100 and $150, depending on the original price and sophistication of the product. If you're serious enough about your craft to devote your time and energy to it, do yourself a favor: get the upgrades, they'll save you time and probably end up saving you money. Besides, it's appealing to clients to know they're working with someone who cares enough to use the best technology available.

Always pay for your software. Piracy hurts all users in the form of increased product cost. In many instances, the documentation and technical support are as valuable as the physical software. We need the software companies to prosper, so they can spend more money researching and implementing great new features, and so we can make better music with the greatest of ease.

# 6 Digital Effects

Many digital effects perform the same tasks as the analog devices of the same name, but they achieve results in a different way. As an example, the analog domain uses voltage-controlled amplifying circuits as the primary operator in dynamics processors. The addition of any amplifying circuit adds a measured amount of noise and distortion, no matter how high the quality of the components and design. Digital dynamics processors, on the other hand, analyze the signal content, then, according to user settings, recalculate the digital information, resulting in a theoretically perfect revision of the original sound wave. No amplifying circuits are needed in the digital manipulation of digital data.

Digital effects aren't always perfect, however. Although, in concept, they offer a mathematically pure procedure, their reputation is often flawed by their sound quality. Inexpensive digital devices, using inferior converters, or errant calculation algorithms often sound grainy. Their sonic quality sometimes lacks smoothness and fullness. Especially annoying are devices that introduce a kind of zing to the audio they process.

In theory, digital processors blow away similar analog devices. In practice, many professionals who care only about sound quality prefer high-quality analog devices because of their smooth and accurate sound. As digital technology has improved over the years, however, dis-

cerning pros are using digital equipment alongside of, or even instead of, their favorite classic analog devices.

## Real-time versus Non-Real-time Digital Effects

In the arena of software-based digital effects, there are functionally two types: real-time and non-real-time.

A real-time digital effect can be continuously monitored while the program source is playing back. It operates much like an outboard effect wherein the dry track continues to play while the recordist blends the effect at will. The effect never becomes part of the dry signal; it always remains separate and adjustable.

Non-real-time effects provide an opportunity to preview the effect, typically for just a portion of the program. The recordist must decide the most appropriate parameter settings based on this preview, then instruct the computer to calculate the entire selection accordingly. Once the track has been processed, the new and separate track can't be returned to its original state. Fortunately, most effects packages that operate this way let the user select whether the newly calculated digital data replaces the original or simply displaces the original, leaving it available in a file for retrieval if necessary.

The most user-friendly digital effects are real-time. They're much more flexible and forgiving over time and operate in a way that makes logical sense to anyone, even the first time they operate a software-based effect.

The disadvantage to real-time effects is that they tend to dominate available processing power. Whereas a combined MIDI/digital audio software package might be able to play back 24 digital audio tracks with no effects, the same system might only play back 12 audio tracks once you implement a complex reverb algorithm. Obviously, there is a trade off when using real-time effects.

Non-real-time effects simply preview, then process tracks. Playback power is not affected, no matter how many tracks you've processed, since, once they're processed, tracks play back as though they were originally recorded that way.

## Hardware versus Software versus Plug-ins

Digital effects are commonly available as both freestanding hardware and computer software. Sound quality only varies between these formats in accordance with the quality of the calculation algorithms, the power and speed of the available processor, and the quality of any D/A or A/D converters included in the process.

Hardware devices are often very convenient when a software-based system is either not available, or is being overtaxed by other tasks. With a piece of hardware, the manufacturer controls the quality of converters and the type of accessible data transfer options. Even though a hardware-based effect has analog inputs and outputs, it's increasingly common to interconnect via digital data transfer means such as AES/EBU or S/P DIF so as to avoid the inclusion of analog amplifying circuits.

Plug-ins are an extension of a software-based system. They typically offer both real-time and non-real-time effects and dynamics controls. In fact, most manufacturers of hardware effects and dynamics hardware offer their software in plug-in form, letting the user operate in a software environment of their choice (Digital Performer, Studio Vision, Cakewalk, Pro, etc.). The plug-in, although it might be manufactured by a competing company, installs as an option available for selection and manipulation within the host software package.

## Digitally Controlled Amplifier

The digitally controlled amplifier (DCA) is an analog amplifying circuit that is controlled digitally. Digital control provides a system whereby the analog signal path can be mixed, automated, and manipulated in much the same manner as a fully digital system. Euphonix popularized the digitally controlled analog concept with the introduction of their CS series consoles. Like digital mixers, the CS consoles facilitate snapshots and automation of all mix parameters: level, pan, mute, EQ, aux sends, etc. This concept is particularly applicable to users who prefer the analog sound, yet require total control over mix parameters.

## Digital Signal Processor

The digital signal processor (DSP) is the muscle behind digital effects. When the recordist decides to apply reverb, dynamic, or special effects to audio in the digital domain, something needs to make all the data calculations to facilitate these effects. That something is the digital signal processor.

Many software-based packages take advantage of the host computer's processing power to perform these calculations. These systems are very powerful and, as the computer industry has progressed, our industry has seen great strides in software-based systems that utilize no additional processors.

Some more professional systems supply additional processing power in the form of DSP cards that physically attach to the expansion slots available in most computers. This additional processing power facilitates a larger recording and processing package. Through this type of system, the user can access a nearly unlimited number of tracks, along with multiple real-time effects capabilities. Systems that utilize these external DSP cards are often interfaced with additional hardware that provides for different forms of digital data transfer, as well as multiple input and outputs for true multitrack recording configurations. These systems commonly offer in excess of 24 simultaneous inputs and outputs, along with professional interface options for Modular Digital Multitrack and modern multimedia applications.

## Pitch Change

Pitch change is a phenomenal feature that can be very useful on any instrument but is especially so when recording vocals. Most software packages allow for multiple types of pitch change, from fixed half-step changes to interval and scale based changes, all the way down to changes in cents (hundredths of a half-step).

Software is available that will analyze pitch and automatically adjust it to the closest half-step. The user sets parameters determining how soon the auto tune feature takes effect, or how far from perfectly in tune it'll allow a note to be.

Manual tuning is often the preferred approach simply because it lets the recordist determine what needs tuning using a musical de-

cision rather than a technical one. It is possible to manipulate the vocals, for example, so that they're so perfectly in tune that in time that they lose life and intensity. I'm usually very willing to tune and tweak to great lengths to get everything just right, but sometimes the intensity caused by one part being almost imperceptibly out of tune is important to the emotional impact of a song.

### Audio Example 6-1 Pitch Change
### CD-1: Track 84

Less sophisticated and less expensive time converters are incapable of controlling the pitch versus time relationship. They function in a way that is similar to an analog tape recorder: decreasing the time increases the pitch and, conversely, increasing the time decreases the pitch.

In order to keep the sample rate constant, these systems change pitch by removing or adding samples based on the ratio between the current and desired pitch. When samples are removed from a digital source, the remaining representation of the waveform plays back faster and higher (Illustration 6-1).

In order to lower the pitch, the original digital signal must be analyzed by the processor. The computer must spread the digital data out over a longer period, then estimate what might have been in the spaces created by the process. This calculating and estimating is called interpolating.

It's typically more difficult to pitch-shift a mixed musical work than to shift a single mono track. Individual vocal tracks are usually shifted with little or no perceivable degradation. A complete mix is much more intricate in its content,

# Illustration 6-1
## Shortening a Sample

Inexpensive digital software deals with sample manipulation in basic way. The result of the procedure is similar to speeding up and slowing a an analog tape machine—whatever gets higher plays back faster and whatever gets slower sounds lower.

In this type os pitch change the original sample (A) has samples removed at regular intervals (B). When the sample plays back at the original sample rate it's faster and higher (C).

Most good digital recording packages allow for pitch shifting and time manipulation, independent of each other. To perform these complex tasks, the samples must be manipulated through variations in sample rate, interpolation and elimination of sample data, and through sample rate conversion.

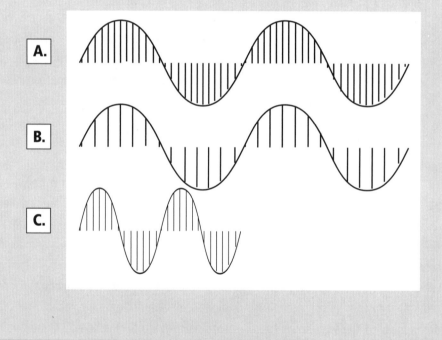

and often the slightest pitch change causes very unsatisfactory results. Some software manufacturers have devised pitch transposition algorithms to increase the likelihood of usable transpositions of full range audio, but even those are not effective in every case.

When pitch adjusting, it's best to:

- Avoid mixing multiple tracks before changing pitch. It's preferable to pitch-shift the individual ingredients, then mix down.
- Pitch-shift dry tracks. Reverb, distortion, and delay effects don't fare well in most pitch change processes.
- Be sure your levels are optimized. Whenever altering digital audio, it's very important to take advantage of every available bit so the

calculations result in the smoothest transformation of the original waveform. Audio that's been recorded at low digital levels will yield the poorest results in any digital manipulation, including pitch change.

---

*Audio Example 6-2 Pitch Shifted Waveform,*
*Recorded at Full Digital Level*
*CD-1: Track 85*

---

*Audio Example 6-3 Pitch Shifted Waveform,*
*Recorded at 50% Digital Level*
*CD-1: Track 86*

---

Most software packages let the user shift pitch an octave or two in either direction, but, practically speaking, large pitch changes are best used for special effects or not at all. Even though it's possible to keep the same time while changing the pitch, a standard pitch shift algorithm sounds very Munchkin-like after a pitch change of a third or fourth. On a lead vocal track, changes of a half-step or whole step create a dramatic change in tonal character—often, too extreme to use. I avoid any changes over a quarter-step on a lead vocal track (50 cents): if the track is that far out of tune, it probably should be sung again anyway.

Transposition features for audio tracks are very convenient. Say, for example, you record all your reference tracks, then determine the song would work better for the lead vocalist a half-step or whole step higher or lower. Audio transposition enables audio and MIDI tracks to change key together. A change of a half-step in either direction usually renders some usable changes, but even the tracks that aren't natural

sounding still come in handy as references when recutting vocals in the new key.

## Formants

Formants represent the tonal character of a pitch. Eight singers singing A 440 produce eight separate and distinguishable sounds. Although they sing the same note, some sound bright, some sound dark, some sound thick, and others sound thin. The ingredient that varies between these singers is the formant content.

Formants are shaped by the vocal tract—everything between the vocal chord, which creates a buzzy, saw-tooth wave sound, and the mouth and nose. The mouth, nose, tongue, and lips all work together to influence the formant content of an individual voice. Aside from the voice, each instrument also contains its own specific formant content.

It's interesting that even when pitch changes, formant content remains consistent. This explains why each instrument or voice retains a characteristic sound no matter what note is being played or sung.

The formant sounds are characterized by the individual vowel sound in the human voice. Variations of "ay," "ee," "eye," "oh," and "oo" demonstrate the specific formant sounds of a particular voice or instrument. In regard to the human voice, these sounds, whether sung or spoken, act as the filters that shape the tonal personality of the raw, buzzing sound that originates at the vocal cords.

Software with formant adjustment controls, independent of pitch adjustment controls, provides amazing power when adjusting digital audio pitch and tone. If a vocal note needs to be altered by a whole step, possibly to match a chord change, the pitch can be shifted without altering the formant content. Therefore, the altered note retains the same tonal character and personality as the rest of the track, even though the pitch was moved up a complete whole step. With this type of feature, pitch changes of a much greater degree produce very usable results.

---

### Audio Example 6-4
### Pitch Change Without Formant Change
### CD-1: Track 87

---

It's also simple, through formant change alone, to change the sound of an instrument or voice without any pitch change. An alto voice can easily be transformed into a tenor, bass, or soprano voice through formant changes alone— that is, if all those voices could sing the alto range.

---

### Audio Example 6-5
### Formant Change Without Pitch Change
### CD-1: Track 88

---

Traditional pitch change adjusts pitch and formant content by the same amount. That's why the higher the pitch goes, the smaller the source sounds, and the lower the pitch goes, the larger the source sounds. This process produces a sound identical to that created by simply speeding up or slowing down a tape recorder.

---

### Audio Example 6-6
### Pitch and Formant Change the Same Amount
### CD-1: Track 89

---

## Time Compression and Expansion

The digital domain offers time compression and expansion capabilities, which are nonexistent in the analog domain. An analog tape recorder can be easily sped up or slowed down, but with any speed increase there is a corresponding pitch increase, and with any tape speed decrease there's a corresponding lowering of pitch. However, digitally, time can be compressed or expanded completely independent of pitch, and pitch can be changed in either direction completely independent of time.

The process of time compression and expansion is simple. First, speed up or slow down the sample playback rate so that the same digital data occupies a new and different amount of time. Once the time is specified, perform a sample rate conversion from the adjusted rate back to the desired rate. For example, if you expand a 44.1kHz digital recording by 10 percent, you end up with a relative playback rate of 39.69kHz. Once that sample rate is converted back to 44.1kHz, your recording can again play back on a standard CD player, but the data will occupy 10 percent more time—its time line will have been expanded.

When we combine the concepts of time and pitch manipulation with a fast and accurate processor, it's possible to perform either function in a way that seems completely independent of the other. In reality, your computer has to perform an amazing number of calculations and recalculations to provide sonically appealing results.

Depending on the bit and sample rate, there is a limit as to how far time and pitch can be changed while maintaining a natural and believable sound quality. Within the specified range of acceptability, though, pitch and time can be altered with little or no perceivable change in audio personality.

Sound quality is also dependent on the source being altered. Voice-only recordings are much more forgiving than full-band tracks. Listen to Audio Examples 6-7 through 6-10 to compare identical time and pitch alterations—one on voice and one on a band.

---

**Audio Example 6-7 Voice Original**
**CD-1: Track 90**

---

**Audio Example 6-8 Voice Up 2 Whole Steps**
**CD-1: Track 91**

---

**Audio Example 6-9 Band Original**
**CD-1: Track 92**

---

**Audio Example 6-10 Band Up 2 Whole Steps**
**CD-1: Track 93**

---

Listen to the following audio examples. As the change in parameters increase, notice the change in audio character.

---

**Audio Example 6-11**
**Time Compression 2 Percent**
**CD-1: Track 94**

---

**Audio Example 6-12**
**Time Compression 6 Percent**
**CD-1: Track 95**

---

**Audio Example 6-13**
**Time Compression 8 Percent**
**CD-1: Track 96**

---

**Audio Example 6-14**
**Time Compression 15 Percent**
**CD-1: Track 97**

---

**Audio Example 6-15**
**Time Expansion 2 Percent**
**CD-1: Track 98**

---

**Audio Example 6-16**
**Time Expansion 6 Percent**
**CD-1: Track 99**

---

**Audio Example 6-17**
**Time Expansion 8 Percent**
**CD-2: Track 1**

---

**Audio Example 6-18**
**Time Expansion 15 Percent**
**CD-2: Track 2**

---

Some particularly powerful software packages provide for completely independent adjustments of pitch, formant, and time parameters. With these features, the creativity of the user is not hindered by lack of control.

## Spectral Effects

The spectral effects feature of Mark of the Unicorn's Digital Perform offers an amazingly simple interface to control time, pitch, and formants with a single three- dimensional control. Illustration 6-2 shows how simply all these parameters can be displayed and adjusted.

## Multiband Compressor/Limiter

A multiband compressor/limiter is exactly like two or more compressors in the same box, with each compressor being sensitive to only a specific bandwidth. The multiband compressor/limiter becomes an amazingly effective tool when compressing a musical signal. In most circumstances where full bandwidth music is patched through a compressor, the low frequencies end up driving the level sensor.

A compressor/limiter is simply an automatic volume control that turns the signal flowing through it down when it receives a certain user set and amount of amplitude, then back up again when the amplitude level decreases. That's all very good, but the normal compressor/limiter doesn't care what type of signal the amplitude is at all—it's just looking for a specified amplitude. In order to make a mix is to sound as loud as it possibly can, mastering houses use a multiband compressor/limiter. With this tool, the lows, mids, and highs can be compressed or limited separately so that each frequency range remains as close to the front of the mix as possible.

## Illustration 6-2
### Combined Time, Pitch, and Formant Control

In this type of system, time, formants and pitch can be easily adjusted by moving the red ball in the three-dimensional grid. You can also type in numerical values or select from preset transformations.

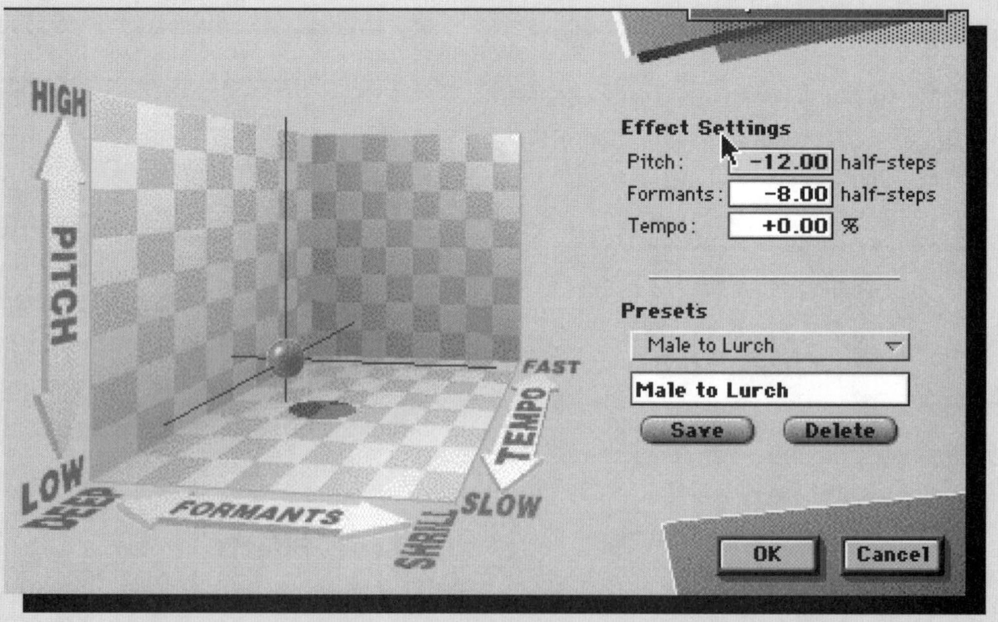

This tool is available in analog, digital, and software formats. Turn to Chapter 10 for further discussion of multiband compressor/limiter as it is used in mastering.

## Peak Limiter

A peak limiter is a very fast limiter, designed to nearly instantaneously recognize and limit waveform peaks. A good, clean peak limiter effectively reduces the level of transients in a way that has minimal negative effect on audio quality. The attack and decay are so fast that they effectively reduce the transient level with very little audible deviation.

Since transients are often several dB above the average level, a true peak limiter can easily assist in adding several dB to the overall mix level. For example, if your music contains transients peaks that exceed the average mix level by 10dB, you might run the mix through a peak limiter and adjust the threshold for a 6dB gain reduction on the peaks. You end up with a mix that can be boosted 6dB, so it's consistently 6dB hotter than it ever could have been without the aid of the peak limiter. As review from *The AudioPro Home Recording Course, Volume I*, a compressor uses a ratio of anything less than 10:1, and a limiter uses a ratio of 10:1 or higher, up to 100:1, or even ∞:1.

Digital compressor/limiters perform the same function as analog devices. The primary difference in the two processes is that the analog gear utilizes one or more voltage controlled amplifiers to control the signal level, whereas digital devices perform a mathematical calculation, altering the binary code to produce the desired results. In the ideal world, digital calculations and alterations have the potential to produce the most amazing results. They change the

audio waves to the closest tolerance in a way that doesn't need to include distortion-causing amplification circuits (Illustrations 6-3 and 6-4).

---

*Audio Example 6-19*
*Guitar with Digital Compression*
*4:1 with 8 dB Reduction*
*CD-2: Track 3*

---

*Audio Example 6-20*
*Guitar With Digital Peak Limiting*
*8 dB Reduction*
*CD-2: Track 4*

---

## Expanders and Gates

Gates, downward expanders, and upward expanders produce the same results in the digital domain as they do in the analog domain. The big difference, again, in the digital arena is the lack of another amplifier (VCA) in the signal chain. Digital calculations and algorithms simply alter the binary data to change dynamics, therefore avoiding any coloration, addition of noise, or distortion. In the academic sense, digital control of audio dynamics is a nearly perfect process. Aside from basic digital audio drawbacks and concerns, digital dynamics processors provide amazing results. The higher the bit and sample rates, the more incredible the results from digital processors.

## Delay Effects

For several years, the most common delay effects have been digital. However, as computers have played more and more into the digital manipulation and storage of sound, delay ef-

# Illustration 6-3
## Digital Compressor

This is an excellent example of a software-based digital multiband compressor. Notice the ease with which crossover points and gain reductions can be selected to fine tune the sound of a mix or instrument.

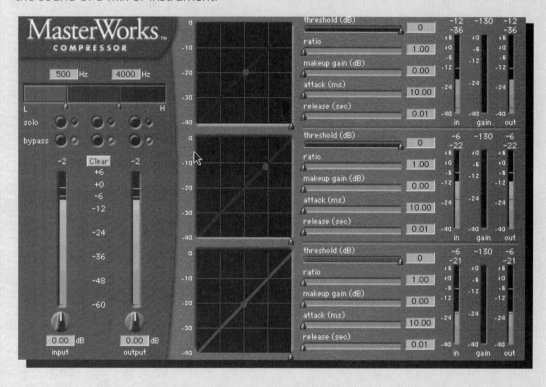

fects have become much more flexible and far easier to adjust. Onscreen adjustments of delay parameters provide amazingly quick and accurate control for all digital delay effects, from typical to bizarre.

Musical needs and stylistic considerations of the day guide the modern day musician to the type of effects that best support the musical vision. Though a simple slapback delay is still very effective in the proper place, many new parameters are available to help the musician fine-tune and adjust innovative new sounds.

Listen to Audio Examples 6-21 through 6-

23 to hear some of the effects possible though the use of the computer-based digital effects available in Opcode's Studio Vision Pro software package.

---

*Audio Example 6-21*
*Lots of Delays Bouncing All Over*
*CD-2: Track 5*

---

*Audio Example 6-22 Whacky Delay Effect 1*
*CD-2: Track 6*

## Illustration 6-4
### Digital Limiter

This limiter is easy to use and shows the frequency balance of the mix. This is a great way to check compatibility between mixes. If the frequency balance graph looks radically different between two mixes, they're probably not going to sound good when played one after the other.

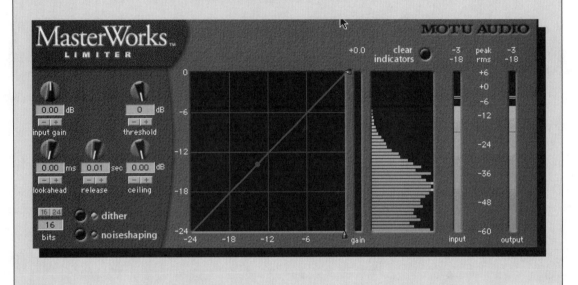

---

*Audio Example 6-23 Whack Delay Effect 2*
*CD-2: Track 7*

---

### Reverb Effects

There are many reverberation parameters. They've traditionally been cumbersome to access because most hardware-based reverbs provide one small window to access the controls. The maze of pages, and scrolling up, down, and sideways through them, are not just awkward and frustrating, they're a hindrance to the creative process. Often, you find just about the right sound in an effect's presets and settle for "close enough" because it's too much of a headache to make the sound "just right." You can't stop the creative flow just to locate the correct page and parameter that will fine-tune the sound.

With computer-based reverbs and other effects, all parameters and controls are available onscreen. They're typically displayed in a way that is easy to understand, follow, and change. In fact, once you see the graphic representation of features you've only scrolled past in an access window, actually understanding the concept is much easier.

Parameters like predelay, pre-echo, diffusion, crossover, filtering, and various room types are easily understood when seen in graphic form (Illustration 6-5).

## Illustration 6-5
### Digital Reverb

Notice how easily the onscreen parameters are to access and adjust. A primary advantage of software-based effects is their amazing ease of use. There's no scrolling through mysterious text windows, just point-and-click simplicity.

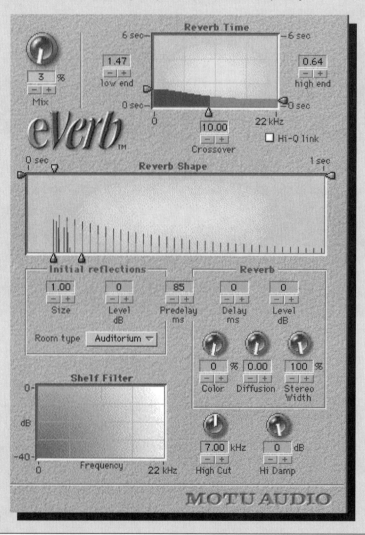

*Audio Example 6-24*
*Changing Reverb Parameters*
*CD-2: Track 8*

### Equalizers

Digital equalization is an amazingly flexible tool. In addition, it involves recalculation of digital data to produce tonal changes, rather than the filtering, amplifying, and phase altering techniques utilized in the analog. Ideally,

# Illustration 6-6
## Digital EQ

This type of equalization is easy to use, however this package doesn't provide real-time adjustment. Though it's cumbersome to process the file in order to hear the results, the benefit is reduced demand on the processor. Real-time effects place constant demand on the computer. On the other hand, effects that must be processed in order to hear them, only demand the processor's attention while calculating the data. This leaves more power for playback and provides for complex effects on all tracks, if necessary.

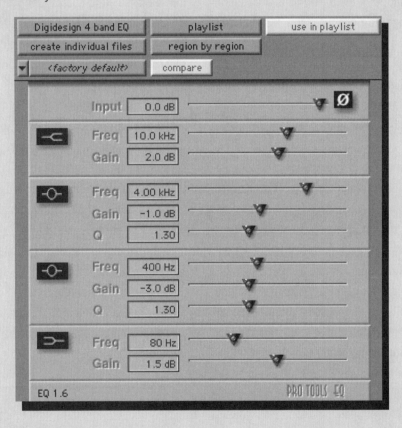

digital equalization is a pure and noiseless transformation.

The controls provided in any digital EQ are essentially the same as an analog device, but, especially in computer-based models, the parameters are easy to set and can be easily recalled and duplicated. Frequency is typically adjustable in 1Hz increments, gain in tenths of adB, and the bandwidth is completely controllable within a hundredth of an octave.

The ability to accurately recall and adjust equalization is a bonus. An analog graphic equalizer is a useful tool. But there's a big difference in creative flow when you can instantly recall a sound you worked a while to get, as opposed to spending time adjusting the analog sliders to approximate what you think you had.

The features and functionality of digital equalizers are amazing, but, sonically, there are several analog devices that are wonderfully smooth and warm in a way that has been difficult to digitally emulate. The original digital equalizers were harsh and grainy sounding. As technology has progressed, we continue to reap the benefit of competition and innovations through the availability of increasingly better tools.

Notice in Illustration 6-6 the instant access to fine-tuned adjustments over a 4-band equalizer. Each band is quite adjustable, in a very precise way.

Be careful about the signal level whenever boosting frequency ranges in the digital domain. If you've been a conscientious modern day recordist, your digital levels are probably almost as hot as they can be before you begin equalization. Boosting one or more frequency ranges can easily boost signal levels above the range of acceptability. Therefore, most digital equalizers provide input and output level adjustments and many provide metering to help you maintain optimum levels.

## Delay

One of the original digital delays was the Lexicon Primetime. It had most of the controls needed to create musical effects. Lexicon has always done a great job providing high quality, musical recording tools. Many Primetime delays are still in studios around the country. As they've aged, they've continued to serve faithfully in spite of some scratchy pots and sliders.

Current software-based digital delays of-

fer the sonic advantage of remaining in the digital domain—no scratchy pots or sliders. We don't need to bus an analog signal to an analog input, which is then converted to digital, effected, then converted back to analog, etc. We can simply maintain digital data integrity throughout the signal chain.

Some digital delays are very simple, offering one or more delays that are easily adjusted in terms of level, delay length, and feedback. Other software-based delays packages perform all the delay type effects, including slapback, chorus, flanging, phase shift, and others.

## Chorus/Flanger

Chorus, flanging, and phase shifting fall within the delay family. Like the modern digital delay, software-based systems offer understandable graphical interfaces, instant recall features, and precise adjustment capabilities.

Notice in Illustrations 6-7 and 6-8 the precision adjustments readily available. Sliders offer a comfortable operating option, yet, for precise changes, parameters can be entered numerically. Audio Example 6-25 demonstrates some of the sounds capable with the digital chorus/flanger.

---

*Audio Example 6-25*
*Digital Chorus and Flanging Sounds*
*CD-2: Track 9*

---

## Invert Phase

Phase inversion is the same process in digital and audio. Inverting the phase of a waveform simply changes every amplitude peak into a valley and every valley into a peak. There is no no-

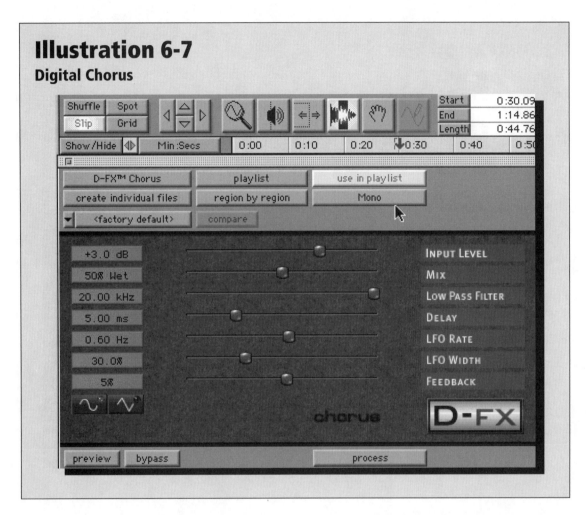

**Illustration 6-7**
**Digital Chorus**

ticeable effect on the sound of a single wave-form after the phase has been inverted. However, if you've combined several tracks, especially acoustically recorded multiple tracks (like a drum set track configuration), inverting the phase of one or more tracks might change the track from very thin-sounding to very full and punchy.

## Reverse

Waveform reversal is a process that lends itself very well to the digital domain. In the analog domain, the tape must be played backward or run through the tape path in a creative way to get reverse sounds and, even at that, they're difficult to position properly. Reversing an au-

dio wave is not commonplace, but it's also not rare. A backward cymbal sound, or a guitar sound that evolves from nowhere and then ends in a crunching release, can be musically dramatic when used appropriately.

The beauty of this technique when performed digitally is the ease of capturing and implementing the audio. Simply record as usual, then select the proper menu item to reverse the waveform, and slide it into place with sample accurate precision. An event that would have taken several minutes in the old days can be accomplished in seconds via modern digital recording (Illustration 6-9).

## Illustration 6-8
**Digital Flanger**

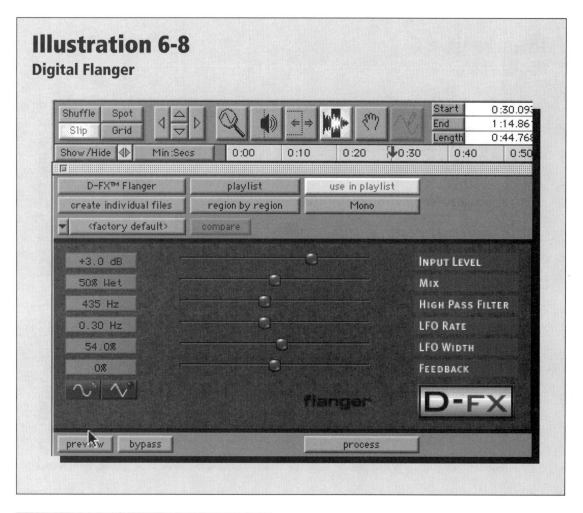

*Audio Example 6-26 Original Guitar Sound*
*CD-2: Track 10*

*Audio Example 6-26 Original Guitar Sound*
*CD-2: Track 10*

*Audio Example 6-27 Reversed Guitar Sound*
*CD-2: Track 11*

### Special Effects

Sci-Fi is a delay and modulation-based effects generator. These types of effects, though sometimes more difficult to place musically, provide a unique and impacting personality. Sounds like these can become a tonal signature, setting a song instantly apart from the pack. The Sci-Fi effects, part of the AudioSuite package included with Digidesign's Pro Tools, provides many special effects. Listen to Audio Example 6-28 to hear a ring modulator, freak modulator, resonator, envelope follower, sample and hold, and trigger and hold.

These effects all utilize combinations of delay, modulation, and harmonic effects. A simple delay, when oscillated—or modulated—and fed back through itself, produces a potentially wild sound characterized by resonator and modulator effects (Illustration 6-10).

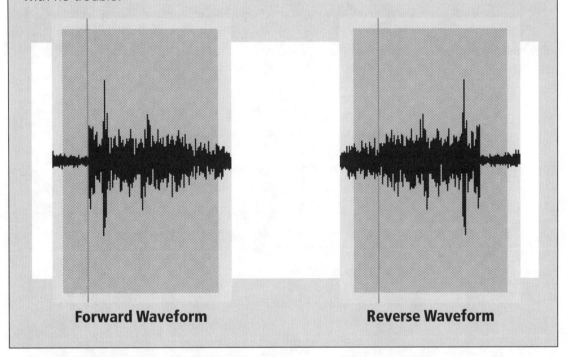

## Illustration 6-9
### Reverse Waveforms

Reversed sounds are difficult to achieve in the analog world. Reels need to be turned upside down or the tape needs to threaded in an unconventional way. Then, the sound needs to be recorded at the correct point while the tape runs backwards. In general, backwards sounds can be a pain to record. However, in the digital domain, a simple menu command produces immediate results—you get instant reversed sounds with no trouble!

**Forward Waveform**                    **Reverse Waveform**

*Audio Example 6-28 Multiple Sci-Fi Effects*
*CD-2: Track 12*

### Variable Speeds
A plug-in like Vari-Fi, included in the Pro Tools' AudioSuite package, simply lets the user increase or decrease the speed of the program material. Pitch remains constant, while the speed changes. Illustration 6-10 shows the simple, straightforward, screen for this easy-to-use plug-in.

Listen to Audio Example 6-29 to hear how

far the speed can change without much noticeable degradation (Illustration 6-11).

*Audio Example 6-29 Variable Speeds*
*CD-2: Track 13*

### Filter
Filter effects, like Filter from Opcode's Fusion Effects series, oscillate (or sweep) a specified bandwidth between two specified frequencies. The rate of the oscillation, or modulation, can

## Illustration 6-10
### Sci-Fi Effects

These effects aren't easy to use in a musically appropriate way. They're often too gimmicky, or cliche, subtracting from, rather than adding to, the power of an arrangement. There are, however, circumstances where these sounds are the perfect answer to a difficult arranging need.

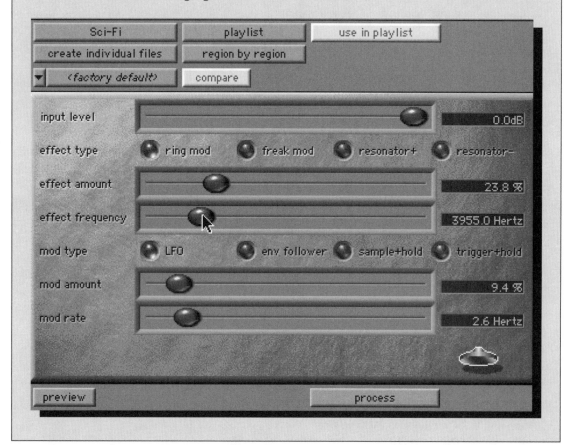

be controlled from none to very fast. This plug-in lets the user determine the effect speed based on musical tempo and rhythmic background unit.

Controls are also simply laid out to vary phase, oscillation shape, and degree of ramp.

*Audio Example 6-30  Filter Effects*
*CD-2: Track 14*

### Vinyl Simulation

Opcode's Vinyl, from the Fusion Effects plug-in library, is a very creative tool designed to simulate the sound character of a vinyl record. Controls range from record surface conditions, including dirt, static, hiss, and wear, to the type of turntable system design featuring adjustments for rumble, bandwidth, compression, and groove depth. Scratches and warp can also be simulated. Though this tool isn't useful on a day-to-day

## Illustration 6-11
### Variable Speed

basis, it offers many creative options for customizing sounds in a musical and emotionally inspiring way.

Illustration 6-12 shows the easy-to-use parameters included in Vinyl. Listen to Audio Example 6-31 and notice how authentic and real these vinyl simulations are. For those of us who actually remember vinyl, this is a blast from the past!

*Audio Example 6-31  Vinyl Simulation*
*CD-2: Track 15*

## Illustration 6-12
### Vinyl Simulation Effects

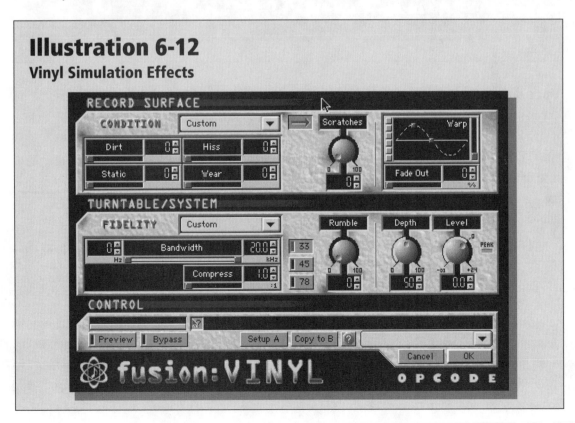

# Illustration 6-13
## Vocode

Vocorder effects like these often sound like they'll be more fun to use than they are. When used in the right place and time, they can be very effective. When overused, they're irritating at best.

## Vocode

Vocode is wild effect from Opcode's Fusion Effects plug-in series. It is a digital version of the older analog vocorder. This device lets the user fuse one sound's personality with another. The most graphic examples of this type of effect are guitar "talk box" effects and keyboard-assisted backing vocals.

In the talk box effect, the guitar provides the sound, but the mouth provides the variations in tone and articulation. The instrument sounds like it's talking. A vocorder performs this type of function in which one instrument seems to be playing out of another.

The other common use for vocorders involves a synthesizer for pitch definition—single or multiple pitches—and a voice for basic tone, pronunciation, and articulation.

Illustration 6-13 highlights the controls available on this flexible tool.

---

### Audio Example 6-32 Vocode
### CD-2: Track 16

---

## Lo-Fi

Lo-Fi, part of the AudioSuite plug-in series from Digidesign, is an amazing tool for determining how low you can take the digital resolution of a particular sound file while maintaining effective impact. In the world of music, we need and want

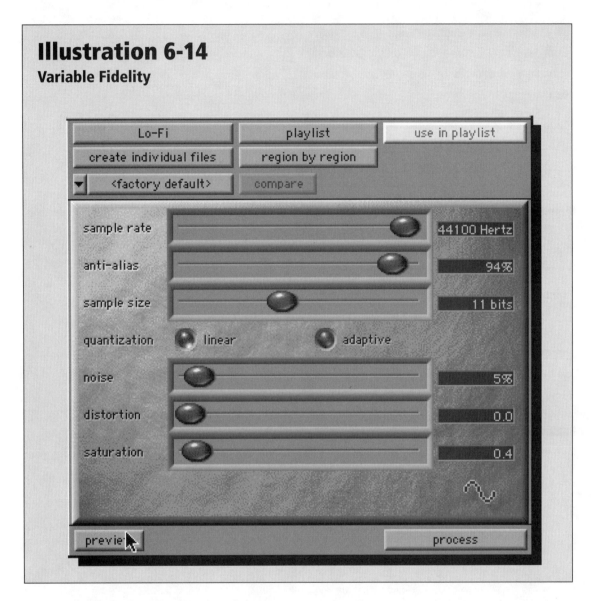

## Illustration 6-14
### Variable Fidelity

more resolution, higher sample rate, and cleaner, smoother conversion. However, when developing audio for a specific purpose that requires either minimal file size or limited bandwidth, a tool like this can be a lifesaver.

The ability to evaluate the audio you've toiled over for countless hours in the form it will really end up in on the final product gives you control over the method used to meet the needs. Should you decrease the sample rate, the word size? What type of quantization should you use

and where exactly should the anti-aliasing filter be set to make your work sound best? What will your product sound like when subjected to the noise, distortion, and saturation specs of the medium in which it will be experienced? All these things can be checked, double-checked, and verified before you release your work to the masses! Illustration 6-14 shows how simple it can be to preview your work before it hits the street.

Listen to Audio Examples 6-33 through 6-

36 to hear the differences between high and low sample rates, 2-bit through 16-bit words, along with varying degrees of noise, distortion, and saturation.

*Audio Example  6-33 16-bit*
*CD-2: Track 17*

*Audio Example  6-34 12-bit*
*CD-2: Track 18*

*Audio Example  6-35 8-bit*
*CD-2: Track 19*

*Audio Example  6-36 2-bit*
*CD-2: Track 20*

# Chapter 7 Random Access Editing

Tape recorders became a reality in the mid-1950s. They offered a feature that had previously been either prohibitively cumbersome or impossible: whatever was recorded on tape could be edited, moved around, or tightened up. Separate takes could even be pieced together. As radio was increasing in size and power, any tool that would help speed up production and increase quality was destined to make its mark.

Bing Crosby was the first real celebrity to try this new medium. He was frustrated with the lack of flexibility in the 78 RPM recording process. Using tape, he could record his radio programs, cutting out mistakes, ill-chosen words, or unacceptable performances. Magnetic tape, an engineer, and a box of razor blades gave him control over production quality and provided a reliable medium for storage.

Digital editing, also referred to as random access editing, has given us a new level of control over production quality, and the digital storage medium has proven to be reliable, affordable, and flexible.

Early digital editing systems were very expensive and the storage medium was either prohibitively costly or it was SLOW! One of the first digital systems I worked with archived short samples to a standard 5 1/4-inch floppy disk. In the operation manual, the manufacturer suggested that the time while the data was being saved could be used for such tasks as learning to fly an airliner or becoming a brain surgeon! They weren't far off.

Current systems are fast, and the storage media is cheap. Very cool!

## The Basics

Most digital editing systems utilize similar terminology. In addition, many parameters, functions, and controls are alike in basic design. There are only so many functions to perform; the course of time and competition has brought technological processes closer and closer together in their performance and practical functionality. The simple fact that competitors in the industry watch each other and copy whoever has the hot hand of the day has an impact on the corporate development of standards. We've definitely seen this phenomenon in the MIDI sequencers manufacturers, and the same thing is happening with the digital editing systems.

Whether or not the recording platform you're operating on uses these exact terms, make yourself familiar with them. As fast as technology changes, you'll probably see these features and functions come across your computer screen soon.

### Nondestructive Editing
Nearly all edits performed in modern digital editors are nondestructive. Nondestructive editing

has no adverse effect on the original waveform. No audio data is ever written or destroyed in the nondestructive digital editing procedure. Audio, which exists on the hard drive, is merely referenced and accessed, leaving the actual data untouched.

Creating a nondestructive data file affords the user the luxury of reordering musical sections, dialogue, or sound effects in as many ways as their creativity can envision. All this is available in an environment that bears no degradation at all to audio quality.

Since this process is only referencing existing audio, it has little effect on the size of a digital audio file. The only thing being written in a nondestructive edit is the reference to data location on the drive, along with reference to in and out points. So, hundreds of edits can be written in one file with little relative increase in file size.

## Destructive Editing

Destructive editing changes and replaces the original waveform, rendering the original irretrievable. This type of editing is rare, though most packages provide a way to perform it. Fortunately, destructive editing normally requires specific actions, procedures, or keystrokes that the user must consciously perform in order for the destructive edit to finalize.

Pencil edits, where the actual waveform is redrawn by the operator, are destructive, though they can be undone immediately after the action if the desired results aren't achieved.

Whenever sections of audio are removed in a destructive way, the computer processor must recalculate the positioning of data, therefore taxing the processor and requiring a fair amount of time. Depending on the speed of your computer system and the amount of data after the edit, this type of destructive editing could take several minutes.

## Regions

A region is simply a defined section of a waveform. If you've just recorded the lead vocal track in one continuous pass, the entire track could be called a region. If you highlight the first chorus, you can specifically define that highlighted area as a separate region. Typically, once you've defined or created a region, it shows up on a list of region, which can be inserted into a playlist at any time. Once a region is defined, it can be named, marked, and edited. New regions can be made from within any region.

Regions can be used repeatedly, if needed. Using a region multiple times takes up no more disk space than just using it once, since the region name simply refers to a specified portion of data located at one point on the drive. Creating and changing regions is a completely nondestructive procedure (Illustration 7-1).

## Playlist/Edit Decision List

A playlist is exactly what it sounds like. It's a list indicating the playback order for specified regions. The playlist is an essential tool in most digital editing packages. Recorders based on specific hardware with a single access window often use a playlist that scrolls in a vertical manner, usually referred to as an edit decision list, or EDL.

A playlist is usually characterized by waveform graphics onscreen, whereas an EDL, in its vertically scrolling list, utilizes text, indicating the track name, as well as in and out points for each list item. These in and out locators are referenced to time code. Crossfade, loop, and play-

## Illustration 7-1
### Highlighted Region in Studio Vision Pro

The gray shaded area in the graphic below can be called a region. Any portion of an audio recording can be designated as a region. A complete recording can also be referred to as a region.

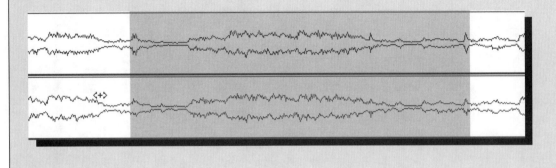

back level information is often included in the EDL. The EDL can be a very convenient way to keep track of certain types of audio programs. Film and video hit points for sound effects are often easy to track this way.

Most software-based systems display the playlist along a horizontal time line, with visual representations of the waveforms scrolling from left to right. In this type of editor, one region naturally flows into the next and they connect, butt together, or crossfade graphically in a way that's easy to understand.

Playlists utilizing graphic representations of each waveform are very user-friendly. Almost anybody can jump into this process and instantly understand what's going on. Once a few terms and tools are understood, editing proceeds in a logical and easy to understand manner (Illustration 7-2).

## RAM Buffer

In order for a hard disk-based editing system to keep up with the demands of random access editing, a storage area for backlogging data is needed. No drive is fast enough to provide continual instant access to regions of audio data, especially as they hop from sector to sector on the drive. Therefore, a clever scheme, like that used by the MiniDisc, allows data to pass into a RAM buffer before it actually flows in the data signal path. Data flows into the RAM buffer—in the correct order for playback—and is streamed out of the buffer, after a slight delay, at the proper rate.

This process is like filling a bucket of water with a hole in the bottom. It buys the drive some time to find a specified portion of audio, stream it into the RAM buffer, then repeat the activity for all the items on the EDL or playlist. The buffer flows the digital data stream at the proper rate, and in the user-determined order, seamlessly (Illustration 7-3).

## Illustration 7-2
### Edit Decision List

The edit decision list (EDL) is a very convenient way to edit audio segment start and end positions. Once you get used to it, this can be the most efficient manner to adjust audio segment timing. Although it isn't as graphic as some screens, it is very efficient.

| | | | | | | |
|---|---|---|---|---|---|---|
| ‖ | 32· 1· 0 | Rec | Mute | Solo | 11 Events | |
| • | 1· 1· 0 | Audio-1 | M Keith's whale | | 17♩+ 135 | 127↓ |
| • | 1· 1· 0 | Audio-2 | M Jamie's lix | | 17♩+ 135 | 127↓ |
| • | 5· 1· 0 | Audio-1 | M Doug's growl | | 22♩+ 413 | 127↓ |
| • | 5· 1· 0 | Audio-2 | M Kerry's Bass Note | | 22♩+ 413 | 127↓ |
| • | 12· 1· 0 | Audio-1 | M Starbucks cup | | 25♩+ 403 | 127↓ |
| • | 12· 1· 0 | Audio-2 | M Spam box | | 25♩+ 403 | 127↓ |
| • | 15· 3· 0 | Audio-2 | M doorbell | | 14♩+ 7 | 127↓ |
| • | 15· 4· 0 | EPS-16+-1 | A2 | 0♩+ 77  18↓ | 64↑ | |
| • | 18· 3· 0 | Audio-1 | M Dog food exitting can | | 14♩+ 7 | 127↓ |
| • | 26· 1· 0 | Audio-1 | M Egg splat 1 | | 23♩+ 123 | 127↓ |
| • | 26· 1· 0 | Audio-2 | M Space Ship | | 23♩+ 123 | 127↓ |

## Gain Change/Normalizing

Gain change is a very simple concept. It applies to digital and analog audio in the same ways. When increasing the gain in either format, you're simply turning the level of everything up or down; the effect of the gain change is global for the selected audio. In analog, you turn the level control up or down. In the computer-based digital domain, the processor simply adds or subtracts equal amounts of level from each sample.

Normalizing is a type of gain change used in the digital domain. The computer searches the selected waveform form for its peak amplitude, then equally adjusts each sample in the wave so that the peak is at maximum amplitude. Some software packages include a percentage parameter in their normalize screen, and the user can adjust the waveform so that the peak is at a certain percentage of maximum amplitude.

We know that when the full amplitude is utilized in the digital waveform we're using all of the available bits. In addition, we know that when only half the available amplitude is used in digital audio we've only really used half our available resolution, or bits. Therefore, it makes sense that adjusting the waveform gain to maximum, or normalizing, would be the right thing to do for the sake of audio integrity and efficient use of the available audio bits. In some instances, this theory holds ground; in others it doesn't.

As the processor calculates gain changes from low-level signals, we run into problems. In the digital domain, low-level signals are best left that way. The resolution in very low-level signals is also very low, so when the gain is changed the result is simply a louder version of a low-

# Illustration 7-3
## RAM Buffer and the Hard-disk System

In Illustration 4-12 we saw the RAM buffer. This concept carries throughout the digital recording network. Whether in a MiniDisc, computer-based system, CD, or DVD, the audio data is passed through a buffer, which can receive the data at varying rates. Digital tape and media don't need to playback at a constant rate; they just needs to spill the data into the RAM buffer in the correct order. As the data leaves the RAM buffer it's clocked to the selected sample playback rate. As long as the buffer doesn't run dry, the audio will playback perfectly free from timing variations.

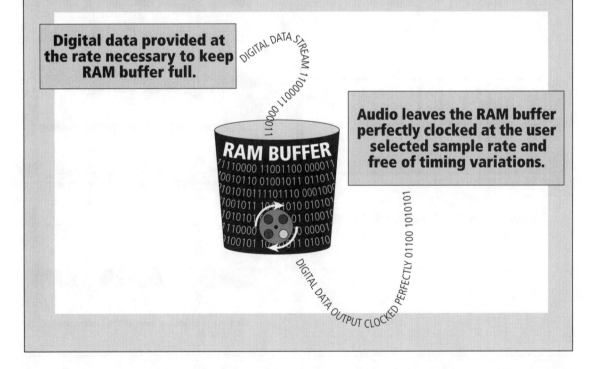

**Digital data provided at the rate necessary to keep RAM buffer full.**

**Audio leaves the RAM buffer perfectly clocked at the user selected sample rate and free of timing variations.**

RAM BUFFER

DIGITAL DATA STREAM 110001 1 00001 1

DIGITAL DATA OUTPUT CLOCKED PERFECTLY 01100 1010101

level, low-resolution sound. Increasing the gain of poorly recorded audio does not increase the resolution. If you only use six bits of a 24-bit word and then turn up the level to occupy the space of a full 24-bit signal, the resulting audio doesn't sound like 24 bits. It sounds like a loud 6-bit waveform.

The very best solution to this normalizing process is to record your original audio as close as possible to maximum amplitude. In this way, the only sounds recorded at very low levels are sounds meant to be there. In terms of waveform amplitude, the only way to optimize the clarity of your digital recordings is to use the full amount of available amplitude (Illustration 7-4).

# Illustration 7-4
## Low Level, Normalized

Waveform A represents a properly recorded digital audio segment. Waveform B is the same example as waveform A, recorded at an extremely low digital level. Waveform C show a 100 percent normalization of waveform B. Notice how the basic waveform shape has been built in waveform C. However, the fine detail and precision have obviously not been rebuilt through the process. Audio Example 7-1 though 7-3 show the sonic correlation to the graphics in this illustration.

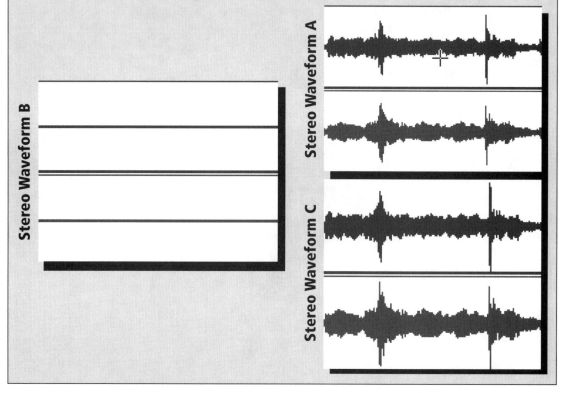

*Audio Example 7-1*
*Audio Recorded at Normal Level*
*CD-2: Track 21*

*Audio Example 7-3*
*Audio From 7-2 Normalized to 100 Percent*
*CD-2: Track 23*

*Audio Example 7-2*
*Audio From 7-1 Recorded at Very Low Level*
*CD-2: Track 22*

## Cut, Copy, and Paste

It's very efficient and convenient that computer-based digital editing software packages utilize many of the same commands as other software. Cut, Copy, Paste, Undo, Redo, Save, etc. are typically performed the same way they are in most word processing, spreadsheet, or database software—and often with the same key strokes.

The nondestructive digital editor doesn't move data in these functions; it merely references sections of previously existing data. Therefore, all these functions are nearly instantaneous. To move or remove a section requires no waiting. Once you select a region and execute a command, it's done. This is an amazing leap ahead from the analog domain.

The addition of these simple computer functions raises the efficiency of the recording process by incredible amounts. The fact that a large chorus with several difficult vocal parts can be perfected within seconds, copied and pasted into every chorus section, is amazing when compared to the alternative. This feature alone could save hours on one song!

## Undo, Redo, Save, Revert to Saved

The Undo command could be the single most important feature in computer-based digital recording—at least it seems like it when you've mistakenly erased a sax solo played by a high-priced virtuoso who's no longer in the country.

Erasing a track, or several tracks, by mistake is one of the worst feelings in the recording process (can you feel my personal pain here?). Once it's gone, it's gone! No amount of weeping, gnashing of teeth, apologizing, or groveling can bring it back.

But the Undo" command saves the day. The computer-based digital recorder lets you undo your last action. So, if you realize that you just taped over the lead vocal track with that triangle part, simply press Undo and the lead vocal lives again! It's an amazing feeling: like finding a lost puppy or realizing you didn't just

run over your vintage Les Paul in your car or that girl making out with Bruno on the beach is somebody else's daughter.

If you undo a recording or other action and then you realize you shouldn't have undone it, you can use the Redo command to redo it. If you finish recording a vocal track and, in your infinite wisdom, decide it was garbage and nobody on the planet will ever want to hear it, you can simply undo, or cut the take, in order to save disk space. Then, when the vocalist starts exclaiming how great the take was and how he could never sing it that well again, you can quietly and calmly press the Redo command—this is a good era to be alive in!

Remember, anytime a computer is involved, save often! Saving is part of my regular functionality—like breathing. In fact, I just saved. Crashes happen, and data gets lost, so save a lot. Some programs have auto-save features. Sometimes that's good and sometimes it's not. The only time I avoid saving is when I try something that involves moving sections of music around. Within a few minutes an arrangement can be tested in different forms and then, if no forward progress is made, I can select Return to Saved. This feature closes down the file and reopens it in its most recently saved form.

## Save As.../Save a Copy As...

If your arrangement is sounding good, but you'd like to try something different and you're not sure whether it will improve or ruin your music, try saving the file as a different name. This way you get to keep the status of your song intact, so you can come back to it if your experiment is a flop.

Use the Save As... command to save your song as another file, under another name. I like to save by the same name, with a different revision number. For example, "My Song rev. 1.1" or "My Song rev. 2.0" is easy to distinguish from "My Song." Try using the same kind of system for numbering revisions that the software manufacturers use for their upgrades. A minor revision gets an increase only to the right of the decimal point; major revisions see a change to the left of the decimal point.

Save As… is different from Save a Copy As…. Save As… simply creates another document icon and a new program file, but all audio continues to be referenced from their original audio folders.

Save a Copy As… not only saves the program file icon as a different name, it also saves all referenced audio files into a new folder. It's very difficult to archive a song with several audio soundfiles without a feature like Save a Copy As… Sometimes, a soundfile that's referenced in your data file never makes it into the folder with the rest of the soundfiles. This can happen when you import audio from another file, or if you've saved a copy as a different name—or sometimes it seems like it's just an inside joke that the computer gets a real kick out of. Use Save a Copy As… any time you want to create a new file containing all audio data related to a specific song. Whether archiving or transporting, if you need to be sure you have all necessary files, use this command.

## Waveform/Pencil Editing

Most digital editing packages provide a facility for waveform editing, sometimes referred to as pencil editing. The pencil tool lets the user destructively redraw waveform data. It's necessary to zoom in to the sample level where just a single line wave is seen onscreen. Once zoomed in far enough, the pencil tool becomes accessible.

Since this is a destructive edit, pre-plan your edits to avoid causing more problems than you repair. This technique is commonly used to repair clicks, pops, and other erroneous transients. These glitches can be seen onscreen as sharp and protruding spikes. They are easily repaired by zooming in, accessing the pencil tool, and redrawing the wave at the questionable point.

Sometimes the spike still looks like a spike in close-up view, and sometimes it doesn't. Often, the waveform that results in a spike in zoomed-out view is really a tightly grouped series of small peaks. The appearance of these grouped peaks can be deceiving in close-up view. However, they're often grouped conspicuously closer together than the surrounding crests and troughs. Redrawing over these grouped peaks to form one wave that occupies the same space as the entire group often solves this problem (Illustration 7-5).

## Smoothing

Smoothing is another technique that works very well when an erroneous peak occurs. This is very similar to editing with the pencil tool. Simply zoom in on the peak in question, then highlight it. When the smoothing task is requested, the processor calculates a smoother wave for the selected area. This technique usually works very well. If, for some reason it doesn't, undo the action, change the selected area to include more or less of the waveform, and try again.

Some smoothing plug-ins provide user adjustable parameters. Some simply smooth the selected area according to preset guidelines. This is a very convenient feature that typically works very well with little tweaking, as long as you've

## Illustration 7-5
### Repairing Clicks, Pops, and Spikes

Waves A, B, C, and D show the repair of a particular pop within a digital audio segment. Notice the peak in A. When zoomed in to view the wave, we might expect to see one big peak. However, often the peak comes from a small grouping (B). The energy accumulates in a small region to additively form a large mass of energy. To repair this type of pop or click, simply use the pencil tool to draw a smooth wave in the place of the jagged ones (C). Typically, this procedure seamlessly eliminates the noise.

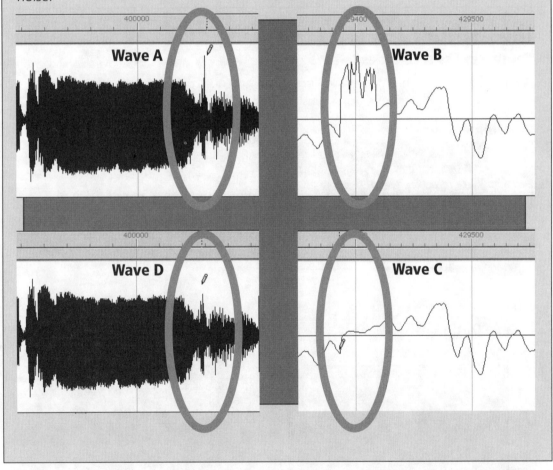

selected the correct portion of the waveform.

### Preview Mode
Preview mode lets the user hear what an edit or other digital manipulation sounds like before committing to the change. Preview often allows you to hear crossfades before okaying them.

When using plug-ins or other effects that either create a new waveform or permanently alter the existing waveform, preview mode is almost always available. Devices that include real-time effects don't have a need for preview mode because they allow effects to be altered at any time without any change to the original waveform.

## Fades

In the analog world, fades are preformed manually through VCA automation, or, at best, moving fader automation. There is definitely an art to the manual fade. Many excellent recordings have faded out (or in) at the hand of the mixing engineer. In most VCA and moving fader automation packages, it's possible to let the computer fade in or out according to a user-defined fade length.

Computer-controlled digital fades are very flexible, smooth, and easy. The length of the fade can be determined by setting the length of the fade onscreen or by highlighting the area the

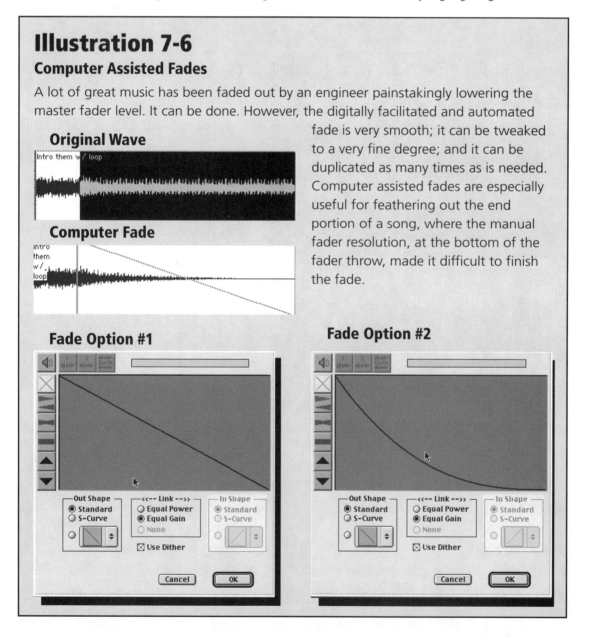

# Illustration 7-6
## Computer Assisted Fades

A lot of great music has been faded out by an engineer painstakingly lowering the master fader level. It can be done. However, the digitally facilitated and automated fade is very smooth; it can be tweaked to a very fine degree; and it can be duplicated as many times as is needed. Computer assisted fades are especially useful for feathering out the end portion of a song, where the manual fader resolution, at the bottom of the fader throw, made it difficult to finish the fade.

### Original Wave

### Computer Fade

### Fade Option #1

### Fade Option #2

fade should occupy. Typically, digital fades can be shaped or drawn within the software package (Illustration 7-6).

---

*Audio Example 7-4 10 Second Automated Fade*
*(Straight Line)*
*CD-2: Track 24*

---

*Audio Example 7-5 15 Second Automated Fade*
*(Gentle Dip Slope)*
*CD-2: Track 25*

---

*Audio Example 7-6 15 Second Automated Fade*
*(Gentle Hill Slope)*
*CD-2: Track 26*

---

*Audio Example 7-7 7 Second Automated Fade*
*(Gentle Dip Slope)*
*CD-2: Track 27*

---

## Crossfades

Prior to the availability of digital editing and features like the crossfade, editing was performed on the master analog tape. The editor, by necessity, was very careful with every cut—the process wasn't nearly as casual as the digital era editing process. When you're cutting the mixed master tape and there's no backup, every cut must be calculated and planned with great precision. A good tape editor constantly listens for the perfect hole in which to make the cut. All sounds are considered, including cymbal decay, reverb decay, every instrument's sustain, room sound, and instrumentation. Once every-

thing has been considered and it looks like you've spotted the perfect edit point, it's time to make the cut, put the tape back together with special editing tape, then listen. Razor blade editing is an art form that takes practice and patience. In the thousands of razor blade edits I've made, I made very few irreparable errors, but I have spent a fair amount of time fixing questionable or downright awful edits. Therefore, I have great appreciation for the digital editing process.

The crossfade, simply an overlap of one region's fadeout with the next region's fade-in, is an amazingly useful tool that's available only in the digital domain. With this one tool, you can regularly perform smooth and undetectable edits that simply weren't possible before its introduction. A crossfade lets the recordist pick an edit point between two musical sections, then fade into one section while fading out of the other.

There are several types of crossfades; each has a place in digital editing that serves a unique function. In application, where one fade type results in a perfectly smooth and unnoticeable fade, another type might not work at all. As you practice applying the different types of fades, you'll soon develop a feel for which type produces the best results for each task. However, even the most experienced engineer needs to experiment with various options for certain more troublesome edit points.

The edit point, where two regions come together, might create a pop or click; one wave might be at the peak of its crest, for example, while the other is at the bottom of its trough. The ultimate goal of a crossfade is to smooth over an edit point so it's undetectable. A listener should never be able to tell that the

## Illustration 7-7
### Crossfading an Awkward Point

The edit point, where two regions come together, might create a pop or click; one wave might be at the peak of its crest, for example, while the other is at the bottom of its trough. The ultimate goal of a crossfade is to smooth over an edit point so it's undetectable. A listener should never be able to tell that the audio they hear has any edits, unless there's a musically creative reason to include the sound of two sections of audio butting together

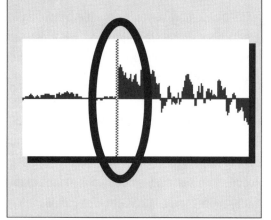

and then, later, to focus in on the edit points in order to perfect each one.

### Linear Fade

Conceptually, the simplest crossfade is the linear fade; it uses a straight fadeout at the same time as a straight fade-in. Many digital editing systems utilize a linear crossfade on every edit to help smooth the transition from one region to the next. The fade duration is typically 10ms or less—unnoticeable in terms of audible fade time—and is often user definable.

A user-controlled linear fade is often 50–100ms in length, though each edit is unique and requires evaluation as to it requirements. Special effects fades might be very long on both sides, but the limiting factor is processing power. Fades are a DSP driven feature. Therefore, total fade length is dependent on available RAM and DSP power (Illustration 7-8).

---

*Audio Example 7-8*
*Awkward Sounding Edit Point (No Crossfade)*
*CD-2: Track 28*

---

*Audio Example 7-9 Linear Crossfade of 7-8*
*CD-2: Track 29*

---

audio they hear has any edits, unless there's a musically creative reason to include the sound of two sections of audio butting together (Illustration 7-7).

Digital edits, including fades and crossfades, are nondestructive, unless you specifically choose to make them destructive. The edit point can easily be changed or the original unedited waveform is always available, in case things ever get really messed up. In addition, digital edits can be fine-tuned later. It's possible to rough a task in, verifying time or musical flow

### Curve Fade

The curve fade swoops in and up or down and out. This gentle curved crossfade works well in an application where the audio must enter and exit the crossfade zone gently. Crossfades with longer durations often produce very smooth music fades. The primary concern, when utilizing linear or curve fades, is a possible dip at the

# Illustration 7-8
## Linear Crossfade

The linear crossfade includes a straight ramp down from one audio segment, in the same time period as a straight ramp up from the next audio segment. These are very common crossfades and they typically perform flawlessly. In fact, many work stations automatically include a 5 – 10 millisecond crossfade on every edit, just smooth over the point where differing audio butts together.

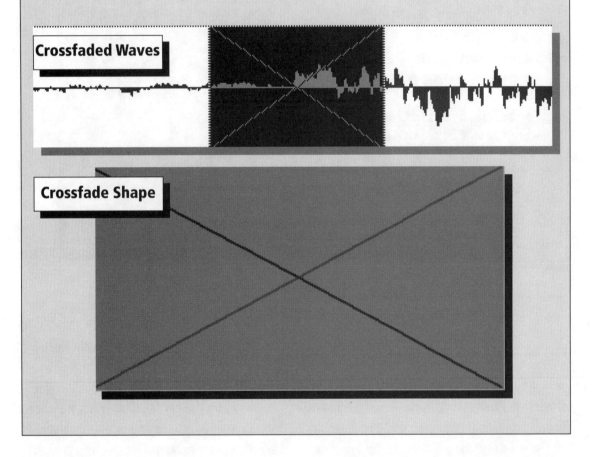

**Crossfaded Waves**

**Crossfade Shape**

edit point. When this happens, an S-curve, equal power, or equal gain fade might produce a better fade.

## S-Curve

The S-curve fades in faster at the start of the waveform and slower at the end. This type of fade curve is particularly useful for material that's difficult to crossfade. It typically helps to eliminate a drop in volume that sometimes occurs at the edit point when a linear or curve fade is used (Illustration 7-9).

*Audio Example 7-10*
*Awkward Sounding Edit Point (No Crossfade)*
*CD-2: Track 30*

# Illustration 7-9
## S-Curve Crossfades

The S-curve fades in faster at the start of the waveform and slower at the end. This type of fade curve is particularly useful for material that's difficult to crossfade. It typically helps to eliminate a drop in volume that sometimes occurs at the edit point when a linear or curve fade is used

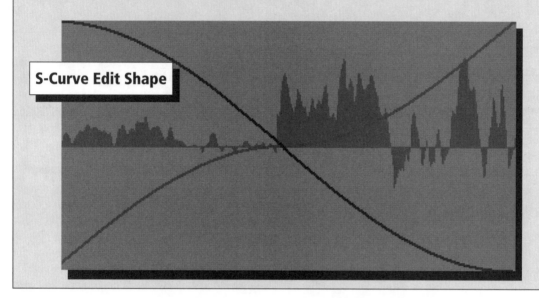

**S-Curve Edit Shape**

*Audio Example 7-11 S-Curve Crossfade of 7-10*
*CD-2: Track 31*

## Overlap Fade

The overlap fade is characterized by an immediate rise in level at the beginning of the fade zone from the waveform fading in and an immediate drop in level of the wave at the end of the fade zone. Both regions maintain full amplitude throughout the fade. This type of fade works well when working from one ambient sound to another, especially when they're both behind other, more important audio. The overlap fade doesn't usually work well for musical crossfades because the combined amplitude of two full strength waveforms often produces dramatic peaks. If two musical sections fade in and out naturally, the overlap fade could be the perfect choice.

## Equal Gain

A linear crossfade often produces a noticeable dip in level as one region fades into the next. Most software packages provide a means to link the fade curves in a way that maintains equal combined gain throughout the crossfade region. The equal gain fade works best when fading between two regions that sound alike—i.e., that are nearly phase-coherent. It also keeps a lid on the level, which helps to eliminate clipping when the equal power link might allow clipping.

## Equal Power

This fade is best used when fading between two totally different sounding regions. It links the two regions together in a way that continually analyzes the amount of energy created by the two regions. The software calculates the combined amplitude so that it maintains equal power throughout the fade range.

## Pre-roll/Post-roll

In the computer-based digital domain, there is no waiting for tape to rewind or fast forward. If you need to return to the beginning of a song, it happens immediately, whether the song is 10 seconds or 100 minutes. However, it's not always efficient to locate to a specific edit point; it's usually best to start a few seconds before the edit and then listen over the edit, stopping a few seconds after the edit.

The amount of playback time prior to the edit point is called pre-roll; the amount of playback time after the edit point is called post-roll. These terms are commonly used in the video editing world where the video tape actually rolls to a specified point ahead of the edit before it begins playback and then rolls after the edit point by the specified post-roll time.

Typical pre- and post-roll times are about three seconds. These parameters usually pertain to preview modes only, though some systems implement a pre-roll every time the transport locates an assigned position.

## Online/Offline

*Online* and *offline* are terms used to denote a digital editor, tape recorder, or other device's status regarding synchronization.

A device that's online will receive and follow the synchronization master device. When the master begins playback, any device that's online immediately locates to the same point in the recording and plays along in sync.

A device that's offline is set to reference playback to its own internal clock, ignoring any other sync reference.

When operating a system that has several devices referencing a master sync source, it's common to go online and offline with a particular device. For example, in a setup including a computer and some ADATs, it's often convenient to take the computer offline to check some MIDI keyboard parts. It's usually a lot quicker and simpler to check parts on one device alone than it is to wait for all synchronized devices to find each other and then to check a part with everything running in sync.

# Editing within the Software-Based Multitrack Domain

Many of the features used by the software-based digital editor are available on the newer modular digital multitracks, like those made by Alesis, Tascam, Fostex, and others. However, the most flexible multitrack platforms are computer-based, hard disk systems. The terms in this section apply specifically to computer-based systems, though many of them transfer to MDM systems. References to specific functions are not intended to be specific to any particular manufacturer.

## Soundfiles

Audio recorded to a hard disk recorder writes directly to the drive. It stays in that form unless the recordist decides to undo the recording or perform a destructive edit. The audio data is typically cataloged on a list of soundfiles, also called, among other things, soundbites, waveforms, audio events, audio instruments, or audio files.

When using a tape-based multitrack, a track is recorded and archived on tape until it's recorded over. Once you record over a tape track, it's gone forever.

In contrast to a tape-based recorder, once audio data is stored on the drive and cataloged in the audio file list, it remains there—even if the user cuts it from the playlist or EDL. Only a blatantly destructive edit removes audio from

the drive, and the software will typically ask once or twice if the audio should really be erased from the drive. Other than saving disk space, there's not normally a good reason to destroy audio data. The fact that it remains on a list provides the user with the option to recall the audio any time.

Since all audio that's ever recorded in a session is available at any time, digital multitrack recording offers an amazing amount of flexibility. If the lead vocal track is just about perfect, there's really no risk in trying it again, recording right over the top of the original track.

# Illustration 7-10
## Visual Assistance from Waveform Editing

In the waveform below the announcer says, "...and the guitar player is about to play his best lick, uh, ever." He emphasizes the "uh" and it sounds unprofessional. With waveform editing, problems like this are very easy to spot and repair. Simply locate the problem word or sound, highlight it, and remove it.

And the guitar player was about to play his best lick, uhhhhhhhhhhhhh, ever.

And the guitar player was about to play his best lick ever.

Audio 1-

**Repaired Speech**

At anytime, the older, almost perfect track can be recalled just as if it had never been cut.

## Waveform View

Most editing and recording packages display audio data in a graphic waveform. This waveform shows exactly what the sound is doing. If it gets louder, the waveform gets bigger; if there's silence, the waveform display is a straight line. Editing becomes nearly as visual as it is aural.

Illustration 7-10 demonstrates how easy choosing an edit point is with the waveform view available.

In the waveform view, it's easy to trim off either end to eliminate unwanted data, or even to remove data from anywhere within the waveform. If the recording went on for a few seconds too long, it's very easy to slide the end of the waveform to the left, trimming the excess. Only the portion of the wave that's seen is heard.

## Punch-in

The punch-in, when using a hard disk recorder, holds a different level of intensity and precision than when using a tape-based recorder. In the tape-based domain, the punch-in is destructive—one mistake and an entire phrase might be ruined.

There is an art to tape-based punch-ins. The operator learns to punch in and out of record with amazing precision. Replacing a word or portion of a word is common. However, one slip of the finger, one note held a little too long by the performer, and the material before, during, and after the intended record zone is damaged, usually irreparably.

With the advent of computer-based recording, the art form of punching in and out of record

is dying. No longer do the recordist and the artist need to work perfectly together in the same "zone" to perform the perfect series of punches repeatedly. Most computer-based systems offer a "fast punch" option, but if you happen to make a mistake, it's no big deal. Simply access the waveform edit window and resize the audio boxes to include whatever you need from the old and new takes. Even if it sounds like you cut off part of the original audio, it can be easily resurrected and positioned to perfection. No problem! (Illustration 7-11)

And while you're at it, if the performance was a little ahead of or behind the groove just move it around in time until it feels great. Then, if it was a little out of tune, just shift the pitch until it's perfectly in tune. With all these tools available to perfect your music, you can concentrate on the important details, like "double pepperoni, double cheese" or "the veggie special" or Subway or Blimpies.

## Auto Record

The auto record feature has been in use for a while in the analog domain—especially in the video and film realms. It provides a means to let the device shift into and out of record mode automatically, in reference to user-prescribed time code locations. This is particularly useful for the solo artist/technician/recordist. Punching in and out while playing an instrument is very difficult without auto record.

Auto record is also very convenient in the video and film domain. If a music or ambience change is required at a very specific point, simply program the auto record to punch in and out at the perfect SMPTE points.

# Illustration 7-11
## Fixing the Digital Punch-in

Even though the punch-in, circled on B, looks like it erases over some of the good part of the take, all is well because the data still exists. Simply grab the end of the waveform blocks to close in or open up the waveform blocks. Once the edit point in B is moved to the right on the new lyric, the original good take can be opened back up to include the portion that appeared to be erased. Digital editing like this provides ample freedom to experiment without the fear of ruining anything. Even when it looks like damage is done, it probably isn't.

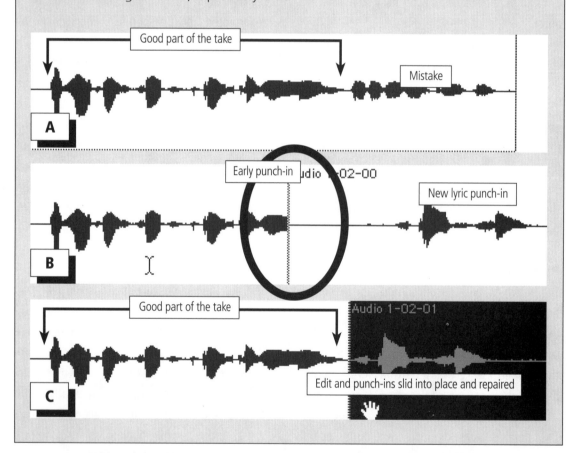

A — Good part of the take — Mistake

B — Early punch-in — New lyric punch-in

C — Good part of the take — Edit and punch-ins slid into place and repaired

## Channels, Tracks, and Takes

A few terms are often used interchangeably, although they refer to different interrelated functions. Tracks, channels, and takes are not all the same. These words need to be differentiated so the concepts can be understood and put into practice.

Channels reside on a mixer. Each of the identical rows of faders, knobs, and buttons is a channel. To say a system has 24 channels refers only to the mixer, not to the multitrack recording capabilities.

Tracks are individual recording zones on a multitrack recorder. A 24-track analog tape recorder has 24 separate portions spread evenly across the width of tape. Audio is recorded separately across the horizontal distance of the tape. A modular digital multitrack operates on the same horizontal track scheme.

The computer-based digital recorder also has tracks. Although there's no tape, a track is still represented on a list and the onscreen transport operates along a horizontal line like the tape-based systems.

A track, in a digital system, typically has provisions for its own level, balance, equalization, and routing control (its own channel) within the software realm, just as it would in a traditional analog setup.

Takes add another dimension to tracks. When a track is created and the instrument is recorded, you're done—in the tape-based domain. The computer setup, on the other hand, provides for multiple takes on each track. Without creating another track, a completely separate take can be recorded. In this way, the track list remains small and manageable, while the possibilities for creating options for each track are virtually limitless—depending on available disk space.

There are many applications for the concept of multiple takes. Takes are particularly convenient on lead vocal tracks, as well as instrumental solo and fill tracks. Most software packages that combine MIDI and digital audio allow for multiple takes on all tracks, no matter which type.

## Comping

Comping is a technique that has been used in the multitrack world for about as long as they've been in existence. The concept is simple—find the best parts from several takes, then compile them into one track that represents the performance in the very best way.

This is a technique commonly used on lead vocals. Since they convey much of the meaning and emotion of a song, the lead vocals should be flawless, if possible: flawless in emotion, rhythm, pitch, sound quality, and impact.

If vocalists could just sing for 16 hours straight with no break, if they'd sing every note perfectly in tune, if they were always rhythmically in the pocket, and if they could keep their energy and emotional fire intact for the duration, their tracks would be simple—and there'd be no need for comping. Realistically, there is a point of no return for most vocalists—a point where their voice and attitude get worse instead of better. There is an art to recording lead vocals, and it requires constant motivation and positive reinforcement on your part. A good producer knows how to keep a singer in the game.

Most vocalists work best when they know they've got at least one track as a backup—a track that's been recorded and is good enough to use in case nothing better comes out. This reassurance is usually enough to loosen the singer up, and sure enough, the forthcoming takes are more relaxed and creative. A vocalist typically needs to take some chances to get the performance to the next level.

Once you've recorded a good take, record another take, but save the old version. The computer-based system allows for plenty of takes, so let the singer fly a bit. Record several takes straight through the song. Stop as seldom as possible. Only stop to focus on a section that you know hasn't quite made it to the perfection of the previous takes. When you have several takes and you're convinced that, somewhere in file, each section has been performed to the highest standards, you've succeeded.

The actual comping process involves re-evaluating each take. Use a lyric sheet to mark the best take for each lyric. Once you're convinced you know where each chunk of brilliance is located, start compiling all the sections to one new track. Simply copy from the source takes then paste to the new comped track.

For each part, record each performance as a separate take on one track. Then, when it's time to comp, create a new track below the original performance track. Copy each desired sec-tion then drag it down to the comped track—preferably locked to a time grid so as to remain in the same groove reference. This technique helps keep the confusion level to a minimum, both onscreen and in your head (Illustration 7-12).

Once all the preferred sections are in place, some adjustments to edit points, level, equal-ization, or pitch might be necessary. There's usu-ally a way to get the comped track to sound smooth and natural, as if it was the only take of the day, but sometimes it requires some effort.

# Illustration 7-12
## Comping the Lead Vocal

It's common to record several versions of a track for review at a later date. Comping is the art of compiling portions from various takes in a way that sounds like one excellent take. When performed with skill, this procedure is transparent—it sounds like the tracks were always meant to be the way they end up. Comping vocal tracks lets the artist keep the best of each take. It also provides a system that lifts a little pressure off singers. They don't have to perform a flawless take. They don't have to second guess whether they can do a better complete performance. Neither do they have to continually experience vocal fatigue from countless tries at a complete performance. Comping is time consuming, but it results in incredible sounding vocal tracks.

| TAKE 1 | The prince and the poet found romance in South Hampton. |
| TAKE 2 | The prince and the poet found romance in South Hampton. |
| TAKE 3 | The prince and the poet found romance in South Hampton. |
| TAKE 4 | The prince and the poet found romance in South Hampton. |
| TAKE 5 | The prince and the poet found romance in South Hampton. |
| COMP | The prince and the poet found romance in South Hampton. |

Crossfading between regions serves to smooth out many rough spots.

If an edit isn't sounding smooth and you've exhausted your available technology and patience, go back the source takes to look for more options. Sometimes this process takes a while, an amazing lead vocal gives the music its greatest chance of success.

## Tuning

A great sounding recording that was made prior to the technological boon we're in commands much respect. There are musical problems that we almost routinely repair and perfect today; our predecessors would have toiled for hours to achieve similar results. We take for granted the minute control available to each of us regard-ing intonation, timing, and all the mix parameters.

Intonation is definitely an attribute that we, as modern recordists, can effectively manipulate. If a note is a little out of tune, we don't need to ruin the singer trying to get it a little closer. We can simply tune it.

With the auto-tune software packages available now, it's not even necessary to have a good ear or perfect pitch to insure that all vocals or instruments are in tune. Simply set the parameters within the software package and process the desired audio; your part will be tuned to your specified perfection. Auto-Tune by Antares provides 19 different scales to reference intonation, along with the facility for graphical interface, vibrato (leaving it alone and creating

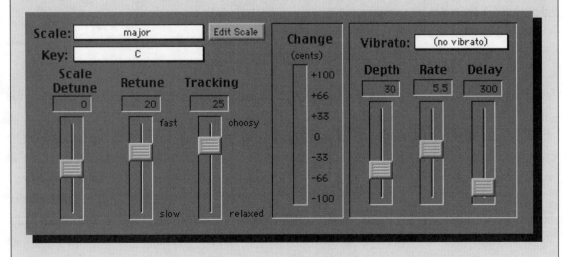

# Illustration 7-13
## Automatic Tuning

Automatic tuning programs offer digital pitch analysis and repair. In the time it takes the player or singer to perform with inaccurate intonation, the processor can analyze the pitch, guess where the tonal center should have been, and repair the problem. This all happens in real-time. Special scale types can be indicated as well as the type and degree of vibrato included, or created.

it), and tolerance settings. Mackie offers an auto-tune plug-in for their D8B Digital Mixer that's also very impressive—and it's right in the console (Illustration 7-13).

---

### Audio Example 7-12 Out of Tune Vocal
### CD-2: Track 32

---

### Audio Example 7-13 Automatic Vocal Re-tuning
### CD-2: Track 33

---

With the depth of technology available today, it's possible to tune a song too much. Stylistically, certain notes and inflections should be slightly out of tune. The "blue" note, for example, often works its way from just above one pitch to just below the next; it's never quite in tune with any one note in our tempered tuning scheme. Since much popular music is based on blues in some way, there are many instances where perfect intonation is simply inappropriate.

Depending on the style and accuracy of the vocalist, I often prefer to tune vocal parts by ear. Great singers working together can create a powerful impact. Much of their natural intonation is driven by emotional and musical tendencies. It's often best to capture a great performance, then tweak as little as possible to get right feeling for the song. Sometimes very few changes are required; sometimes an amazing change must be made. Everything depends on musical considerations.

## Finding the Groove

Shifting tracks in time is a feature unique to the digital era. In the analog, tape-based domain, a singer or instrumentalist is required to control the performance relative to the groove. In the digital domain, though ideally the musician will produce the very best possible performance, if a portion is a bit out of the pocket (not in time) it can be easily slid into place.

When vocals are recorded along with a MIDI sequence, finding the groove becomes extremely easy. The MIDI beat grid is typically right there onscreen. With graphic waveforms built along with the sequence, the beginnings of notes and words are simple to spot at a given location. Slide the audio waveform back and forth until the feel is right.

With controls like these available, it becomes increasingly important that the recordist have musical skills, understanding, and opinions. A technical engineer with no basis for making musical judgement calls must rely on the expertise of a skilled and experienced musician to effectively use the features and flexibility available in today's musical tools.

Listen to Audio Example 7-14 and notice the hyperactive feel of the guitar part.

---

### Audio Example 7-14 Hyper-sounding Guitar Part
### CD-2: Track 34

---

Now listen to the same musical example used in Audio Example 7-14 , this time with the guitar shifted backward in time. This type of change is simple and instantaneous. Producing the same results in the analog domain would require a lot of time and at least one generation loss in quality. Digital manipulations like this produce absolutely no loss in audio integrity and require insignificant amounts of time and energy.

---

*Audio Example 7-15 Repaired Guitar Groove*
*CD-2: Track 35*

---

## Quantizing Audio Segments

Though quantizing is known primarily as a MIDI function that is capable of conforming MIDI notes and data to a specified time grid, this capability is also applicable to audio segments within combined audio/MIDI software packages.

Since, as a rule, the beginning points of digital audio segments aren't consistent, quantizing audio isn't a common function. However, when building a percussive instrumental track from many repeated segments that have been carefully trimmed, audio quantizing is very usable. Like MIDI data, audio segments can be quantized to varying amounts, degrees, and percentages of user defined note values.

Listen to Audio Example 7-16. It uses voice and percussive natural sounds to create a rhythmic groove. The individual ingredients were laid into the edit window so they were close to their intended beats, but little attention was paid to precision.

Next, listen to Audio Example 7-17. The audio segments have been quantized to the closest sixteenth note at 85 percent strength. The effect of this quantizing technique is dramatic.

---

*Audio Example 7-16*
*Percussive Sounds with Loose Groove*
*CD-2: Track 36*

---

---

*Audio Example 7-17*
*Percussive Sounds with Quantized Groove*
*CD-2: Track 37*

---

# Moving Audio Segments

There are some basic ways to move audio segments. The specifics depend on the software you use, but most packages offer some version of each of these features.

### Spot Mode

Spotting lets the user enter a specific start or end time for the audio segment. For example, entering a start point of 01:01:00:00 places the selected region on the time line so it begins at that SMPTE time.

This feature is very useful in the film and video realm. The sound designer's video work copy contains a SMPTE time code window onscreen, which displays the correct time code throughout the program. If you've recorded a sound effect of an egg hitting the ground, which needs to be added at the precise time the egg begins to splat, the procedure is simple if you use spot mode. Simply roll the video, frame by frame, to the splat point. Then, type that SMPTE time into the start time window with the egg splat sound selected, and it's placed precisely where it should be—no trial and error, no guesswork.

For length-specific programming, like radio and television programs, end spotting is an important feature. If you need the last bit of reverb to trail out at 59 seconds, simply enter 00:00:59:00 in the end time window. This type

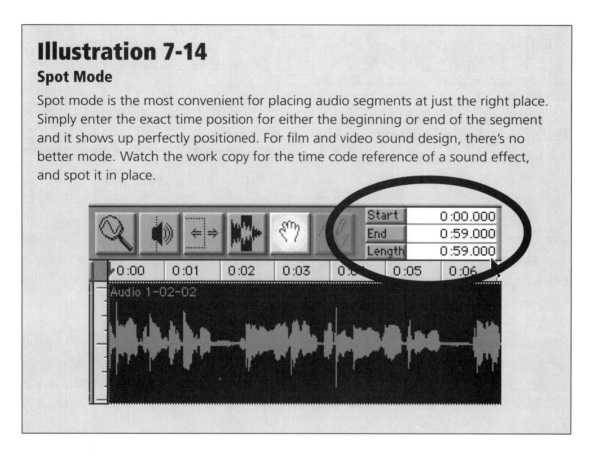

## Illustration 7-14
### Spot Mode
Spot mode is the most convenient for placing audio segments at just the right place. Simply enter the exact time position for either the beginning or end of the segment and it shows up perfectly positioned. For film and video sound design, there's no better mode. Watch the work copy for the time code reference of a sound effect, and spot it in place.

of spotting, called *back placing* is commonly used in the broadcast field (Illustration 7-14).

## Slip Mode
Slip mode lets the user slide an audio region smoothly along the time line. This is a wonderful mode when adjusting timing. If the drummer was pushing the groove all the way through the song, simply select the entire track. Then, zoom the view in as far as possible so that you can see the smallest of time shifts. Then manually slide the track back a little in time. This might require a bit of experimentation and time, but the effort is well worth it when the groove tightens up.

As previously discussed, the same procedure works well on any track. Vocals and instrumental solos especially benefit from the avail-

ability of this feature.

Slip mode is also a very convenient way to rough in dialogue, music, and sound effects for slide presentations, radio programs, and documentaries.

## Grid Mode
Grid mode is similar to slip mode in that audio regions can be slid along the time line. It differs from slip mode in that, instead of sliding smoothly, the regions click along a user-selected grid. If the grid is set to quarter notes, regions will only stop on beat one, two, three, or four.

This mode is especially useful when developing rhythmic patterns with audio regions.

## Shuffle Mode

Shuffle mode forces regions to butt together; it's particularly useful in speech editing. If a word or phrase is cut, instead of a space remaining where the phrase was, the phrase following the cut snaps over next to the phrase before the cut.

This mode is also very useful in song editing where entire sections are removed. With this type of editing, it's necessary to bring the remaining regions together, so this automatic shuffling is very convenient.

# Multitrack Backing Vocals

Backing vocals are very important to a song's impact. If they're done well, they can help the song convey its message in a stronger way. If they're performed, recorded, and edited poorly, they become a distraction and indicate a shabby project.

Tightening the performance during recording helps save time in the editing process and helps keep the quality standards high. Even when the vocals are very clean and tight, there are still several places the editor can help. Breaths, entrances, releases, and intonation are all factors that must be perfected to facilitate a professional-sounding product.

It's very common to double and triple backing vocals. For the following considerations, we'll assume all parts have been at least doubled. When a group sings tracks together, these factors should be addressed during the performance, since they're sometimes difficult to cover up during mixing. If the vocal group, or individual, sings with energy, life, and precision during tracking, the recordist should be able to quickly tighten any loose ends to create an im-

pressive sound.

## Breaths

The worst thing to do on any vocal track is to take out all breaths. For a track to sound, natural, real, and believable, some breaths need to be heard; they make the recording sound alive. However, they shouldn't be so loud that they're distracting to the lead vocals or to the instrumental bed.

With a digital editor, breaths during backing vocals can easily be turned down, left out, or repositioned. The most important consideration is the groove. If the breaths are left in as part of the track's life, they need to be in time with the groove. If they're not, move them, turn them down, or eliminate them. Musical judgement is the key.

Listen to Audio Example 7-18. Notice how the breaths are out of time and a little too loud.

---

*Audio Example 7-18 Breaths Out of Time*
*CD-2: Track 38*

---

Next, listen to Audio Example 7-19. Notice how the breaths have been shifted in time and adjusted slightly in volume. Now they maintain life but add to the rhythmic feel of the arrangement.

---

*Audio Example 7-19*
*Breaths Placed Rhythmically Correct*
*CD-2: Track 39*

---

## Illustration 7-15
### Sloppy Entrances

Notice how the backing vocals (A, B, and C) don't line up perfectly with the lead vocal. In the analog domain, this scenario is difficult and time consuming to correct. In the computer-based digital domain repairing this problem is as easy as clicking on the waveform and sliding it into perfect rhythmic alignment.

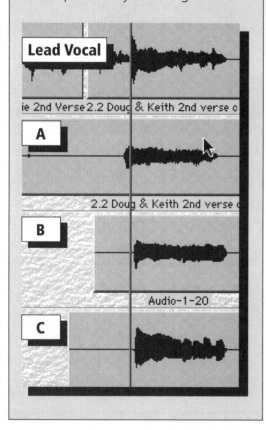

### Entrances

One of the primary indicators of well-sung, cleanly performed backing vocals is the precision of the entrances. If every part starts together, they'll probably stay together, often all the way through the release.

Entrances are easy to place. It's always clear where the waveform begins and, when the backing vocal tracks are lined up vertically,

## Illustration 7-16
### Cleaned Up Entrances

These are the same vocal parts as in Illustration 7-15. However, they've been slid into position so all backing vocal tracks (A, B, and C) line up rhythmically with the lead vocal. Now all parts work together as a unit and the sound is impressive and powerful. It's always ideal to get the vocal parts as close to perfect as possible during tracking. But, if the singers are having a difficult time and the session is growing long, this technique can be a life saver.

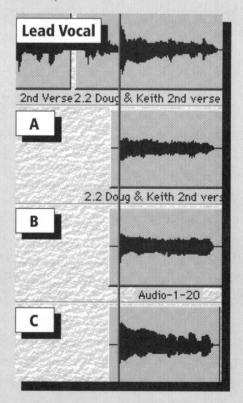

any part that's slightly out of time is instantly detectable. The computer-based digital recording system is laid out perfectly for fine tuning these details. Illustration 7-15 demonstrates how easy it is to see when tracks are out of the groove. Illustration 7-16 shows the same tracks after they've been slid into place to produce a precise vocal performance.

Audio Example 7-20 demonstrates the sound of a backing vocal with sloppy entrances (Illustration 7-15).

---

### *Audio Example 7-20 Sloppy Vocal Entrances*
### *CD-2: Track 40*

---

Listen to Audio Example 7-21 to hear the same piece of music with all entrances clean and precise (Illustration 7-16).

---

### *Audio Example 7-21 Cleaned Up Vocal Entrances*
### *CD-2: Track 41*

---

## Releases

Releases are nearly as important as entrances to the polished feel of a song. The most critical releases are transient releases. Words that end in *s*, *t*, *k*, *sh*, and *ch* sounds are very distracting when the tracks lack precision.

With a digital editor and some patience, these ending sounds can be easily lined up with great precision after the fact. As with breath placement, these sounds should fit together nicely with the groove. Transients act like additional percussion instruments in most cases, so they should be placed with that in mind.

Audio Example 7-22 has some sloppy

releases that distract from the groove (Illustration 7-17).

---

### *Audio Example 7-22 Sloppy Releases*
### *CD-2: Track 42*

---

Listen to Audio Example 7-23 to hear how much better the backing vocals sound when they're working together on the releases (Illustration 7-18).

---

### *Audio Example 7-23 Cleaned Up Releases*
### *CD-2: Track 43*

---

## Intonation

Tuning is very important to the impact and professionalism of the recorded sound. As indicated earlier in this chapter, it's unrealistic to expect a work to command respect in the music community if care hasn't been taken to insure appropriately precise intonation.

One of the problems in backing vocals is fading intonation over the course of a long note. Since the vocalists are often singing along with themselves or others, it's easy for them to lose track of pitch as they hold long notes—so they go flat or sharp.

This problem can be dealt with manually by retuning just a portion of the note and burying the edit point in the mix; some software packages also address this problem. For example, Opcode has a feature called Audio-to-MIDI, which analyzes the audio data and creates MIDI parameters to correspond to note value, velocity, volume, tone, and pitch bend. With this feature, it's possible, once the MIDI

## Illustration 7-17
### Sloppy Releases

Precise releases are an important ingredient in a well sung arrangement. In a computer-based system they're easy to slide into place. Depending on how rhythmically consistent the entire phrase is, some cutting and sliding might be needed to keep the groove constant throughout the phrase.

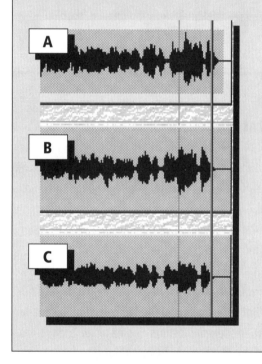

through the MIDI-to-Audio command and the vocal track will play back with perfectly consistent intonation. As previously mentioned, Auto-Tune and the Mackie D8B plug-in could also address this problem. Each system has advantages in particular situations.

### Detuning

In the digital domain, it's a simple task to detune an entire track. In *The Audio Pro Home Recording Course, Volume II*, I discussed varying the

## Illustration 7-18
### Cleaned Up Releases

With the releases tightened up, not only does the entire phrase sound better, but the phrase that follows has the opportunity for greater impact if it's precise. Notice how audio segments A, B, and C finish together.

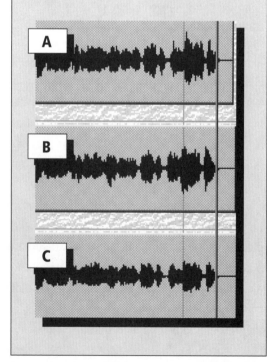

parameters have been created, to adjust any parameter as if the audio had always been MIDI data.

With this process, if a note slides flat, then sharp, then flat again, that movement is registered as pitch bend data. The recordist can simply redraw the pitch bend data as a straight line at "0," therefore eliminating any variance in pitch. Next, the edited audio can be recreated tape speed between takes by one to seven cents to create a bigger vocal sound. Digitally, the same effect can be created in a nondestructive way. Raise or lower the pitch of one or more vocal tracks, then evaluate the effect. If it doesn't sound fuller, undo the action. Try another pitch change amount and evaluate again.

With Opcode's Audio-to-MIDI process, you can draw in a slightly varying pitch bend parameter, then convert back to audio for a realistically floating pitch reference.

Listen to Audio Example 7-24 to hear a doubled backing vocal track, first as it was originally sung, then with the backing vocal tracks detuned by five cents.

---

**Audio Example 7-24**
**Detuning the Vocal Track by Five Cents**
**CD-2: Track 44**

---

## Readjusting Formants

Detuning fattens because it changes the overtone structure of the vocal sound, simulating the effect of a different vocalist or group on the altered track. With modern digital editing packages, formants can be adjusted separate from pitch. Since formants control the apparent size of the voices, independent of the pitch, this adjustment can produce some amazing vocal effects. Alter the formant slightly on one of the backing vocal tracks for a fat sound.

Audio Example 7-25 demonstrates a tripled backing vocal track with the center as recorded, left with raised formants, and the right with lowered formants.

---

**Audio Example 7-25**
**Tripled Backing Vocal with Altered Formants**
**CD-2: Track 45**

---

## Fills, Frills, and Licks

The digital domain is wonderful for recording, moving, altering, and comping solos and licks. It's very convenient to just let the soloist play. Let them fill the track. Have them perform multiple takes—keeping them all, of course. Once you're sure you have enough to work with, thank 'em kindly and pay 'em highly. They'll be on their way, happy to receive your call another day, and you'll have lots of material to work with. It's better to have too much than too little.

Only select the necessary frills. It's anticlimactic to include too many hot licks. However, just the right amount provides a powerful musical addition. It's common to assemble solos and licks together from different takes or to use a lick that was originally performed at the end of a song in the early part of the song. With the incredible flexibility available in modern technology, you can make your decisions based on musical considerations rather than performance positioning.

# Broadcast Audio

## Voice-Over/Editing Speech

The digital editor is an incredibly powerful tool! We've been given control over almost every imaginable voice and music parameter. You can let your creativity run free in this medium. Musically, instrumentally, or in speech, you can usually produce anything you can imagine.

To alter a recording in a way that puts words in someone's mouth is child's play. Converting a public speech from a nervous and bumbling state to a slick and polished form is not difficult. The responsibility given to the editor is awesome. Listen to Audio Example 7-26.

---

### Audio Example 7-26 Original Statement
### CD-2: Track 46

---

Now listen to Audio Example 7-27. Notice how different the content is from Audio Example 7-26, even though it's simply an edited version of the same audio segment.

---

### Audio Example 7-27
### Edited Version of Audio Example 7-26
### CD-2: Track 47

---

## Application of Voice Editing

The advertising, radio, and television industries are built around speech. Narration, dialogue, and monologue are key forms of communication in these mediums. Dialogue replacement is commonplace in the world of film and video. An amazing number of movies utilize absolutely no field audio. Often, all speech, ambience, and sound effects are added in after the film has been edited. The world of multimedia uses speech as a common thread to hold the video, picture, and text together.

Speech editing is a huge part of the audio industry. Many engineers work their entire career without ever recording music. A voice editor, who is both easy to be around and can per-

form high quality work quickly and efficiently is a valuable commodity.

## Voice-Over

The voice-over is simply a recording of one or more voices over a music, ambience, or sound effects bed. The person speaking the voice-over is referred to as the *talent*. Good voice talent is valuable. The ability to read the voice-over text (called *copy*) in a fluid, natural, and believable way is not an inherent gift, built into our species. In fact, inexperienced talent makes for an excruciating voice-over session. Excellent talent makes for a great day in the studio.

Even the most capable and experienced talent makes a mistake now and again. For the recordist, mistakes turn into edits.

## Timing

One of the characteristics of prime talent is the ability to pace copy in the way that will be the most powerful. Delivery timing is fundamental to the voice-over's impact. Often, however, the talent must adjust the delivery timing, simply to fit the copy within specified time constraints.

It's more likely that there'll be too much copy for the allotted time than too little. The editor's challenge is to fit the copy in while maintaining a natural flow. Always leave at least a couple spaces where the listener could imagine talent taking a quick breath. Small breath spaces serve to punctuate the copy, drawing the listener in.

Eliminate unnatural pauses. Keep the flow moving ahead. Don't be afraid to tighten everything up so the copy has momentum. With only a small breath space or two, copy can flow quickly and still impact the listener.

## Ambience

Voice-overs are usually very dynamically compressed, but they're typically recorded in a very quiet voice-over booth. This small recording room is designed to minimize reflections and to provide a warm, smooth speaking sound. Most professionally recorded voice-overs have no problem with ambience changes from take to take—their recording environment is designed to minimize ambient influence.

Field audio, however, is captured on location. Recording a speech in front of a crowd offers special challenges. The sound reinforcement system adds to the character of the voice; feedback can be an issue; crowd noises are always a consideration; and other background noise is often changing constantly. Smoothing together phrases or eliminating stammers and false starts are easy in the controlled environment of the studio, because there's no ambience change. Audio from the field contains continual changes in ambience; the simplest of edits are often complicated by a sneeze or a baby's cry.

# Problematic Edits

When confronted with problematic edits we have a few options that can serve very well to hide, obscure, or eliminate them. Try these features, one at a time, until you're satisfied that the edit is satisfactory.

## Crossfade Ambience

With a little experimentation, crossfades can often smooth over an ambience change at an edit point. Adjust the crossfade length and shift the edit point until you find the right combination.

## Music Bed

When the situation calls for a music bed under field audio, try positioning the music bed so it strategically swells or so that an instrument enters at the ambience change. Music adds cohesiveness to almost any speaking part. It also helps smooth over edits.

## Add Ambience

If the edit point sounds too abrupt no matter what you do with music or crossfades, listen closely to the ambience change. Once you hear the sound of the loudest ambience, try to find a portion of the recording that has that ambience sound alone. When the proper ambience is located, copy a few seconds, then paste it onto another track at the same point as the edit in question. Fade the ambience up and then down at the edit point. This technique is very effective in most cases (Illustration 7-19).

*Audio Example 7-28*
*Adding Ambience to Match Takes*
*CD-2: Track 48*

## Reconstruct the Scene

Film and video sound presents these ambience change problems all the time. If a line simply must be heard and understood but there's a distraction like a huge truck rumbling in the background over the first half of it, you might need to rerecord the line. Try reconstructing the scene. Either go back on location to record the questionable portion in a cleaner ambient environment, or assess the ambience sound and recreate the recording electronically. It's amazing how well a field voice texture can be replicated in

## Illustration 7-19
### Adding Ambience to Match Takes

Often, separate parts of a dialogue are recorded in different places and at different times. Ambience changes between recordings can be distracting and annoying. It's good procedure to record a few minutes of silence each time you record voice. This silence, called *room tone,* can be used to feather ambiences together. In the graphic below, differing ambiences are represented by changes in shading. If we've recorded some gray ambience, it's simple, using a digital editing system to lay it in under the white ambience track to provide a constant room feel. Version A plus additional Ambience A (Version B) produces constant ambience (Version C).

| Voice A<br>Ambience A | Voice B<br>Ambience B | Voice A<br>Ambience A | Voice B<br>Ambience B |
|---|---|---|---|
| The music police entered the room. | What did they say? | They said, "Stop! You're busted! Don't ever play that skanky country lick in a heavy metal song again. You have the right to remain silent!" | What did you do? |

**Version A**

| Voice A<br>Ambience A | Voice B<br>Ambience B | Voice A<br>Ambience A | Voice B<br>Ambience B |
|---|---|---|---|
| The music police entered the room. | What did they say? | They said, "Stop! You're busted! Don't ever play that skanky country lick in a heavy metal song again. You have the right to remain silent!" | What did you do? |

**Version B**

Sampled Ambience     Sampled Ambience

| Voice A<br>Ambience A | Voice B<br>Ambience A | Voice A<br>Ambience A | Voice B<br>Ambience A |
|---|---|---|---|
| The music police entered the room. | What did they say? | They said, "Stop! You're busted! Don't ever play that skanky country lick in a heavy metal song again. You have the right to remain silent!" | What did you do? |

**Version C**

the studio. Try to equalize the sound to match. If possible, use the same mic setup that was used in the field. If the field audio had some natural reverberation, try to simulate it digitally. As the final ingredient, copy some field ambience from the original recording. Place it on another track at the insert point and use it to bridge the gap between the real audio and the reconstructed audio.

## Live with It

If the nature of the program material is primarily informational, it might be appropriate to just accept the abrupt edit. All good editors try to do the very best job possible, but there are applications where an obvious edit isn't the end of the world. Judgement calls are the norm in the day-to-day world of audio production. Sometimes the details are in control; other times the deadline is in control.

## Breaths

Speech is often very compressed to keep each syllable at the forefront of the mix. The drawback, technically, in this approach is that along with every word that's enhanced by the compressor's level adjustments comes every breath, lip smack, and tongue clack. In many applications, these distracting sounds must be diminished or removed. Notice in Audio Example 7-29 how pronounced the breaths and mouth sounds are (Illustration 7-20).

*Audio Example 7-29*
*Pronounced Breath and Mouth Sounds*
*CD-2: Track 49*

Some breaths and mouth sounds should simply be eliminated. Other sounds just require a gain adjustment. If you remove all breaths, you're recording will lack life, authenticity, and believability. Practice various techniques and approaches until you have a feel for what it takes

# Illustration 7-20
## Pronounced Breath and Mouth Sounds

It's best to deal with these sounds before they hit the airwaves (radio or television). If they're irritating on the master, they'll be even more pronounced after the broadcast compressors have emphasized them further.

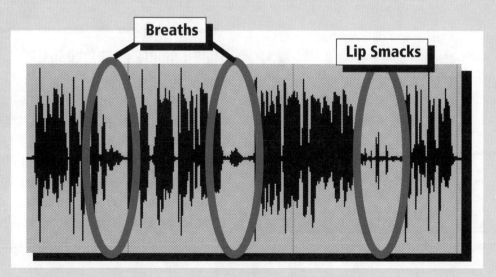

## Illustration 7-21
### Repaired Breath and Mouth Sounds

Sometimes it's best to eliminate unwanted mouth and breath sounds; often it's best to simply turn them down, either through a processed gain change or an automated volume control. If a breath flows normally in the recording, it's usually preferable to turn it down rather than remove it. If a sound seems awkward or out of place, it's common to remove it. There are always exceptions, so taste and educated discretion remain of great value. In the example below, the breaths should be turned down. However, notice that the lip smack have been eliminated.

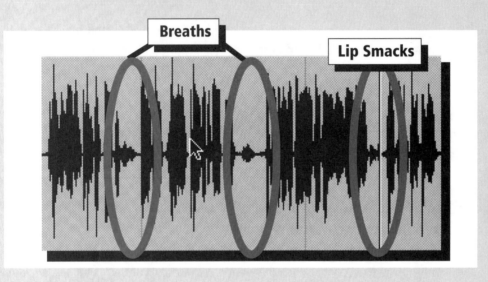

**Breaths**

**Lip Smacks**

to produce a real-sounding voice edit.

Now listen to Audio Example 7-30. Notice how much more impact the text has with the distracting breaths and mouth sounds turned down or eliminated (Illustration 7-21).

---

*Audio Example 7-30*
*Repaired Breath and Mouth Sounds*
*CD-2: Track 50*

---

## Time Compression/Expansion

Time compression and expansion are used commonly in the broadcast world. A thirty-second commercial needs to end in between 29 and 30 seconds. If a spot is short and runs at 26 or 28 seconds, it not only messes up the programming, it's an inefficient use of airtime. Total production cost for an ad is typically several thousand dollars, so the motivation is to use every valuable second.

Voice recordings can usually be compressed or expanded by 10–15 percent with little adverse effect on the impact of the text. Whenever time-adjusting audio, act primarily on the voice. When speech is altered and the music is left in its original state, the results are more consistently satisfying.

Listen to Audio Examples 7-31 through 7-35. The voice has been time-adjusted by varying percentages, which are indicated in the recording. Notice the character of the voice at each degree of compression or expansion.

---

*Audio Example 7-31 Original Voice-over*
*CD-2: Track 51*

---

*Audio Example 7-32*
*Voice-over Expanded by 10 Percent*
*CD-2: Track 52*

---

*Audio Example 7-33*
*Voice-over Expanded by 20 Percent*
*CD-2: Track 53*

---

*Audio Example 7-34*
*Voice-over Compressed by 10 Percent*
*CD-2: Track 54*

---

*Audio Example 7-35*
*Voice-over Compressed by 20 Percent*
*CD-2: Track 55*

---

# ADR/Foley

ADR and Foley are two terms commonly used in the film and television worlds:

- ADR stands for *automatic dialogue replacement*. The process involves rerecording dialogue that's already been filmed or video taped.
- A Foley soundstage is designed to support the replacement of natural sounds like footsteps, door slams, and creaks and other things that stomp, squeak, thump, or bump.

### ADR

The need for ADR arises from three primary factors: poorly recorded field audio, a desire to project more intimacy with the character than the ambient field audio allows, and line changes.

Capturing high-quality field audio is an art. It's difficult to capture the intimacy of a scene from outside the camera view; sometimes it's impossible. When the field audio is not effective for the scene, the actors are required to come to the studio. In this controlled environment, an intimate sound is easy to capture. The process involves actors watching themselves on a video monitor while they r-speak the dialogue. Each actor tries to recreate the correct inflections, pacing, and emotion for the scene.

This is sometimes a tedious process, but it's amazing how convincing the rerecorded audio is. It's also amazing how many movies use ADR for all spoken parts. Next time you watch a movie, try to imagine whether the ambient sound of the voice matches the indicated ambience of the setting.

It's common that the film producer or director wants the audience to feel like they're intimate with the actors in a given scene. Therefore, no matter what the surrounding ambience or quality of field audio, ADR is needed.

Any film recordist deals constantly with text rewrites. At the last minute, an important line in the film might be changed. Line changes seldom involve reshooting the video or film because of budgetary reasons, but they often involve ADR and some creative scene editing. An attempt is made to obscure the actor's mouth during a scene with a line change. A distant, side, or rear shot might be selected. However, often the production staff decides to rely on the audience's inattention to detail. Watch movies with an alert eye. You'll see many scenes where the actors are saying something different than it looks like they're saying. This is a judgement call. The production team must decide if the line change is strong enough to warrant a visual discrepancy that most people will never notice.

ADR is typically done in reference to SMPTE time code. A scrolling image of the correct SMPTE time code is burned in to a video tape reference. With the digital editor locked to time code, the actors' lines are rerecorded as they try to match the picture. The reference videotape often includes the field audio for an audible reference, too.

Once the dialogue has been rerecorded and is very close to matching, the digital editor takes over. It's simple to slide the new audio into place. The nudge keys are very convenient. Simply select the nudge resolution that seems right for the job and slide the audio into place. It's best to use the nudge feature once the new audio is closely positioned, because it gives the operator a frame of reference. If the audio is moved six nudges early but then seems a little too early, it's easy to guess that it might need to be moved back two or three nudges. If the audio is simply slid around, there's no frame of reference, and the task will take longer than it should.

## Foley

The process for Foley recording is similar to that of ADR. Someone on the Foley soundstage watches a videotape of the program, trying to match the steps, slams, or squeaks with those onscreen. With waveform graphics and onscreen SMPTE time code available, placing most Foley sounds is a simple task. At the contact of the shoe with the ground, for example, you can note the time code reference and spot the rerecorded footstep perfectly in place. Most Foley sound effects can be easily positioned this way.

In the major film and video markets around the world, there are several highly skilled Foley artists who are very accurate in their placement of sounds. If you hire excellent Foley talent with an impressive arsenal of sound creating gadgets, this process will go very smoothly, and you might not need to do much shifting or nudging at all.

# Getting the Program Ready for the Air

## Normalize

Once the voice is recorded and positioned, whether in radio, television, or film, it needs to be readied for presentation. First, be sure the levels of the audio are strong and full. If the track needs to be normalized, now is the time. Be sure that, if there are several edits within the voice-over, the entire track is normalized as

## Illustration 7-22
### Normalizing by Region

When normalizing by region, the processor has no real way of telling which regions should be adjusted differently. It simply takes each region and normalizes it to the set specification—usually 100 percent level at the peak. When normalizing edited dialogue it's best to normalize the entire file as one event, then to save it as a continuous file.

Especially in sections like the one marked below, normalizing by region results in artificial loud sections. Regions meant to be heard at low level get boosted to full amplitude.

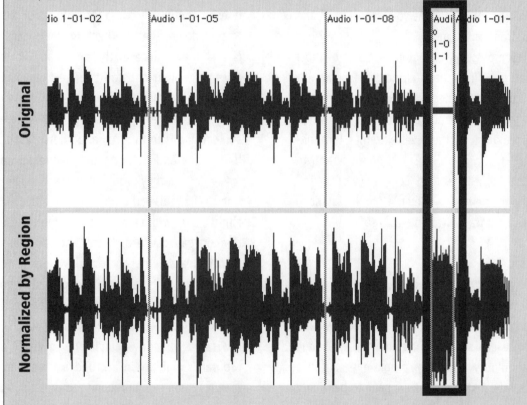

one item. This mode looks for the peak across the entire track, then moves all levels up relative to the peak. Another mode normalizes each item separately. This is the wrong mode for normalizing a complete voice-over.

See Illustration 7-22 for an example of a voice-over normalized two ways: one way as an entire track and the other as individual regions.

*Audio Example 7-36 Edited Voice*
*CD-2: Track 56*

---

*Audio Example 7-37*
*Edited Voice Normalized by Region*
*CD-2: Track 57*

---

## Compress

If the voice-over track has a substantial difference between the loudest and softest portions, compress the entire track for the most natural, though consistently present, voice sound. It's very important to keep the voice level strong and in the front of the mix.

Compression is a standard part of most digital recording software packages. Some utilize a preview mode; with these, you must select the preview region according to its overall representation of the level extremes throughout the track. There'll usually be an option to replace the original track completely or to simply add the new, processed track to the list. Keep the original track available as a safety.

## Music

Usually music needs to be feathered in throughout a program to add to the flow and emotion of the presentation. Match the music level and the voice level so they both sound strong. Though you should try to keep the program level at 0VU constantly, certain sounds appear to be louder than others, even at the same level. For this reason, always use your ears as well as your meters to predict how well a show will project.

Adjust the volume of accompanying music so that it is well below that of the voice. Always guess low on the music level; it should be under the voice-over level. A couple of things happen in the broadcast process that affect the final balance between the music and voice:

1. Multiband compression is used on most broadcast transmissions. A multiband compressor divides the audible spectrum into discrete ranges. Most broadcast compressors divide the transmission bandwidth into two or three frequency ranges: typically highs, mids, and lows. Each of these bands is compressed separately. The advantage to this process is that the bass, which contains the most energy of any frequency range, isn't always hitting the main threshold. Therefore, the bass doesn't continually cause the entire program to turn down. The drawback to this process is that the balance of the music and voice doesn't remain constant. Since the voice should be the strongest signal in its frequency range, it's constantly activating the compressor, causing it to turn its range down. If the bass range and treble range compress to a lesser degree, they probably increase in relation to the mids—the prime vocal range.

2. Limited bandwidth in the radio and television domain can cause a discrepancy between what is heard in the studio and what is heard on-air. It's for this reason that recordists who work with broadcast often, use a speaker or speakers designed to reproduce the sound of AM radio or mono television. To verify a program's viability in a broadcast medium, monitor through a multiband compressor and small, inexpensive speakers.

# 8 Synchronizing

Synchronization has become an increasingly complex process as technology has evolved. Modern day equipment has so much flexibility and so many sync capabilities that constant study and updating is required of any serious recordist. We're in a constant state of anxiously awaiting the next amazing tool. Keeping current with technology is no longer good enough; we must continually be in preparation for what's coming.

The basic concept of synchronizing hasn't changed since its inception. Musicians have always appreciated sharing the same groove—I'm sure of it. Synchronized swimmers know what each member of the team intends to do, and they keep track of each other without any of the audience realizing it so they can remain synchronized throughout the entire program.

Synchronizing recording equipment is similar to synchronizing musicians and swimmers:

- It's ideal if all gear is in exactly the some groove. It's easier to get everyone working together if all participants speak the same language.
- Some players, swimmers, and recording equipment are better at synchronizing accurately than others.
- Every once in a while, even the best have a bad day and, for unexplained reasons, mess up everybody that they're around.

In this chapter, we'll cover several different types of synchronization and how they might or might not work well together. Our goal is to understand all the ingredients in order to make informed and insightful decisions regarding system configurations and equipment purchase options.

## Synchronizing Basics

Any synchronization system needs a master transport, which all others follow. Devices that follow the master are called slaves, and they must follow the master within the tightest sync tolerance possible. Different types of synchronization schemes offer varying degrees of accuracy. Some systems are relatively loose, with machines fading back and forth in relation to the master speed. Other, newer systems are able to remain locked to sample-accurate perfection. In a sample-accurate synchronization system, the machines are locked so tightly together that they act like one. If the master machine plays back at a sample rate of 48kHz, so does the slave. The slave verifies at each sample that it's still in sync, and it doesn't drift at all.

In its infancy, the synchronization process was primal compared to our current capabilities. Early schemes, like pilot tone, were an attempt to control film transports so that audio and film images could be combined after the final film print was completed. As the film and television industries grew, SMPTE became an industry standard for synchronizing image to picture; it provided much more flexibility. The simple ability to start, stop, and resume playback at any point in a program while maintaining sync between all SMPTE-savvy machines was a boon. With modern synchronization methods and protocol, not only can many machines sync quickly and easily, but they can sync in a sample accurate manner. Modern systems can synchronize many devices, representing hundreds of audio tracks, together so that they act and sound like a single machine.

For an explanation of the basics of pulse sync, SMPTE, and MTC refer to *The AudioPro Home Recording Course, Volume I*, Chapter 6.

### Why Bother?

This question has become increasingly valid with the advent of powerful new digital audio/MIDI sequencing software packages. If you have a huge hard drive and you record only within your computer domain, you probably haven't needed to worry too much about synchronizing concerns yet. If you simply bounce your mixes to disk, then save them to CD or DVD, you're probably still immune to the sync plague. But, if you need to record your mixes to DAT, if you're jumping into the digital mixer world, if you want to get the most out of your outboard digital effects, if you ever plan on interconnecting to the professional world, or if you think your music has any chance whatsoever to make it to the next level of industry greatness, you're going to need to address synchronization in a serious way.

The power and flexibility of interconnecting the computer-based recorder with the any of the Modular Digital Multitrack recorders and digital effects processors is amazing. You won't want to miss it.

## MIDI to Audio Sync

MIDI to audio sync has made great strides in the area of convenience. Compared to manual sync, pilot tone, sync pulse, song position pointer, and FSK, the SMPTE based system (often referred to as LTC [Longitudinal Time Code]) is fast, accurate, and fairly simple to master. SMPTE/MTC offers compatibility across the industry and serves us well in many cases.

### Timing Discrepancies

MTC and SMPTE are good standards, but they're definitely not precisely accurate. The SMPTE to MTC translation is slow. It's dependent on the integrity and quality of the time SMPTE code. It often has to interpret what it thinks the time code should have been, and it's not always right.

Devices syncing to SMPTE/MTC float back and forth in time depending on a several factors:

- Is the data transfer to and from the MIDI device going through a bottleneck, or can it flow freely and uninhibited?
- Is the device's processor fast enough to keep up with the demand of the MIDI sequence data?
- Is there digital audio data competing for the internal clock or computer processor power?
- Is the MIDI interface keeping up with the demand for multichannel data transfer?
- Is the master MIDI device running from its internal clock, or is it chasing another SMPTE-based device?
- Is there a grand master system clock acting as the time base for the complete system? If so, what kind of timing clock is it?

Many recordists feel that the SMPTE/MTC

synchronization system is a perfect synchronization environment. It's not. The best accuracy factor we can hope for whenever using a SMPTE/MTC based master is ±1/4 frame. That might not seem unreasonable at first glance, but if we calculate the delay, we soon recognize a significant sync variance. If we assume a frame rate of 30 frames per second, it's easy to calculate that, since each frame occupies 1/30 of the 1000ms in a single second, a single frame is about 33 1/3ms. Each quarter frame is about 8 1/3ms. A variance of ±1/4 provides a net error of up to 16 2/3ms, and that's touted to be about as good as it gets.

This degree of error is not too disturbing until you begin to combine devices, transfer data, and interconnect various systems over the course of time. With a ±8 1/3ms error factor, the recordist can't be certain that every pass of every take in every generation will respond to synchronization in exactly the same manner. It's possible for the margin of error to compound over the course of a project, especially whenever combining recording formats and sync devices. The quarter frame error factor can multiply throughout the life of a project, resulting in a musical feel that is much different from the one you slaved to create in the beginning.

Audio Example 8-1 demonstrates the rhythmic effect of the error factor in MTC and how it can compound over the life of a project.

---

*Audio Example 8-1*
*Panned Clicks Simulating MTC Error Factor*
*at 0, 8.333, 16.666., and 33.333ms Delay*
*CD-2: Track 58*

---

Audio example 8-2 through 8-4 demon-strate the sound of a drum track rushed and laid back by the potential margin of error in the MTC-based system.

---

*Audio Example 8-2*
*Original Drum Part*
*CD-2: Track 59*

---

*Audio Example 8-3*
*Drum Part Delayed by 33 1/3 ms*
*CD-2: Track 60*

---

*Audio Example 8-4*
*Drum Part Moved Ahead by 33 1/3 ms*
*CD-2: Track 61*

---

There is no solution to this lack of accuracy as long as the master clock device is SMPTE/MTC based.

# MIDI to MIDI Sync

MIDI to MIDI synchronization is a reasonably simple process. MIDI Time Code (MTC) is simply transmitted through the MIDI cable connecting the synchronized device. Modern MIDI devices include an option to sync to an external source. Once that option is selected, it waits to receive MTC, then plays along in near perfect time (Illustration 8-1).

MTC is a very common time communication format. Many digital devices and recorders synchronize according to MTC language. From previous study in this course, we know that MTC is the MIDI equivalent of SMPTE time code, ref-

## Illustration 8-1
### MTC Connections

Most software packages provide a way to send MTC and other synchronizing information to any machine or MIDI device in the system. Simply drag from one device to another to connect them through the digital, onscreen patching system.

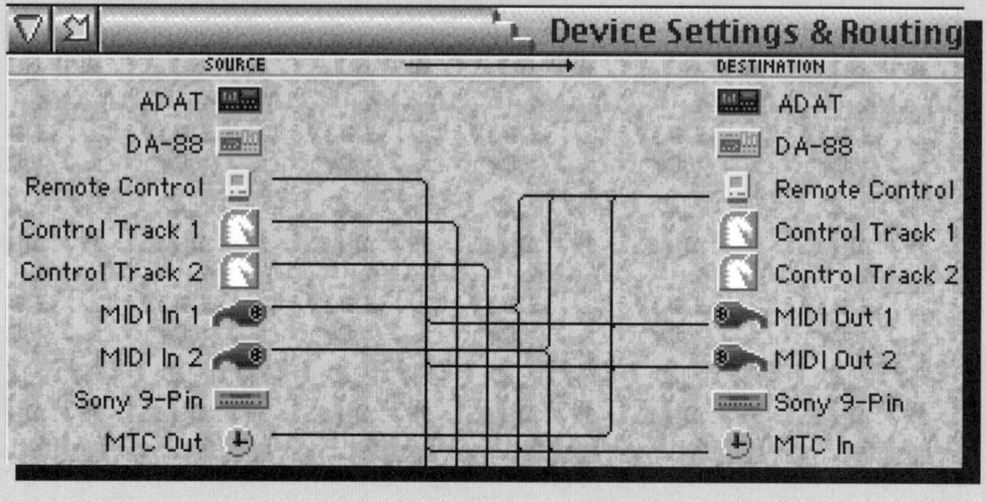

erenced to hours, minutes, seconds, frames, and subframes.

## Accuracy

The accuracy factor of MTC in the MIDI to MIDI communication domain is much more solid than SMPTE-based audio to MIDI sync. An accuracy factor of ±1 tick can be expected in most cases (a tick is typically 1/480 of a beat). Therefore, the accuracy is dependent on the tempo of the song. At 120 quarter notes per minute, we can expect accuracy to within ±1.04ms (500ms/beat÷480 ticks).

Accuracy in MIDI to MIDI sync (MTC to MTC) is still dependent on the same type of factors noted in the previous section: data bottlenecks, processor speed, time clock source, etc..

## Logjam

If a MIDI transmission contains a lot of controller motion, like pitch bend or modulation, the bulk of data can cause a MIDI logjam. As all the data flows at once, sometimes it gets stuck, causing what sounds like a timing hiccup. The short pause, as the data regains its flow, renders the particular playback useless.

The logjam can be eliminated in a couple different ways. First, consider purchasing an interface with a higher data transfer rate. This solution can save you a lot of heartache later. Second, look for an option that lets you thin the controller data. This command might be called Thin Continuous Data or Thin Controller Data, or some similar rendition. This command eliminates a percentage of the data. If you set the command to 50 percent, it will remove every other controller command, dramatically decreasing the bulk of the data. Most of the time, thinning data has no real effect on the sound of the performance, and it usually eliminates the MIDI logjam.

## Processor Speed

Processor speed is very important, especially when using a digital combined audio/MIDI sequencing software package. It's likely that a large file with a substantial amount of digital audio will occupy the processor to such an extent that the timing clock bogs down. With this, the tempo and time feel go up in smoke. The solution to this type of problem is to either buy a faster, bigger, meaner computer; thin out your files so there aren't any unnecessary competitors lurking in the wings; or turn all nonessential system extensions off.

# Analog to Analog

Analog to analog synchronization typically involves reel-to-reel recorders. In fact, most of these analog principles apply to synchronizing digital reel-to-reel recorders, though there are other considerations we'll cover later that are unique to digital synchronization. In dealing with reel-to-reel machines, there still has to be a master and a slave device.

In this type of system, each machine has SMPTE striped on one track, providing a means for the synchronizer controller to evaluate the time address position of each member of the synchronization network.

## LTC on Each Machine

Modern reel-to-reel recorders allow for external control of their playback, fast forward, and rewind motors. Typically, the motors are controlled by variations in voltage. The sync processor keeps track of the SMPTE (also called LTC or longitudinal time code) on each machine. It adjusts the speed of each motor so all transports run together with the master so that their SMPTE clocks are running along at identical addresses.

Therefore, with this system, there's a constant assessment of the individual slave speeds and LTC addresses. This continued assessment of position and adjustment of transport motors causes a phase shift effect between the synchronizing machines. There isn't usually a problem with this phenomenon unless there's identical material on two or more machines. If there is identical data, the resulting sound of simultaneous playback is a very pronounced phase shifting.

A system where a slave machine chases and synchronizes to a master machine is called a chase-locking synchronizer.

## Verifying Sync

In fact, one way to verify the degree of sync between machines is to record identical material on each, then play both machines and listen to the identical material. As the machines run closer together, the phase shift gets tighter and tighter, but it never gets completely synchronized to the point where the resulting sound is smooth and wobble free.

## Offsets

It's typical that all devices in the synchronizing network run referenced to the identical address throughout the reel. If each reel starts at

01:00:00:00 and they always run together, everything makes more sense throughout the project and things seem to run smoother. If, however, you have multiple reels that all were striped with different starting addresses, you'll need to quickly master the offset.

An offset is simply a calculation of the difference in time address between the reels. If reel one starts at 01:00:00:00, but reel two starts at 01:00:45:00, there is a 45-second offset for reel two. On the synchronizer controller, simply enter an offset of +00:00:45:00 for machine two. The synchronizer will calculate the difference in time addresses throughout the reel, keeping the two reels locked together in relative sync.

Sometimes, in a system where sync has drifted over the course of a project, it might be necessary to search for perfect sync. It's usually with the offset control that you'll slide the machines into a tighter sync relationship.

Whenever possible, record a track with a very sharp percussive sound, like a clavé, onto a track of each machine while they're being simultaneously striped. This percussive sound will act as sync verification down the road, if things start to go awry. After the reels have been striped, I like to run a sequencer, generating the percussive click, in sync with the both multitracks, while recording the click to both. This way, if the sync starts to sound out of sync later in the process, I can solo the clicks on each device and easily hear if sync has been maintained or lost somewhere.

Try panning the two clicks hard left and right. If sync is still okay, the clicks might sound a little phased, but they'll seem to come from the center. The tighter the sync, the more centered the click will sound.

If the clicks are out of sync, it could be because one of the devices is being overworked and just can't keep a steady pace. It's also possible that, somewhere along the line, the MTC/SMPTE margin of error exceeded acceptable boundaries, or it could be that corrupt code was recorded in the early stages of the project. For whatever reason it happened—and it does happen—bad sync needs to be addressed.

If devices aren't properly synchronized, the offset control can help slide them closer together. If you recorded percussive sounds on each device when they were verifiably sync-locked, play them back, soloed and panned apart. Adjust the offset of the slave reel by subframe until the clicks move to the center and the phase shift is tight and clean (Illustration 8-2).

## Regenerating Time Code

Whenever copying from one tape or recording medium to another, regenerate any time code that's being transferred. Part of the problem in translating SMPTE to MTC lies in the inability of tape to accurately capture the SMPTE square wave. If the SMPTE wave wasn't recorded accurately to start with, rerecording it from tape to tape only compounds the problem.

Regenerating time code is a simple process. Almost any time code generator outputs identical code to what it receives at its input. So, simply plug the output of the tape into the input of the time code generator. Then, patch the output of the code generator to the input of the machine being copied to.

Code that's been regenerated is as good as new time code. Most generators can even compensate for any time code dropouts that might have developed on the original track (Illustration 8-3).

## Illustration 8-2
### Offsets

Offsets provide a means to adjust timing between machines. If you come across two reels of tape, or devices, that must be synchronized, the time code references on each might not exactly match the other. In this case, the proper difference between the two time code positions must be guessed, then finely adjusted until the devices or machines work together in an efficient and musical way.

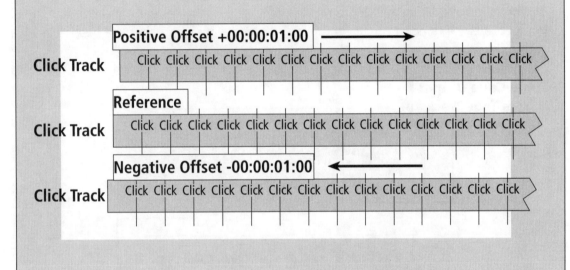

## Free Wheeling

Most sync controllers offer the ability to free-wheel. Whenever there's a dropout in the flow of time code, the sync controller naturally wants to assume that the machine with the dropout has gone offline. In the harsh world of absolutes, a time code dropout causes the machine to stop and then, when it sees code again, the controller chases and relocks to the master. If this happens often in the middle of concentrated creativity, it's very irritating and displeasing to the masses.

The freewheel option lets the user determine how many frames can drop out before the controller assumes the machine is offline. During the dropouts, when instructed properly, the controller continues playback of the machine at the same rate as before the dropout. If the code comes back before the prescribed number of missing frames is up, nobody knows the difference. The machine keeps playing like nothing ever happened.

If the freewheel dropout boundary is set too high, the machines will take an unnaturally long time to stop once the stop button has been pressed. There's usually a good middle ground for this setting that minimizes undue stopping because of dropouts, yet keeps the session pace going by stopping relatively quickly after stop is pressed.

## Jam Sync

Occasionally, the end of a song just comes too soon. If the time code stops near the end, you

## Illustration 8-3
### Regenerating Time Code

Time code that comes from a tape track often loses it's precise definition in the recording process. Sometimes bits of code will be lost or damaged. Therefore, it's advisable to regenerate time code anytime it must be recorded from one tape track to another. It's a good idea to regenerate the code even when it's coming from a tape track into a computer-based system.

The generator simultaneously outputs the exact code it receives at its input. In fact, it compensates for minor dropouts in the incoming code which might have been caused by tape anomalies or wear.

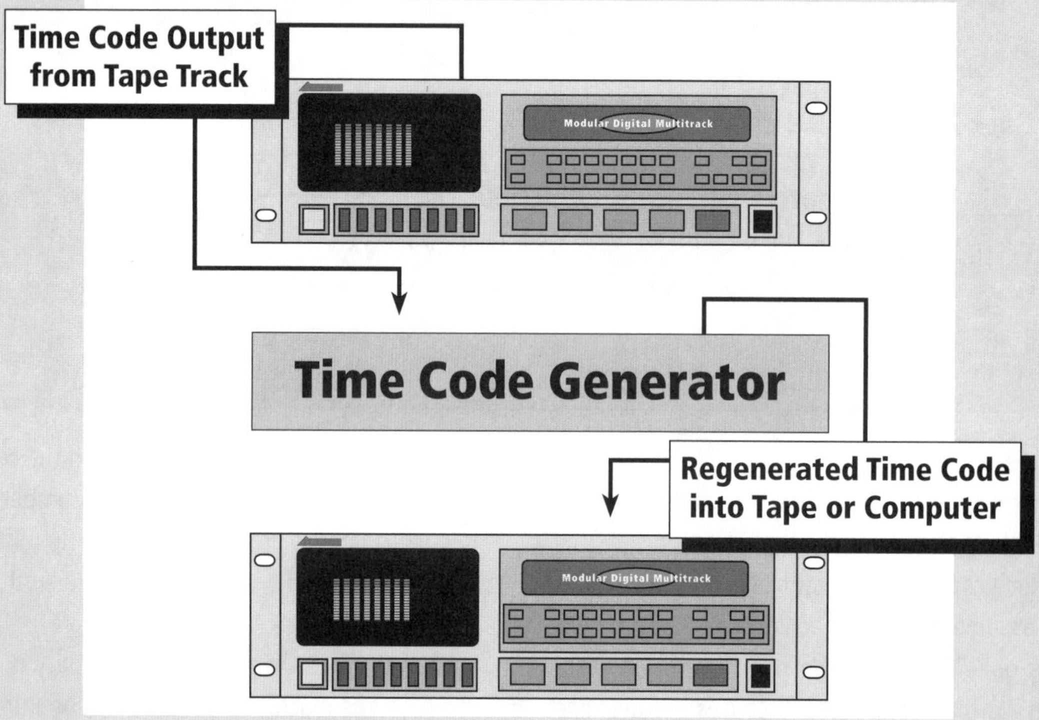

**Time Code Output from Tape Track**

Modular Digital Multitrack

**Time Code Generator**

**Regenerated Time Code into Tape or Computer**

Modular Digital Multitrack

might be in a bind. If you've already got the early portion of the song sequenced, recorded, and synchronized, it's not practical to start over with new code.

This problem can be easily overcome through jam sync. Jam sync is like infinite freewheel. It follows the original LTC, regenerating fresh time code that can be printed on another track. Once the LTC runs out, the generator keeps generating code, even when it loses the reference code. If you keep the machine in record on the new code track, the generator will keep generating as long as you desire. With the newly generated fresh time code track, you can complete your recording and add any additional music you'd like.

# Digital to Digital Sync

Digital to digital sync is similar to regular analog or reel-to-reel sync in many ways. There's a master and slave machine, or several slave machines. The machines follow a time base reference and can chase SMPTE, LTC, VITC, MTC, and most other types of sync codes.

Though its similar to LTC sync, digital sync offers a much tighter and absolute synchronizing scheme. Digital to digital synchronizing is typically capable of sample accurate sync.

Sample accurate sync has no drift and no phasing. It is as accurate as if the two recorders were one. The digital sync device analyzes sync at the sample level, maintaining a perfect lock at all times. This is a very cool feature!

# Components of Digital Sync

Digital synchronization operates through the continuous control of three parameters:
• Time Base
• Address
• Transport control

## Time Base—Word Clock

Any time digital transfers are made, both the source and the record machines must reference the same clock. Word clock, which is simply the flow of data at the speed of the sample rate, acts as the timing constant between a source and record deck. If the record deck isn't referencing the word clock of the source deck, the digital data can't transfer accurately—each sample is not seen completely, or maybe two are seen at once. Word clock must provide a stable, accurate measure of time passage.

When a record deck is set to external sync, it receives each sample in order from the source deck, at its rate. Therefore, each word is transmitted accurately and in a timely manner. The two machines remain locked together sample by sample.

The concept of word clock isn't too different from the concept of the earlier pilot tone and sync pulse. In each system, word clock, pilot tone, and sync pulse, the slave deck moves ahead at the same rate as the pulse, cycle, or sample of the source device (Illustration 8-4).

Word clock can synchronize through any digital communications/transmission route including S/P DIF, AES/EBU, SDIF-2, DA-88, ADAT, or proprietary control track. Devices that require word clock communication for proper sync are digital mixers, stand-alone hard-disk recorders, computer-based digital audio workstations, and computer-based audio cards.

When devices are not referencing the same clock source during a digital-to-digital recording, the audio typically contains unwanted clicks, pitch wavers, and pops. These occur because of an abnormally high error rate due to data confusion as the data send gets out of sync with the data receipt.

## Word Clock Rate

The word clock rate equates to the sample rate. The standard audio CD rate of 44.1kHz is typically used for digital audio recordings that need to be released on CD. Although higher sample rates yield higher fidelity, the negative effects of sample rate conversion offset the benefit. Digital recordings, destined to be mixed down to analog or through analog processing are best recorded at the highest available sample rate.

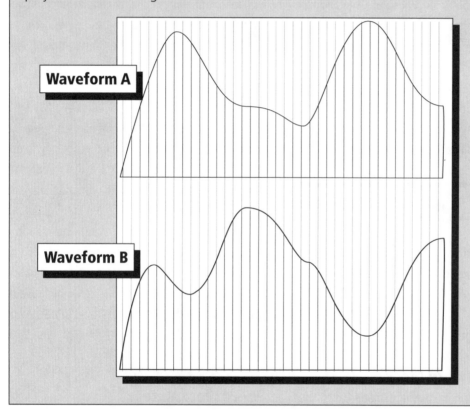

# Illustration 8-4
## Sample-to-Sample Synchronization

Sample-to-sample sync provides absolute synchronization between multiple devices. This type of system contains a master clock that runs all digital devices; every time a sample is played back on one device, a sample is played back on all devices. It's important, therefore, that each device contains material recorded at the same sample rate. For example, a device containing audio recorded at 44.1kHz will playback fast and higher-pitched when locked to a master device playing back at 48kHz. Each sample in waveform B waits to playback until receives the go-ahead from the sample playback clock driving waveform A.

**Waveform A**

**Waveform B**

Therefore, word clock time base reference could also be 48kHz, 96kHz, or even 192kHz.

## Pull-Up/Pull-Down

Pull-up and pull-down affect the sample rate, either by increasing or decreasing it by 0.1 percent. Therefore, a 44.1kHz sample rate pulled down actually progresses at only 44055.9Hz; if

it's pulled up the sample rate becomes 44144.1Hz.

NTSC video runs at 29.97 frames per second. Notice that 29.97fps is 0.1 percent less the 30fps. There is a correlation between these two relationships.

There is a timing difference at each transfer stage when film is transferred to video for post-production and then transferred back to film again. Film runs at 24fps. In the transfer process from film to video, every 24 film frames is mapped onto 30 video frames. However, the video then plays back at 29.97fps. Since playback is 0.1 percent slower than the original transfer speed, any audio that's synchronized to the work video must be pulled down in speed by 0.1 percent. When the audio is transferred back to film, it will again play from the video at 30fps. Since the audio was recorded at the proportionately slow speed, it will transfer in perfect sync to the film image.

If you're working on a film that's been transferred to video, select a pull-down rate on your sync controller. This will help insure sync throughout the end of the film project.

## Address Code

Word clock acts to synchronize the sample rates between two digital devices. However, in order to run together in both relative sync and at exactly the right time musically, there must be an address code. The address code can take on several forms in digital communication.

MTC, SMPTE, VITC, Sony 9-pin, ADAT, DA-88, and Proprietary control track all have address information built in. Keep in mind that digital sync allows for combinations of time base and address code. As long as you're using a time hub that can read and write all of these forms of sync and time code, it only matters that, at all times, there are cross-compatible time base and address masters.

## Transport Control

Whether using a hardware- or software-based transport, digital sync performs and feels like analog sync to LTC or VITC. The master control-

ler calls the shots and the slave machines chase to a location, then they follow in perfect sync. All playback, fast forward, rewind, stop, and cueing functions are mirrored by the slave machines.

## MIDI Machine Control (MMC)

MIDI Machine Control uses specific MIDI commands for controlling transport and cueing functions. Most modern recorders like those made by Alesis, Tascam, Sony, Fostex, Otari, etc. can be controlled through MMC. These machines must be connected, through standard MIDI cables and an interface, to the MIDI controller. The specific controller could be a software-based sequencing/digital audio package, a dedicated hardware controller, or a master tape machine.

Whether hardware- or software-based, MMC controls look and act like tape-deck style transport controls. In a typical setup, the MMC controller sends transport commands to another MMC device, which serves as an address master. The address master generates and distributes time code information to all recording and playback devices, which, in turn, chase and lock according to the MMC commands. It's not necessary that post-address master devices and machines respond to MMC commands; they must simply follow the timing commands supplied by the address master (Illustration 8-5).

# Variations in Accuracy

Not all devices support the same degree of synchronization accuracy. You might have purchased a device promising sample accurate sync. Then, when you connected it to your system, the sync seemed somewhat loose. That's probably be-

# Illustration 8-5
## MIDI Machine Control

MIDI Machine Control is a very convenient means of controlling physical transports from within your computer-based digital recording system. The screen below controls multiple machines while the MIDI sequence plays along. All sequence transport and record commands are functional for the connected tape machines as well.

cause your system's sync is being controlled by the lowest common denominator. Devices that claim sample-accurate sync provide it only when connected to other devices specifically capable of sample-accurate sync.

There are four basic type of synchronization. Each type has a completely different degree of timing accuracy.

## Sample-Accurate Sync

When devices run together in sample-accurate sync, they progress together on the sample level. They play sample 1 together, then proceed to sample number 2, then 3, then 4, and so on. Therefore, at a sample rate of 48kHz, the devices track together at each of the 48,000 samples; this continues throughout the recording. This continuous tracking together results in the best possible synchronization.

The process of tracking together, sample by sample, also describes word clock. Sample-accurate sync, however, also keeps track of each sample throughout the recording. If the master machine starts at sample number one, all devices start at the very beginning of the recording. If the master device starts at sample

35,000,001, all devices go to that specific address and begin playing perfectly together. Ideally, no machine will be even on sample out of sync with the others, and that sync will be maintained without variation or phasing throughout the duration of the playback or recording.

A slight bit of skewing, or deviation from absolute tracking, might occur due to analog filter delays. But the delay will be very slight and absolutely consistent, so no phasing or adverse effect should arise.

## Frame-Accurate Sync with Phase Lock

The term phase lock refers to the process described above, where the slave device tracks together with the master, sample by sample. When phase lock is achieved, there is no drift between the devices. Frame-accurate sync, however, is bound to the accuracy of LTC/SMPTE time code. Most systems using SMPTE and MTC are capable of phase lock, but their fundamental limitation resides with in the quarter-frame accuracy factor of the SMPTE to MTC relationship. Although phase-locked, devices in this system cannot be trusted for sync accuracy closer than ±1/4 frame. The net accuracy from take to take is therefore ±1/2 frame.

The difference between sample-accurate and frame-accurate sync is only in the accuracy of the start point for playback—it will only be within ±1/4 frame. But, once the devices are synchronized, they'll stay as tightly synchronized, sample to sample, as sample-accurate sync. In the scope of precise musical feel, groove, and emotional impact, ±1/4 frame accuracy is disappointing and frustrating, though it's practically functional.

## Frame-Accurate Sync with No Phase Lock/Continuous Sync

The accuracy factor for this type of sync within one frame is about 1/30 of a second—plus or minus 33ms. The variance factor of frame-accurate sync with no phase lock is substantial and continually changing. Since there's no link to word clock locking devices together once they achieve their relative sync status, the device transports are continually accessing sync status. As they assess their relation to the other devices, the only way to maintain sync is to speed up and slow down. An analog device continually varies the transport motor speed to maintain sync. A digital device must continually adjust the playback sample rate to keep pace. Within the software domain, this is often called *continuous sync.*

The continual speed change as the transports adjust to maintain sync causes a pronounced phase shifting effect between any two machines. A chorus-like sound occurs whenever identical material is being played back from different machines. Though it's not normal to play identical material from two sources at the same time, it's disturbing that the subtleties of the combined musical groove are continually varying. Especially considering that when a musical ingredient shifts within a pattern, sequence, or groove by a few milliseconds, the emotion and feel change dramatically.

## Frame-Accurate Trigger Sync

Frame-accurate trigger sync has none of the continuous tracking or updating characteristics of the previous sync forms. Trigger sync is a very simple process; the master device tells the digital slave to start playing a specific sample at a specified frame. The slave plays the audio at its own pace, totally independent of any other timing source. Any audio over a few seconds long is prone to drift out of sync, and there's no way to keep it in sync within this format. Trigger sync was used by early versions of most of the digital editing packages. It's a fairly useless system for anything other than triggering very short audio regions to play within one frame of where they really should end up. Frame-accurate trigger sync is archaic by modern standards.

# Various Sync Formats

There are several different types of synchronization formats and schemes. One ingredient of a complete synchronizing system doesn't ordinarily make a complete package. Time base, address code, and transport controls are fundamental to a rock solid synchronization setup.

## Internal

The internal sync clock for any digital device is pretty solid and consistent. Some devices can even play back over long periods of time, staying fairly close together with no synchronization other than a precisely timed press of both start buttons. However, internal sync is primarily for playback and recording within a one-device closed system.

Some devices have a relatively inaccurate and inconsistent internal timing clock. If a device like this can be controlled by word clock or another very accurate external sync source, it's usually worth the effort. An inconsistent timing clock can have an adverse effect on audio quality. Synchronizing to a more reliable time base reference will result in higher quality digital audio.

## MTC

MIDI Time Code is not a bad choice for synchronizing a MIDI sequencer to another MIDI sequencing device. The resolution of accuracy is ±1 sequencer clock unit (often called a *tick*). It's common for computer-based sequencers to divide each beat into 480 ticks. However, when synchronizing digital audio devices, MIDI Time Code provides the least amount of time base stability. Using MTC as a master source for time base and time code is unadvisable. Even if MIDI Machine Control is required for system completion, you'll get much better results if you use another, more accurate time base and address source.

## SMPTE (LTC) 30fps, 29.97fps, 29.97df, 25, 24fps

SMPTE (Longitudinal Time Code, or LTC) is commonly used as a time base in the analog multitrack domain. One track of the multitrack—typically the track with the highest number—is striped with SMPTE. SMPTE time code provides the address information for a synchronizing system. When used in conjunction with MTC and MMC, timing resolution and accuracy isn't exceptional. As stated earlier, the accuracy within ±1/4 frame can have an adverse effect on the musical feel.

LTC to LTC synchronizing systems are fairly accurate within the analog multitrack domain. The sync controller typically keeps the machines within a subframe of each other. This accuracy is dependent on the integrity of the time code and the ability of the transport mechanism to maintain subframe accurate sync. Although, LTC to LTC sync is relatively accurate, the slave transport still continually varies its speed while searching for perfect sync.

## Video Sync

Video sync, also called *house sync* and *blackburst*, is a constant timing reference used in situations where multiple video tape recorders, switchers, edit controllers, and audio devices must interconnect accurately and reliably. The clock frequency of house sync is exactly 15,734.2657Hz.

Without a timing constant like house sync, video devices do not interconnect well; they'll produce image glitches, rolling pictures, and other time-related inconsistencies. House sync serves to insure that the leading edge of each video frame and time code address happen at the exact same time, therefore continuously controlling the accuracy and stability of the system.

Audio devices also benefit from house sync. Resolving all audio devices to this constant time source, though it doesn't increase the initial accuracy of a time address system, helps them lock together accurately. Once relative sync is achieved, all devices run smoothly together without drift because each transport tracks the crystal generated blackburst.

## VITC

Vertical Interval Time Code (or VITC, pronounced *vitt'•see*) encodes the same SMPTE address and code structure information as LTC into the video signal itself. With VITC, there's no separate LTC track. The time code information resides in a portion of the video signal, called *vertical blanking interval*, that's outside the visible video image.

Since the time code information is part of the video signal, a professional VTR can accurately read it at all speeds: fast, slow, and still framed. A VITC system provides for quick and accurate placement of audio segments and sound effects in relation to the video image.

Normal work-copy video, called a window dub, contains an actual scrolling image of the exact time code reference throughout the video. VITC systems are accurate enough to eliminate the need for such a dub.

## Word 1x

Word 1x is standard word clock. It serves as the master time base for most digital audio systems. Systems that resolve word clock maintain rock-solid sync, free from inter-machine phasing and drift. Using word clock as time base doesn't, by itself, insure sample-accurate sync. But it does insure that, once sync has been achieved within the address code limitations, it will remain stable and constant.

## Word 256x

Word 256x, also called super clock, is used by Digidesign hard-disk systems as their time base. Like Word 1x, this time base reference serves as a guide clock.

## S/P DIF and AES/EBU

S/P DIF and AES/EBU are similar to word clock in that they act as the stable time base in a digital recording setup. These sync protocols specify one device as the master and one as the slave. The slave tracks the master, typically in phase lock—the digital data flow is perfectly in sync—though there's no address code information. S/P DIF and AES/EBU synchronization protocol do, however, have provisions for embedded time address information, though it's not typically implemented.

S/P DIF and AES/EBU are different from word clock in that they contain digital data, as well as time base.

## SDIF-2 and MADI

SDIF-2 and MADI are digital connecting systems that separate the word clock time base reference from the digital audio data. Word clock reference is typically connected through a separate BNC connector.

## Proprietary Sync Systems

Several proprietary sync formats are in common use. Manufacturers develop synchronization schemes that they feel offer prime support for their specific product needs. Alesis, Tascam, and Mark of the Unicorn, Digidesign, and others have sample accurate sync systems for their equipment. Although these platforms are proprietary in their development, other manufactures occasionally support or borrow them in their product designs.

## ADAT and DA-88 Sync

These proprietary sync systems are very stable and precise. Sample accurate sync information, including time base and address code information, is transmitted in the data stream along with the audio information. Complete sample accurate sync is achieved between ADATs or DA-88s through direct, unit-to-unit communication. Only in the older ADATs is an external control required to attain sync.

ADAT and DA-88 sync is so precise and rock-solid that sync ports can be daisy chained with no loss. Standard configuration limits on complete systems are capable of utilizing up to 16 units chained together for 128 tracks.

# 9 Digital Mixing

Whether in the '60s or the third millennium, mixing is a subjective art form. However, with the amazing progress of technology, it takes little foresight to forecast the coming of the completely computer-formulated mix. In the scope of what software and hardware can now accomplish, it seems like a piece of cake to develop an algorithm capable of taking into account the relative levels, EQ, panning, and effects for the various mix ingredients. In fact, why not just add another menu to the digital console—the Mix menu? Simply call up the Bruce Swedien mix, or the Bob Clearmountain mix, or maybe check out how your music would sound if it had been mixed by George Martin! (Illustration 9-1)

Maybe plug-ins like these would be instructive, but music is art, emotion, feeling, and expression. It should be built from the ground up, with the soul of the artist and music fused together.

The technical flexibility available for mix assistance is incredible. On many mixing systems, everything can be automated; the automation has no intrusive sonic affect; and effects, ease of use, and sonic integrity are unsurpassed. One person can develop a mix that's tremendously complex, by previous technological standards. However, it seemed more exciting with 12 folks standing around a console that was about the size and shape of Tennessee. Each person had a list of prescribed tasks that had to be completed at the perfect time, in order to perform a corporately perfect mix…

…Nahh! It's more fun now. Creativity knows no boundaries, nor does it want them. We can always get 12 people around a great big table and come up with much cooler creative things to do than to perform primal commands off of a sloppily scribbled task list. "At 00:22:33:15 move fader 12 to –4…" Let's move on!

## How Are Digital and Analog Mixers Different?

### The Analog Mixer
The analog signal path contains several transducers that change from acoustic (sound source) to electric (microphone) to magnetic (recorder) to electric (mixer, amps) and back to acoustic (speakers). As soon as the signal leaves the microphone, it's on its way to degradation. Each component sucks a little more life out of the original waveform; then, after so much loss, the signal is amplified back up to line level. However, the signal that's amplified lacks the original definition. Then the signal passes through more circuitry. Maybe it's equalized, compressed, gated, and trimmed up to the optimum level— there are two or three amplifying circuits right

## Illustration 9-1
### Mix Engineer Menu

Wouldn't it be fun to hear what the legends would do with your music? It might take some of the sparkle out of creating the magic on your own, but maybe someday this'll be an option in a software manufacturer's package. It could provide a good starting place for further creativity.

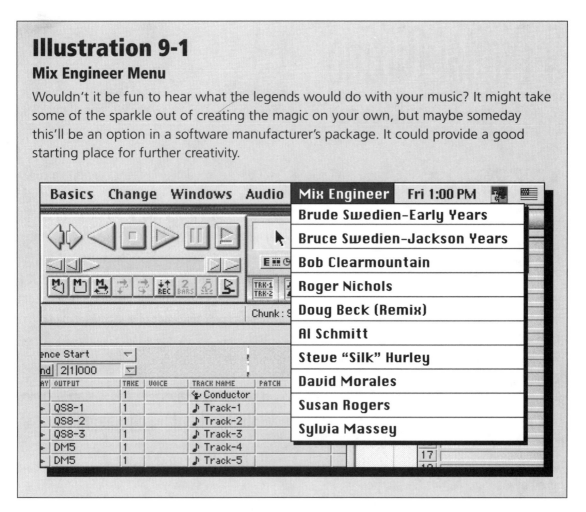

there. All these stopovers for the precious signal suck more life out. Then, it's often automated using a VCA-based automation package. Yet another amplifier sucks more life out of every track!

The journey of the analog signal from the microphone to the speaker is much like carting a fine ice sculpture across Phoenix in July with three or four vehicle changes. It starts out finely and intricately carved. Each time it leaves the refrigeration truck and is carried 100 feet, the ice melts a little. By the time it gets to the next refrigeration truck, it's still the same sculpture, but the edges aren't quite as sharp. Then it's frozen solid again, but at the next vehicle

change, the sculpture is carried 200 feet in the afternoon sun. No matter how quickly it's carried, the sculpture isn't quite the same by the time it's frozen solid again. Once it reaches its destination, the sculpture is probably still impressive—it might even win some awards—but it's not nearly as spectacular as when it was first completed.

The fact that analog systems sound good at all is amazing. But the fact that high-quality classic and modern analog gear often sets the standard for sonic quality is an homage to the gutsy persistence of designers and artists who are unwilling to settle for anything less than perfection. We all owe them a debt of gratitude.

## The Digital Mixer

The digital mixer is unlike the analog mixer in many technical and functional ways. The mission of most manufacturers is to create a physical environment that's intuitive, convenient, familiar, and relevant to the creative mind—incredible functionality is assumed. A digital mixer only needs one knob, one button, and one access window—the knob and button scroll through and set parameters that are viewed in the access window. The rest is just for us, so we'll feel comfortable and creatively uninhibited.

The digital mixer does not use amplifiers at each processing stage because the functions don't degrade the digital data, or they shouldn't, if the math has been done properly. There's no need to amplify the signal; it's binary data, not analog signal. If all is well throughout the data transfer bus, there should be no change to data that flows through unprocessed. In addition, if it's processed 1 or 20 times, there should be no degradation: only data changes according to the mixing engineers specifications.

In relation to our previous ice sculpture analogy, digital mixing is ideally like staying in the freezer with the artist, simply whittling away a little, shaping, or adding as your musical choices dictate. The angles never lose their edge, unless you want them to. Details aren't melted off—if anything, they might end up to be more finely honed through the actions of the engineer.

Mix automation holds many new possibilities in the digital domain. Whereas a good automation system in the analog world offers assistance with levels and mutes throughout the mix, digital automation typically offers full computer assistance of every parameter on the mixer! This kind of unrestricted control lets the creative mind focus on musical details. It allows each of us to build the music we hear in our souls as we go. There should be no time or technical limitations or boundaries. If you really need to hear the bassoon fly around the entire perimeter of the room in the middle of the chorus, you can make it happen every time the song plays back. It never has to be any other way. The system enables the bassoon pan to be a part of the musical structure. Other mix ingredients can play off its emotional impact from the time it enters the mix.

## Hardware versus Software

Most software-based digital recorders have digital mixing functions built in. The onscreen graphics usually look like a straight-ahead analog mixer, but the tracking, processing, and automation functions are phenomenal. Digital mixing hardware is no more than a control surface for a dedicated software-based mixer. Most recordists work more efficiently with a certain amount of control immediately accessible. In addition, a hardware mixer provides multiple inputs and outputs. Any system needs mic inputs, line ins and outs, inserts, and machine interfaces for various recording devices, among other interconnect capabilities for digital and analog equipment. Find the mixer that fits your working style best. Functions are becoming very similar from mixer to mixer, but the size and arrangement of the workspace varies greatly. Stick with a brand name you've come to respect and trust. Try to buy gear from a manufacturer that you think will be in existence five years from now—past that, you'll probably need something newer and cooler anyway.

# Automation

## The Basics

As we discussed earlier in this course, automation provides a means for computer-assisted mixing. Almost all automation systems provide automated control of channel levels and mutes. Most of the systems of yesteryear—maybe *yesterweek* is more appropriate in this era—used one of two methods to control the mix: VCA (voltage controlled amplifiers) or moving faders. The moving fader system is sonically more highly regarded because it eliminates the need for a VCA by including a voltage-controlled motor at each channel fader. The motor physically moves the fader as you would if you had 56 hands and a mega-multitasking brain.

Any automation system needs a way to keep track of parameter changes, fader moves, knob twists, etc. Some of the original automation systems printed data right onto one of the multitrack tracks. That data contained all the information about fader moves and mutes printed on tape at the instant of the change. The mix processor simply responded to real-time data changes as read off the tape.

Other automation systems refer each move to a specific time reference based on time code. SMPTE is the standard time address reference. The mix moves and changes are stored in the computer; data is transmitted at the precise time prescribed by the time code reference. If channel 12 must move up 4dB at SMPTE reference 01:22:33:15, the change data is transmitted at that precise time reference. In fact, most digital mixers let the user access the edit decision list for all mix data. This list accounts for each pa-

rameter change listed with the time code reference. If a move happens too early, the operator can quickly enter the EDL and then correct the time code reference by entering the correct value in the time code field.

## Automation Types

Automation is divided into two basic types:

**Snapshot** – Snapshot automation enables instant recall of the console configuration, including all parameter settings controlled through automation. The user has the option to select snapshots at any time, but continuous real-time fades and parameter changes are not supported. Fixed, or static, positions are recalled when a snapshot is selected. A snapshot is a singular global event. Though it can be used within a dynamic mix, it's usually best to keep it separate and to select either dynamic or snapshot automation.

**Dynamic** – Dynamic automation provides for real-time recording and playback of any automation-controlled parameters while referenced to time code. Data for fader moves, mutes, pan, EQ, and effects can all be stored within memory and replayed at the correct time code reference. The digital controllers then recreate the mix moves precisely as they were performed by the mix engineer. There are typically five modes of operation in dynamic automation: Auto Read, Absolute (or Auto Write, Update, or Replace), Auto Touch (or Auto Latch), Trim Levels, and Bypass (or Auto Off or Rehearse).

# Dynamic Automation

Dynamic automation describes a mix procedure that overwrites (completely replaces) all previous events for a changed parameter, in reference to continuously running time code.

Dynamic automation is the most commonly used form of automation for building a strong and powerful mix. Quick control changes, along with smooth musical transitions impact musical expression in the mixing domain. The following automation modes are typical of any system. The terms might adjust slightly between manufacturers but the concepts are consistent.

## Auto Read

Auto Read is playback mode. It reads any automation data that's been recorded. It's important to remember that automation data represents the time code referenced status of controlled mix parameters. When a digital mixer reads automation data, the functions are mathematically calculated for the mix changes. The binary data is altered to represent the mix changes. In contrast, the analog mixer simply varies an analog control through which the analog signal passes. Digital mixing is a much more pure form of waveform manipulation, since it uses no analog signal path or amplifying circuits.

## Absolute Mode/Auto Write/Replace

This mode operates much like a multitrack recorder punching in. You must first select parameters to change or update, then, once the button is pressed to write or record automation, all selected parameters overwrite the existing setting for those parameters only. You can manually punch in and out; plus, most automation

packages let the user change parameters and repeat the punch-in process while the mix is running. This is one of the primary mix building procedures. Mixes often start with a single pass all the way through the song to establish data boundaries. Then the individual moves and intricacies are entered through this mode and Auto Touch mode.

## Auto Touch/Auto Latch

Auto Touch mode is similar to Absolute mode. In Auto Touch, all data is in playback mode until a controller is touched or moved. Once the controller is touched, that particular parameter goes into record mode.

In some systems, the controller remains in record mode until it is manually turned off or time code stops. This method is often called Auto Latch, since the record mode latches on until the user physically turns it off. Other systems that have conductive faders capable of sensing touch go in and out of record as the controller is touched and released. This is typically Auto Touch mode.

## Trim Levels

Trim Levels mode retains all relative moves on a particular controller but adds or subtracts user-specified amounts of change from all moves in a specified region. If you'd simply like to turn up the entire track by 1dB, adjust the parameter control by the appropriate amount on the mixer channel, then press Trim Levels. The mix automation computer will add 1dB to all levels on the selected track starting when the record/write button is pressed and time code is running.

When you adjust the fader for a 1dB up or down trim, the entire track level changes by the same amount, as long as you leave the fader in the same spot. However, the true functionality of the trim process is a merger of previously recorded data with new data being recorded. If the trim moves are active, the resulting levels will be the sum or difference of the original data with the new data.

To trim levels, it's necessary that the controls, typically faders, are set at a unity point. The unity point is essential a controller position that the computer and user agree is a "zero change" position. Moving fader systems often move a fader to unity gain position the instant the trim level button is pushed. In this way, it's easy for the user to discern how far the level has changed from its original position, and it's easy to get back to unity for a smooth transition from trim to the previous status. Faders that don't automatically go to unity setting when the trim button is pushed simply assume that wherever they are at the time is unity. If this is the case with your automation system, get in the habit of setting the fader at unity gain (typically the 0 level setting close to the top of the fader throw) before entering trim mode. This provides the most reliable and easy method to trim levels up or down.

## Bypass/Auto Off/Rehearse

This mode stops all automation playback and recording. With the automation off, or bypassed, it's much easier to set up a basic mix to start from. In addition, tracking is typically best done with the automation off, to avoid any inadvertent automation writing. Automation can be bypassed for the entire mixer or for individual channels.

Rehearse mode is very similar to Bypass or Auto Off mode in that automation data is not recorded. In Rehearse, however, the write but-

ton will switch the status from automation playback to record-ready, reading the selected controller at its current manual status. This is a great way to test your settings before actually printing them as automation data. Once you're sure the moves are close, switch to Absolute or Auto Touch mode and record the mix changes.

## Mutes

Mute status is written like other automation data with the exception that it's not updated or trimmed—it's simply rewritten. Some automation systems deal with mutes differently. The most convenient systems continuously monitor the mute status; if the user makes a change, it's registered and the data proceeds normally from that point. Other systems regard the mute as a relative change. If the mute status is on, the next status is off. Once the user makes a change in mute status, the rest of the mutes in the song might be changed. Some early automation packages were not user-friendly and had features that seemed to be poorly thought out. Most modern systems are relatively intuitive with operating procedures that have been developed and refined in the field.

## Pan

When pan automation is selected alone, all other moves are ignored. In a practical light, most panning remains consistent. An occasional change is necessary, especially if one track contains two or more instruments. It's usually most effective to record the basic pan data along with the first pass automation data throughout the entire song. Then, when the mix details are forming, punch in any pan changes at the desired locations. In practice, including too many sweeping variations in pan position is distracting.

Though it seems like fun at the time, it usually calls attention to itself rather than supporting the emotional impact of the music being mixed.

## Function of Fader Motors in the Digital Domain

Moving faders on a digital mixer—faders that play along with the mix—serve primarily as an automation tool. They provide the user with a visual reference to the status of each fader. For example, when the engineer touches the fader in Auto Touch mode, the data is seamlessly transitioned from the computer status to the user status. If you don't move faders, it's difficult to punch an automation move in without creating a jump in level that might distract from the mix. Many systems don't have physically moving faders. Instead, they utilize onscreen faders that the user can match with the physical fader. There's typically an onscreen fader representing the computer playback fader and another colored fader showing the manual fader status. The user simply matches the computer fader with the manual fader before punching into record, avoiding any unwanted level jumps. Moving faders are more intuitive to use, but the onscreen process is also very efficient.

Aside from assisting the intuitive nature of mixing automation, moving faders are functionally unnecessary. They don't have any effect on the audio quality. They only indicate the status of digital data. No audio actually passes through fader circuitry because there is no audio circuitry, only controller data that indicates a mathematical variation in the binary data stream.

Also—and this can't be discounted, considering the nature of the music business—moving faders are fun to watch. They provide a wow factor that might turn a client's head and make you some money. I remember working on the original Euphonix CSII. It confirmed for me that digitally controlled audio was the only way to fly, but the thing that all the clients thought was really cool, was Vegas mode. The board scrolled quickly through all its lights—and it had a lot of them. It was very impressive, especially with the studio lights turned down.

## Mix Editor Functions

Most modern automation systems provide a mix edit window. This window contains the list of all moves and typically includes the channel number, type of automated event, specific value for each controller, and time code reference. Any of these values can be individually edited by typing in different values. Some fader moves or parameter changes contain a lot of data, so provision is usually made to select a region of data that can be changed in a relative fashion together. For example, in the verse, all the fader moves can be boosted by 1dB or copied to another place in the song.

The mix editor is a very powerful tool, especially for precise changes through complete musical sections. It's common to print several different versions of a mix— vocals up 1dB and then down 1 dB, instrumental, a capella, etc. A careful and precise change in the mix editor is not only easy to accomplish, but it can be quantified and undone. If 1dB up is too much, simply type in a 1/2dB change and see how that sounds.

Even though these tasks are simple to accomplish in the mix editor, they're often cumbersome and not quantifiable in the typical mix automation screen (Illustration 9-2).

# Illustration 9-2
## The Mix Editor

The mix editor let's the user change any mix automation parameter with great accuracy and without needing to run the mix again. Simply find the mix parameter that needs to be changed and enter the desired value. Screens like the one below, from the Mackie D8B, offer an easy to use graphical interface, where parameter setting can be changed by reshaping, re-sizing, and repositioning.

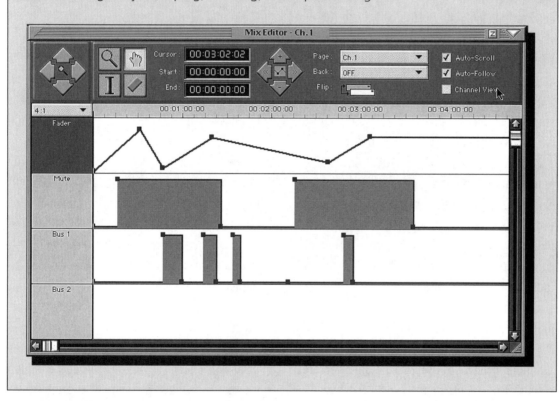

## Snapshot Automation

Snapshots are typically saved as a specific number between 0 and 99 or 0 and 999, etc.. The data that's stored with the snapshot number represents the global status of the mixer at the time of the save. Every controllable parameter is part of the snapshot. Snapshots are very convenient for tracking. Once you've found a great sounding set of EQ and processor settings for a drum set that you'll be recording over the course of several days, simply save the snapshot of all settings. This way, each time you need to remike the kit, you'll have a good starting point. All the settings you slaved over on day one will instantly return for your tweaking pleasure.

Snapshots also serve as an excellent means of comparing mix concepts. Set up a guitar-heavy mix and call it snapshot 1. Then, set up keyboard-heavy mix and call it snapshot 2. Finally, try a percussion-heavy mix. Then scroll through the snapshots as the song plays back. The difference in emotional impact is obvious when the mix approaches are compared in this real-time way. You'll soon recognize the sound you've been looking for.

Snapshots can be integrated into the dynamic mix, but this technique should be utilized with caution. Once the dynamic mix sees a snapshot number, it automatically switches to that snapshot as if someone had actually pushed the snapshot number. For example, if the mixer is told on the chorus to switch to snapshot 10 but you've since changed snapshot 10—or it's somehow gotten lost in the ether—the mix might be ruined at that point.

Also, since a snapshot represents a complete global change in mixer status, there's more of a chance that switching to a snapshot will cause an audible pop or click. Instantly changing the status of all the controls frequently results in an audio change that's drastic enough to be noticeable, which will sound amateurish.

Snapshots can be used very simply and effectively to create subtle changes between sections. They provide the user the opportunity to step through the duration of a mix and select scenes tailored for each musical section. In some cases, this simple scrolling concept provides plenty of control and personalization for the entire mix. Simply create a snapshot for each musical section, then select each scene at the appropriate time while the mix plays.

Listen to Audio Example 9-1. Notice the different sounds as I scroll through the snapshots.

---

*Audio Example 9-1 Scrolling Through Snapshots*
*CD-2: Track 62*

---

# Operational Procedures

## Saving

I've said it before and I'll say it again: Whenever dealing with any computer, whether for sequencing, digital audio recording, video recording, or automating a mixdown, save all the time. I make it part of my regular procedure. I save very often, unless I'm really in a zone and I forget for 10 or 15 minutes. Some programs utilize auto-save architecture. This feature can be a lifesaver in case of an untimely crash, although some recordists like to disengage the Auto-Save feature so they can decide when to keep the current mix status and when not to. However, with the Undo and Save As... features that are available, I recommend using Auto-Save. If you have a mix that you really like, you should save it as a separate file for safekeeping or print it to whatever mixdown storage medium you've selected—before it gets away. Then you can go off on a completely different tangent with the mix free from anxiety. Developing a new mix approach is stimulating and fun if you know you have a great version already in the can. Save often!

## Undo

The Undo command is one of the biggest advantages the software-based digital recorder has over analog recorders. How many times does the vocalist nail a take, then, out of great confidence, want to record over it to make it just a little better? Everyone on the planet, except the singer, knows it won't get any better, but still, against everyone's better judgement, you go for it. It never comes back—not even close. With

Undo available, you can let the singer try again, then, if it's not better than the previous take, undo it—and you're back to the great take.

Undo is also available in mix automation mode. If you make a series of unacceptable moves, undo them. Then you'll be back to the previous status. Some systems have multiple levels of Undo and you can keep pressing Undo until you get back to the preferred status.

## Building Automation

There are several valid approaches to creating a mix with automation. The right method is the one that results in the musical and emotional impact that you feel is best for your music. Any suggestions about mix procedures are just that: suggestions. Try several approaches until you find one that matches your musical and working style.

Often, after all the tracking is completed, the mix process begins. The mix is built from scratch. All the blends and textures are recreated and meshed together from the ground up. Sometimes this is the best approach because it gives the mix engineer a chance to step back and reevaluate all of the mix ingredients. Upon scrutiny, the parts might be panned, equalized, and processed in a completely different way from the original intent. That might be very good for the music, or it might destroy the fire and spontaneity of the original performance.

Some engineers prefer to build the mix as they go, from the first note of the first tracking session. I've noticed several times that the basic tracks feel great when they're recorded. The mix and balance has life and energy. Then, at the next session, the life doesn't seem to fully return. Moreover, at the following session, the same thing happens.

This process doesn't have to happen too many times for you to realize change in procedure is needed. If you have a digital mixer with automation, try automating the mix from the first session on. Capture the life of the original session by saving the mix so it can be completely recalled at a later date. Write down some of the effects processor settings, if you need to. Anything that's not automated should be documented and saved with the master files.

If you work in this way, you'll find that the mix builds as you go through the creative process. Those beefy drum sounds that you got on day one of tracking become part of the song, and everything builds around them. That guitar pan that inspired the keyboard sound is simply part of the song's fabric. It doesn't need to be recreated during mixdown, because it remains an integral part of the song's growth.

Working this way is only possible with modern technology. Since the affordability of high-tech gear has come of age, even the smallest home studios will soon have access to all this flexibility and more.

Several important mixing considerations are presented in *The AudioPro Home Recording Course, Volume II*. As new technology becomes more readily available, our options increase. We can do more with audio now than we could ten years ago. Build your knowledge by keeping up with all the new gadgets and gizmos. However, don't lose sight of your previous standards. Take what applies to you and try it out on your music. As you combine techniques, technological mix procedures, and musical passion, you'll find the way that works best for you. The methods will assuredly vary from song to song. Different music calls to be treated according to its need, not technology's.

## Software Plug-ins

Gates, compressors, limiters, expanders, delays, reverbs, and special effects commonly reside within the digital mixer. The audio quality of the "stock" onboard effects is very good, especially as sample rates and word sizes increase. Moreover, in this technical era of specialization, many small but focused companies are growing in the audio industry by providing software-based plug-ins for a handful of hardware manufacturers. In fact, most of the industry leaders in effects processors also offer software-based versions of their hardware. These plug-ins are compatible with the industry's leading digital audio workstations like Digidesign's Pro Tools, Opcode's Studio Vision Pro, Mark of the Unicorn's Digital Performer, and others.

Plug-ins provide the means to customize a digital setup for your needs. The user gets to pick the emphasis of the mixer's feature set. If everyone bought the mixer du jour and was then locked into all the same effects and dynamics, individuality and personality would soon fade away from their recordings.

Plug-ins utilize the built-in computer or control surface architecture. Whereas the digital mixer is a computer-based data router with several converters, a plug-in uses the power of the computer to create different processing effects.

If a particular plug-in requires extra processing power or if it extends the capacity of the mixer with more inputs, outputs, or processing power, a card can easily be inserted into one of the computer's expansion slots.

Manufacturers who take advantage of the incredibly cost-efficient way to distribute their products utilize the existing computer functions and architecture included in the digital mixing

system. Therefore, hardware costs are minimal or nonexistent, and their products are distributed as data on an inexpensive storage medium. Many manufacturers even minimize their printing costs, sending a minimal start-up manual with the product, then referencing "read me" files on the software disk or technical support sites on the Internet.

What does all this do for the end user? It just gets us more, better, quicker, cheaper. That's all! (Illustration 9-3)

# Mix Procedure Using Automation

Digitally controlled automation adds a completely different dimension to mixing. It gives the mix engineer incredible flexibility and creative freedom as well as providing for a custom designed work environment. Much of the outboard equipment that used to be patched into the mixer is now internal. Less patching is not only convenient, but, with digital processors, the sonic clarity is much more consistent. Dirty contacts and sloppily wired patch bays are often audio's worst nightmare. With the advent of plug-ins, the digital mixing system is very easy to customize. It can be made as powerful as you can afford to make it.

## Inserts

Any good digital mixer contains inserts. There have been so many great analog devices developed through the years that it would be unthinkable to not provide a means of including them in a system. Inserts on a digital mixer provide the same function as they do on an analog mixer. Each digital mixer manipulates audio as data. However, audio from a microphone or line source

# Illustration 9-3
## Plug-ins

Software plug-ins make audio manipulation very convenient. Almost any process that's been dreamed up can be performed within the confines of your primary digital audio software package. Third party manufacturers are supporting more and more platforms. In fact, most hardware effects and dynamics processors are available in plug-in form.

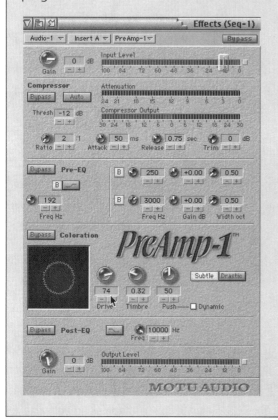 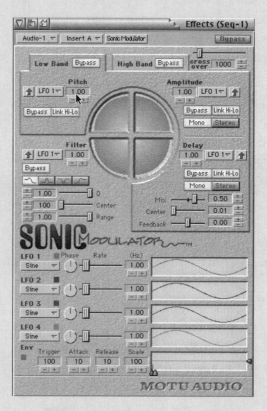

enters the mixer in its analog form. The signal is converted from analog waveforms to digital data once it has passed the gain trim stage. The insert is positioned just prior to conversion. While the signal is still in analog form, it is sent from the insert output to the processing device. Then the signal flows from the output of the processing device back to the insert's input. Immediately after the signal enters the mixers signal path, it's converted to digital data for

further treatment, shaping, and mixing (Illustration 9-4).

Devices, whether analog or digital, should be considered as important as any musical instrument. The sound of a vintage mic through a classic tube compressor can be as sweet and inspiring as the sound of a Les Paul lyrically wailing through a Marshall half-stack. In addition, the sound of a complex and carefully shaped digital reverb can be as stimulating and

# Illustration 9-4
## Inserts to the Digital Console

Any serious digital console needs to provide insert capability. One of the many appeals of a digital console is its ability to combine digital accuracy with classic analog sound. Inserts provide an analog patch point for the efficient inclusion of outboard gear.

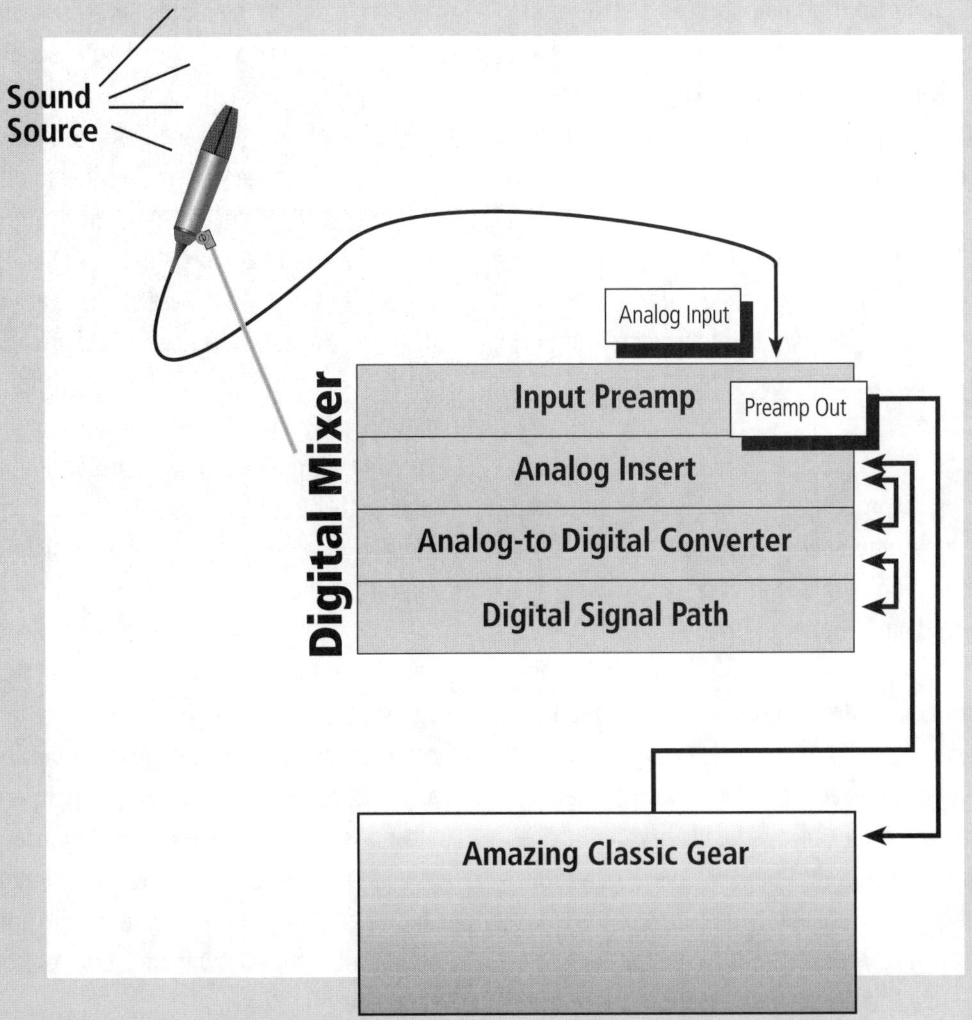

**Sound Source**

**Digital Mixer**

Analog Input

**Input Preamp**    Preamp Out

**Analog Insert**

**Analog-to Digital Converter**

**Digital Signal Path**

**Amazing Classic Gear**

intriguing as the ambience in a natural concert hall. None of these instruments or devices should be held in higher esteem than another. They are simply tools to help us create better music—music that evokes passion and emotion.

## Write Mutes

The first step in most automated mixing sessions is to write all the channel mutes. The mute function is typically separate from the level function, so levels can be written after the mutes have been carefully placed. On any given track, it's best to leave the mutes on unless there's audio on it that's part of the mix. This procedure helps minimize unwanted sounds in the mix that might originate as electrical clicks, electronic blips, or dweeblike titters.

Careful muting eliminates any noise that might come from analog sources at the input: effects processors that have been inserted, headphone leakage, drum mic leakage, or extraneous noises on vocal tracks. This technique helps create a feeling of intimacy and closeness, whether there's 1 track playing or 40.

Once the mutes are all written, it's time to build a mix. Refer to *The AudioPro Home Recording Course, Volume II* for more information on the mixdown process.

## Drums

If you've recorded live drums to the multitrack, there are some special considerations to take when dealing with automation. All actions depend on the microphone configuration. If you've used two or three mics, their channels will probably all need to remain on and up throughout the mix.

If you've used a close kick drum mic along with a stereo pair of overheads, try gating the kick mic. Most digital mixers have a gate built into each channel. Eliminating some of the leakage from the rest of the kit into the kick mic might give the entire drum sound a more intimate and immediate feel.

If you've used several mics on the kit including individual drum mics along with overheads and room mics, it might be necessary to perform several automation moves to keep the drums sounding intimate, while at the same time sounding massive. The individual tom micro-

phones often pick up a substantial amount of rumble even while the toms aren't being played—a perfect example of sympathetic vibration.

Sometimes, if there's too much rumble from very open drums, it's appropriate to gate the tom mics so they're off whenever the toms aren't playing. If the mutes are too abrupt when they switch on and off, try riding the tom faders, turning them down, but not off, unless the toms are being played. Turn them up for the tom fills, then fade them back down. This technique helps create a very punchy drum sound while providing a close-miked and intimate tom sound.

These techniques are simple once you get the hang of them, and they're a tremendous aid in creating good drum sounds. Without automation, these moves would be difficult or impossible to pull off. With automation, they're simple to build, and, once you've completed them, they provide a solid and consistent foundation for the rest of the mix.

If you've included a stereo pair of overheads or room mics, try running them through a stereo compressor—either the built-in digital compressor or an outboard compressor. Both approaches help you get a very punchy and everpresent sound from the kit. The compressor can provide increased attack, increased length, or a smoother sound on the cymbals and toms, depending on the amount and type of compression used.

If you use the digital compressor that's built in to the digital mixing system, try automating the compressor controls at various times to help augment the drum sounds. More compression during the tom fills and less during the basic groove might help highlight the tom fills while minimizing the room sound during the groove. Or, try simply automating the mix of the compressed mics.

Classic tube compression on overheads or room mics typically provides a very warm, smooth, and punchy sound. Often, digital compressors aren't able to provide that warm, almost distorted sound that naturally comes from a tube compressor.

---

**Audio Example 9-2 Original Drum Track**
**CD-2: Track 63**

---

**Audio Example 9-3 Drum Track Through**
**Digital Compressor 4:1 Ratio, -8dB**
**CD-2: Track 64**

---

**Audio Example 9-4 Drum Track Through**
**Tube Analog Compressor 4:1 Ratio, -8dB**
**CD-2: Track 65**

---

**Audio Example 9-5 Drum Track Through**
**Digital Compressor 12:1 Ratio, -12dB**
**CD-2: Track 66**

---

**Audio Example 9-6 Drum Track Through**
**Tube Analog Compressor 12:1 Ratio, -12dB**
**CD-2: Track 67**

---

## Documenting the Mix

Any time you include an outboard processor, it's important to document the settings—*all* the settings. In the likely case that you might need to reconstruct the mix later, you'll be very glad you did. If you're using devices with presets, simply store the preset in the sequence, or, if you didn't use a sequence, create one for archiving device settings. Almost all MIDI devices allow for patch storage and retrieval. Keep the archive with all your mix files.

If you've used several analog devices with no facility for patch storage or retrieval, write down the settings for each knob or parameter. Be as precise as possible. If you're repeatedly using a device, make a template for it with all knobs, numbers, and switches. This will help speed up the record-keeping process. Try contacting the manufacturer at their Web site; they might already have a perfectly drawn template for you to download and print out.

It might seem like a bother to archive and document all your settings and sounds, but it's the only way to guarantee easy reconstruction of the mix. Even at that, it still takes a lot of tweaking to recapture the feel of the original mix.

## Bass

Automating the bass guitar during mixdown helps keep the basic tracks punchy and interesting. Once the overall bass level is set, listen to the track along with the drums. Turn up the vocal track for reference, then listen for the low-end feel. There are often places the bass guitar can bring new life into the track with a slight level boost. Try highlighting any extra licks that the bassist added, or listen to the interaction between the vocals and the bass. Determine whether the musical flow might be more effective with the bass muted in a few essential spots. Try to create a bass track that makes musical sense while creating interest and momentum throughout the song.

This kind of detail is often not an option when mixing without automation. There are too many other things for the mix engineer to consider. However, with automation, this types of detail becomes part of the song. It takes practice creating different types of mixes to develop an ear for what to try using automation. Nevertheless, once you create a few very interesting mixes that would have been impossible without it, you'll soon feel comfortable making musical and arranging decisions during automated mixdown.

## Lead Vocal

Once the drums and bass guitar are working very well together, add the lead vocal. For many styles, this is a great point to make sure that the lead vocal sounds clean, understandable, present, and appropriately equalized all the way through the song.

The mutes should have already been written so that the lead vocal track is only active when there's singing. With the drum and bass levels up, blend the lead vocals so they're evenly balanced. Find a good overall level for the track. Then, write it into the automation for the duration of the song. Only adjust the level if there's an obvious spot you know needs it. In this way, you should be able to count on the average level staying about the same throughout.

Next, listen to the entire song, updating the lead vocal level any time it gets too loud or too soft. This process will provide a good starting point for your vocal mix even before the primary vocal effects are designed.

Find the perfect effect for the vocal, then reassess the blend with the rhythm tracks. Once the effect is in place, you might need to adjust certain parts of the track, or you might even need

to trim the entire track level up or down. When the track is smooth throughout the arrangement, you'll probably be able to rely on trimming large sections to blend in the vocal perfectly.

Be very meticulous with this process. The automation helps on every pass, so there's no reason to let even one syllable fly by at the wrong level.

If you're using a digital mixer, listen to the song for consistent equalization. Sometimes the singer backs away from the microphone, causing a thinner sound, or sometimes they move in too close, causing a thick sound. Automate the EQ at points where the sound seems to need it. Often, quiet, more open passages are screaming for a little low end to fill out the sound. Other times, especially on loud and unrefined passages, the vocal character takes on a sharp edge, so rolling off some highs or mids might perfectly blend the sound without a level change. There are many instances where an EQ change is the perfect solution. Where a level change might adversely affect the mix level, an EQ change might leave the mix level virtually untouched and add understandability to a soft passage or warmth to a loud passage. This concept stands true for all channels in a mixdown.

## Guitars and Synths

Guitar and synthesizer sounds are typically handled the same in automated recording as they are in analog mixing. There are, however, many more options readily available when using powerful automation. Any good digital mixer allows for automation of equalization, gates, compression, limiting, pan, level, etc.

A simple pan sweep placed appropriately during the guitar track is very effective as a highlight. Automation makes a move like this simple, and you hear it for the rest of the song. It's common during a guitar or synth track to find one spot that's too shrill, too loud, too soft, or too harsh. A simple EQ change for a split second might make the difference between holding the momentum and emotion of a song and losing it. These changes are difficult to make in the analog mixing domain—they're simple to perform with digital automation.

Listen to the guitar in Audio Example 9-7. Notice how the chord in bar two sticks out. This level is hot enough to adversely affect the mix amplitude, and the tone is unduly harsh. In Audio Example 9-8, I've lowered the level at the problem spot and changed the equalization so the track flows better throughout the take.

---

*Audio Example 9-7 Original Guitar Track*
*CD-2: Track 68*

---

*Audio Example 9-8*
*Level and EQ Change to Repair Track*
*CD-2: Track 69*

---

# Backing Vocals

Great sounding backing vocals are characterized by several attributes, including the following:

## Intonation

This particular characteristic is key to a great sounding backing vocal. In the days of old, if the singers couldn't sing in tune, you were sunk. Now, however, software and hardware that's capable of tuning individual vocal tracks is commonplace. Some digital mixers having tuning aids built in. Most software-based digital systems either have tuning plug-ins as a part of their package or can easily accept one of the amazing tuning plug-ins available from third-party manufacturers.

Automatic tuning plug-ins work best on mono single-voice tracks or on unison harmonies where the entire group follows the inaccurate pitch center together.

Tuning applications have changed the world of vocals in general—especially backing vocals.

## Expression/Dynamics

If backing vocalists don't all feel the same excitement and emotion in the music they're singing, they rarely work well together. If the singers are all in the same mindset, powerful things can happen. Swells and texture changes are typically style-driven. If everyone is into the style of the music, these things should flow naturally. If only the producer or the leader understands the emotional impact required to authentically and powerfully convey the passion in the song, backing vocal tracking is typically a time consuming and tedious process.

As a recordist using digital technology, you can help drive the dynamic expression of the tracks by riding levels and tightening releases and attacks with automated gain control and mutes.

## Blend

Excellent blend comes from a few different vocal characteristics. If not all singers pronounce the lyrics in a similar fashion, blend is difficult or impossible to achieve. When all singers use precise pronunciation but use incompatible vocal textures, again, achieving an excellent blend is difficult. If the singers aren't sensitive to the volume of the other backing vocalists, they usually will not blend well.

Excellently blended backing vocals demonstrate consistent unity in pronunciation, enunciation, tone, vocal texture, and level. These are largely traits controllable through digital automation. In tracking, be sure the singers are together in their pronunciation and enunciation of the lyrics. Tone, texture, and level are characteristics we can adjust.

Listen to each backing vocal track. Select one track as a reference for the others. Then, start building the overall sound by blending each part with the reference. Adjust the equalization of each new track so that it locks in with the reference in a way that seems to create one sound that happens to consist of two ingredients. Then add all the parts together and adjust them all for a strong blend. When backing vocals are blended properly, they sound like one entity instead of three or four that coexist in the same time and space.

Once the vocals are blended for a particular section, print the mixer status into the automation system. I've achieved stellar results by setting up a section so that it has an excellent blend with relatively few moves, printing it in automation, then moving to the next section, printing that, and so on. Nothing says you have to print the entire track in one pass. Automation frees the user up to perfect each section. Digital mixing systems typically provide a means of copying and pasting automation data throughout the duration of the music. If you've perfected the automation moves in the chorus, for example, try copying the automation data to all the rest of the choruses. It'll at least provide

an excellent starting point and will probably work splendidly as is.

Listen to Audio Example 9-9. Notice how some parts stick out of the group, lacking a blended, unified quality.

### Audio Example 9-9 Poorly Blended Vocals
### CD-2: Track 70

Audio Example 9-10 presents a much more blended and unified feel from these backing vocals. The level and equalization are working together throughout the pass to provide a solid vocal support.

### Audio Example 9-10 Blended Backing Vocals
### CD-2: Track 71

## Accuracy

Typically, groups of singers working together to perform a single pass can accurately attack and release each phrase. When double- and triple-tracking, especially when recording inexperienced vocalists, each track tends to start and stop at a different time. Words that end in *S*, *T*, or some other sibilant sound are usually difficult for singers to perform precisely the same on each pass. Using a digital editor, these details are easily repaired after the fact.

Always strive to achieve the most accurate performance during tracking—attention to detail at this stage helps unify and solidify the singers. If, however, there are some details in need of attention, don't hesitate to clean them up. If the backing vocals are completely clean and blended, the entire song takes on a polished, professional sound.

Audio Example 9-11 demonstrates backing vocals that aren't completely together. In Audio Example 9-12, the vocals have been polished up a bit. Notice how the sibilant sounds have been moved on some of the tracks so they line up together. This process of cleaning up attacks and releases is common, and it helps provide a more powerful and convincing vocal sound. Illustration 9-5 shows the difference between two waveforms before and after they were adjusted by the editor. If a final transient sound doesn't match between tracks, simply move one of the releases so it's together and tight (Illustration 9-5).

## Illustration 9-5
### Cleaning Up Releases

Previously we cleaned up the end of a vocal phrase by simply sliding one audio segment so that the last syllables of the tracks ended together. However, often the process is more complicated. In Set A below, the tracks start together but their finish is sloppy. The only way to clean up the end is to cut some material from the longer note. Sometimes, simply removing a portion of the longer waveform, then sliding the end into place, works wonderfully. In other instances a little more effort is necessary.

In Set B, I cut some material to get the phrases to end together. Next, I slid the edit point back into the phrase, where the waveforms and sounds matched. Finally, I placed a crossfade over the edit point to feather the two parts together. This technique is very effective and quite common.

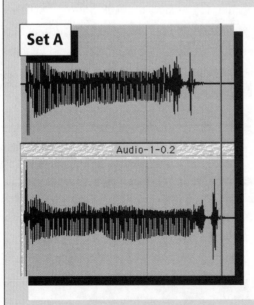

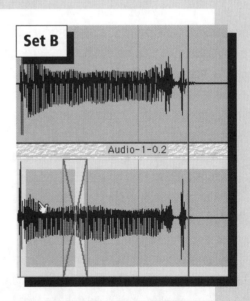

---

**Audio Example 9-11**
**Backing Vocals with Sloppy Articulation**
**CD-2: Track 72**

---

---

**Audio Example 9-12**
**Backing Vocals with Repaired Articulation**
**CD-2: Track 73**

---

# The Rhythm Section

Since automation provides virtually unlimited control over the rhythm section balance, blend, mix, and texture, the mix engineer needs to be in complete understanding of the musical vision for the song. Each orchestration and arrangement is flexible in the mix. The recordist has the power to make or break the excitement and musical impact.

When you're recording your own music, it's easy to realize the musical vision. When recording someone else's music, strive to understand the intent and reasoning behind the lyrical and musical momentum at the heart of the song. A complete understanding and agreement among all interested parties is fundamental to a happy, healthy, prosperous working situation.

Work up several snapshot versions of the mix. Store each so that all parties can hear the differences as the snapshots are selected during playback. Try to get everybody to agree on the vision. Different snapshot concepts might apply more aptly to different musical sections. Once everyone agrees, begin to work through the mix in a precise and calculated manner. Go after the details—don't hide from them. If some-

thing stands out as not yet perfect, focus on it with intent to make it perfect. This kind of attention to detail not only produces better music, it sharpens your aural and technical senses. Listen to Audio Example 9-13 as I scroll from snapshot to snapshot. The orchestration and textures change dramatically, while the musical integrity and character remain.

---

**Audio Example 9-13 Contrasting Snapshots**
**CD-2: Track 74**

---

Each piece of music should have its own momentum throughout the song. Once you understand the direction of the musical momentum, you can highlight and help drive it with your mix. Don't be afraid to thin out part of the orchestration. A factor that contributes to musical power is contrast. Often, the mix demands contrast even if it wasn't planned in the onset. Muting an instrument or set of instruments might be the perfect choice during a section designed to set up a musical climax. The change from a thinned out texture to a powerfully thick and crafted texture is dramatic. Audio Example 9-14 demonstrates the power of a contrasting texture between musical sections.

---

**Audio Example 9-14 Contrasting Mix Textures**
**CD-2: Track 75**

---

## Locate Points

Automation, software-based digital systems, and modular digital multitrack machines work together in a nearly seamless manner. This, along with a powerful automation package provides a working environment that is amazingly efficient, fast, and creatively freeing.

Locate points are the key to working efficiently. Most systems provide for numeric locations throughout a recording. Each number (typically from 0 to 99) is tagged to a specific time code reference. The user simply types in a number and presses the locate button. All devices then chase to the referenced time code point and join in perfect sync. The digital mixer plays along with the recording devices. All its moves are also referenced to the running time code. In fact, most digital mixers have transport control built in so that the mixer and recording devices run together through the duration of the mix.

Many automation systems allow for text descriptions of each locate point. So, instead of remembering that locate point 11 indicates the beginning of the second chorus, the user simply enters some text to represent the musical section (e.g., "Second Chorus—Beginning").

Using these text-driven auto-locate points streamlines the mix process. There is no need to repeatedly search for the proper point in a song. Once you label each section, your location problems are solved. Most systems let the user either click the onscreen text, enter the location number, or type in the first few letters of the section name to move the mixer and all recording devices to the correct song position.

## Copy Moves and Settings

Digital mix automation facilitates application of the same kind of Cut, Copy, and Paste functions found in any word processor. If you like the mix settings in one portion of a musical work, simply copy them to another similar section. Even if they don't work perfectly, they'll probably be close enough to provide a good stating point.

## EQ

Equalization in the digital mixing domain offers great flexibility, convenience, and ease of use. The best an analog EQ could offer is graphic sliders, but digital onscreen equalizers let the user see the actual curve they're shaping. Concepts like bandwidth, frequency, and extreme cuts and boosts are self-explanatory. Look at the onscreen equalizers in Illustration 9-6. They are easy to read, easy to understand, and they're adjustable by merely clicking and dragging the portion of the waveform that you'd like changed. Equalization curves like this are not only straightforward to set up and use, they can be stored for future use or copied to different channels in the same mix.

Most digital equalization packages offer a way to compare changes from previous EQ settings. A simple bypass function lets the user switch between a flat (not equalized) signal to the current settings. Always check the signal in bypass mode so you can verify the effect of the equalization. Sometimes we play with equalization too much. Later, when we hear the original sound in bypass mode, it's easy to hear that it contained more interest and life than the equalized sound.

Many systems let the user set a couple of EQ settings then switch back and forth between them. This is a convenient way to check the musical effect of a particular setting and to try the effect of two extremely different equalization approaches. Some systems let the user morph between two settings at a user-selected speed. These changes are stored in automation data, so a special section can be switched smoothly to the proper EQ and then switched smoothly back to the original EQ later in the song.

There are often portions of a track where the sound takes on an unpleasing character for a brief moment. Without sophisticated automation, the operator typically has to let the part go in the interest of time. It's also possible that, lacking extra hands or feeling overwhelmed by too many mind-boggling moves, the operator might choose to figuratively sweep the glitch under the rug.

We have the capability through digital automation to fix a momentary harsh sound by simply automating as we equalize the problem spot. With repair techniques like this available, it's possible to keep perfecting the mix and arrange-

## Illustration 9-6
### Digital Mix Equalization

Every parameter in the screen below is capable of real-time automation. If a note needs special EQ, simply make the move once while the automation data is being recorded. From that point, the move will happen automatically. Digital mixers that combine creative freedom with intuitive graphic interfaces are helping remove the blockades between what's in the musician's soul and the listener.

ment until they the best they can be. Time and patience become the primary limitations (Illustration 9-6).

## Dynamic and Special Effects

Compression, limiting, expanding, gating, and special effects sounds use most of the same parameters and controls found on their analog counterparts. In fact, many software-based dynamics and effects control screens look like classic equipment, complete with onscreen VU meters, knobs, switches, and buttons.

# Format

Once the mix is completed in the automation, storage is still a consideration. Some systems allow for mix storage within the digital recording system itself where simply printing the mix to two tracks of a digital multitrack is an option.

## Hard Disk

Some systems provide a means to digitally bounce the mix, along with all its mix adjustments and parameters, directly to the hard drive. This method provides for a clean data transfer. Once the mix is on the hard drive, it can be stored accurately on any digital storage medium such as CD, DVD, or other optical cartridge. One of the truest means of storage for playback utilizes transfer of data directly from hard disk to the playback medium. Avoiding the transfer to DAT or analog tape is typically preferred, unless the user specifically prefers the sound and accuracy of high-quality analog tape.

## DAT

DAT offers a low noise recording medium that has served the recording industry well. Many amazing recordings have been mixed to DAT format—recordings anyone could be proud of. However, the error correction scheme used in this format can produce inaccuracies and anomalies that degrade the audio quality—this can be frustrating to the recordist.

When DAT was originally introduced, it was advertised as the end to all noise problems. Supposedly, it wasn't necessary to maximize levels, because even at lower levels it was far superior to analog tape. Having been plagued by analog tape noise, most engineers basked happily in the silence between notes. Then, upon scrutiny, it became apparent that something wasn't exactly right. Analog tape offered warmth, clarity, accuracy, and a feeling that wasn't quite there in DATs. Hence, the beginning of the big debate: is analog better than digital, or is digital better than analog?

Over the years, better understanding has developed throughout the industry regarding format comparisons. Increases in sample rate and word size have produced great strides in digital audio integrity. At the same time, analog holds its own in the industry because of the purity of the process. There's no quantization, no discrete samples, and no error correction. In theory, it provides the most completely accurate version of the original waveform.

The debate will continue over which format is better as long as there are options. The nature of the creative mind is to push the limits—to create the very best version of art. If the recordist and the artist pour their passion into a musical work, they'll always care about the form of delivery to the public. I enjoy the debate process, the experimental process, and the creative development of art through technology.

Listen to your work on as many systems as you can and mix it in as many formats as you can gain access to. There are definitely differences; one format might be the perfect choice for one song while yet another format excels for another. Your decision are most valid for your music.

Mixing in the third millennium brings seemingly countless options. The question at nearly every economic recording level is no longer, "How can I possibly get a musical and professional sound with the few tools I have?" Now the question has become, "How can I ever use all these professional sounding tools to get a musical sound?"

# 10 Master Preparation

Once the final mixes are complete, the fun begins. It's always an exciting point in a project when the songs are mixed and in their final forms. It's at this time that the evaluation process often relaxes, but, in reality, this is the time for it to increase.

You've probably mixed several versions of each song—at least you should have. After the mixes are completed, it's good to spend a few days listening and evaluating your work. There's no doubt that, especially in a competitive world like music, our best work should always go forward. Anything less than the very best we can do is unacceptable. Let's raise the standard. The better your job, the better job I have to do, and so on.

Upon evaluation of your mixes, chances are that you'll like part of one mix particularly well but you'll prefer another mix during a different section. Computer-based digital editing makes combining these different mix portions a breeze.

In the days of analog tape and razor blade edits, we had to be very careful when performing each edit. The editor listened for the tiniest sounds in each hole to confirm the perfect edit point. Was a cymbal crash holding over causing an awkward transition? Did the vocal track release at an inappropriate time on one side or the other of the edit? Should the edit be on the beat or off the beat? Can the edit happen in the middle of a synth pad? All these considerations rushed through the editor's brain until the per-

fect spot made itself known. Then the cut was made!

With current hard disk–based editing systems, the operator can be much more casual. We can take a little of this and a little of that just to see how they might sound together. Nothing is at risk except a few minutes of time. If our first guess is bad, we simply slide the pieces around until they feel okay, then maybe add a little crossfade. Before you know it, the edit sounds so smooth that no one would ever know it wasn't that way on the original master tape. All edits are made in a nondestructive way with no effect on audio quality. The user can develop as many different edits as are needed in a quick, easy, and stress-free manner.

## Editing the Mixed Master

### The AM Version

This is the version that ends up on the radio. It's typically the shortest of all versions. Most radio stations are reluctant to play much more than three minutes or so from any song. This is because there's a difference in performance royalty for long songs in relation to shorter songs; in addition, they typically want to broadcast the most music in the shortest time to make room for the most advertisements.

Practically speaking for the recordist, providing the AM version of a song usually means cutting some parts out. Anything that could remotely be considered extra, is removed. If an intro starts out as eight measures long, it'll probably end up four or two measures long in the AM rendition. A solo section might be cut completely or shortened. Digital editing is particularly useful for changing a solo length. Since the soloist often plays over the beginning of a phrase, shortening a solo section is usually much more involved than a simple phrase removal. Most editing packages let the user set an edit point to determine the length of a passage; then, the edit point can be slid forward or backward to find the smoothest transition.

## The Album Version

The album cut is usually the originally recorded version as it came out of the creative recording process. Typically four or five minutes long, it often reflects the artist's emotional intent. We are quick to cut a song down for commercial radio play, but some of what we cut can have great musical purpose. The album version often fades later than other versions, and it usually includes full solos and breakdowns. This sometimes equates to the director's cut in the film industry. This version really reflects the musical intent of the producer—it's artistically inspired rendition.

## The Dance Mix

The dance mix is often an afterthought of a successful release. Some songs, however, are intended to be dance songs from the onset. As you might guess, this mix is designed for a dance situation. Usually, a DJ at a club or party plays the dance version of the song because it's been mixed and edited to provide rhythmic and dy-

namic interest. The drums and bass are almost always highlighted—sometimes it seems like they're the only instruments in mix.

Often, the dance mix engineer adds a few different sounds to provide a new textural and dynamic interest. Musical sections are commonly shifted around, looped, elongated, or combined. Digital recording provides great ease in designing the dance mix. It's common to remaster and re-edit the original mixes, but the flexibility of current digital multitracks allows you to reload and totally reconfigure the original multitrack files.

Dance mixes are fun for the recordist. They're a chance to step back from a song and breathe new life into it. Creativity is the key. There's one mission during a dance remix: to create excitement and energy—the recordist can put everything else aside.

Most dance mixes are at least five minutes long. Depending on the song's popularity, this mix might go even longer. After all, the DJ always has the option to fade to the next song.

Listen to the following audio examples. The first portion of a song is edited in three different ways.

*Audio Example 10-1 The AM Version*
*CD-2: Track 76*

*Audio Example 10-2 The Album Version*
*CD-2: Track 77*

*Audio Example 10-3 The Dance Mix*
*CD-2: Track 78*

## Creative Restructuring

Some musical groups use the recording process as if it was another musical instrument. From the beginning of the song's development, they use the edit process creatively. Extremely blatant edits are jarring and abrupt in the wrong context, but if they are used for their emotional effect and impact, they can be quite powerful.

Practice editing your music in different ways. Push the envelope. When using nondestructive edit procedures, you can afford to take chances. Push the limits of your creativity.

# Mastering

## What Is Mastering?

Mastering involves the final preparation of the musical program for duplication. Several changes in the material can be made at this stage, or, if everything is already perfect, there might be no changes. The mastering engineer listens for consistent levels from song to song. If a song or two is slightly louder or softer than the rest, levels can be matched in the mastering process.

This is also the point where global equalization might take place. If one song sounds weak in low-frequency content, for example, the mastering engineer selects the low frequency to boost, which helps the deficient song match the others in overall sound. These equalization moves typically affect the entire mix in an identical way on both channels of the stereo mix.

Limiting and compression are commonly used during mastering. A hard limiter lets the engineer add decibels to the overall mix level. If the limiter registers a 6dB reduction in gain during the mix and the levels are optimized so as to achieve a maximum signal level, the mix has been made 6dB louder in comparison to its pre-limiting status. That's typically very good, since commercial music is often compared in relation to how powerfully it's transmitted in a broadcast, dance, or environmental application. When a song is effectively louder, it is typically perceived as stronger and more appealing than the songs heard before or after it.

Listen to Audio Examples 10-4 through 10-6. The same mix is played with three different limiting levels. The first is normal, as mixed. The second demonstrates 3dB of limiting, and the third demonstrates 6dB of gain reduction. Remember that once the gain is reduced on the limited portions, the levels are brought back to optimum, where the strongest section peaks at zero on the digital meter.

---

*Audio Example 10-4 Normal Mix*
*CD-2: Track 79*

---

*Audio Example 10-5 3dB louder*
*CD-2: Track 80*

---

*Audio Example 10-6 6dB louder*
*CD-2: Track 81*

---

The mastering engineer also takes into consideration the flow of the album. A good engineer creates a flow where the songs actually grow slightly in level. This pulls the listener more effectively through the album. If the songs grow in perceived volume throughout the album, even if it's nearly imperceptible, the listener follows the musical progress from beginning to end more comfortably.

This creation of continuity and flow doesn't only include level. It might involve a bit more limiting toward the end of the album, which can make an apparently constant level sound as if it's increasing—the songs at the end will seem louder even though their peak levels are the same as that on the early songs.

Spacing between songs can also be decided during mastering. Most songs flow best with two to four seconds between them. However, there should be continuity and flow considerations that drive the decisions on spacing between songs. If a very slow song follows a very fast song, it's typically a good idea to leave a little more space after the slow song just to let the listener settle down. Sometimes it works great to fade one song directly into another.

When adjusting spacing between songs, listen to the transitions to verify how comfortably they flow. Even if you don't quite know why, you'll be able to discern much about the effectiveness of a movement from one song to the next.

## To Master or Not to Master

With today's technology, anybody can prepare his or her musical product for duplication. You can send a master that will serve as the production master for your final product. You can compress, limit, equalize, effect, shorten, lengthen, space, and insert subcodes and indexes all from the comfort of your bedroom studio. However, should you? What's the advantage to doing your own mastering at home? What's the advantage to sending your work out be mastered by someone else in another facility? How can you develop the skills needed to do a good job of mastering?

Should you do your own mastering? I believe the answer to that question is entirely subject to the goal of the project. If you're recording your best buddy's band, they just want a product they can sell at their gigs, and they're down-and-out-broke, go ahead and master the album yourself. However, do it in a way that is instructive. Research the best way to work with the equipment and software you're using. Research the art of mastering. Try different versions of your work and, above all, compare your work to the real world.

What's the advantage to doing your own mastering at home? The obvious answer is cost. For the price of some mastering software, you can create your own production masters, ready for duplication. The more important advantage to mastering at home is educational. At any level, it's advantageous to learn mastering terminology, techniques, and possibilities. After you've mastered a few of your own projects, you'll not only have a better idea of what the mastering process entails, you'll look at the entire recording process differently. You'll set levels, equalize, use effects, and probably arrange and orchestrate differently. You'll operate according to insider information; you'll see the final picture more easily, even from the first recording of the first note. After completing several projects from the recording of note one to the mastering of the last track, you'll find that your tapes need less and less mastering. They'll be closer to perfect than they ever would have been if you hadn't experienced the mastering process yourself.

What's the advantage to sending your work out be mastered by someone else in another facility? Competitive edge! When you record music that you feel strongly about and think is competitive, you owe it to the music to get a second opinion. Mastering engineers are the recordist's link to the real world. Once your project is complete and mixed, it's comforting to hire an engineer who has mastered successful albums that you think sound good. It gives your hard work a better chance to be held as worthy, relative to its competitors. I've mastered many products myself, but when I produce a project, I always write mastering into the original budget—and not as an option. I want the very best mastering engineer to listen to my material to verify its competitive edge. If there are some radical changes needed to get everything just right, I breathe a sigh of relief that they were caught before the product hit the shelf. If the mastering engineer does very little to my mixes, then that's great, too. Confirmation from another experienced set of ears is just as good as radical changes. In fact, the less they do the better I usually feel about the process. I've sat through several mastering sessions with a handful of the best mastering engineers in the business, and, even though I've learned a lot through the process, I still prefer to have someone else master anything I produce.

If you want to pursue mastering as a passion or vocation, or if you just want to get good at it for your own use on your music, go for it. But how can you develop the skills needed to do a good job of mastering? Every good mastering engineer has an excellent set of monitors that are efficient throughout the audible frequency range. They also have an accurate and stable monitoring environment. Their studios sound good and there isn't a lot of change in them throughout the months and years. Since this is the final stage before product production, be very fussy about the details. All compo-

nents and cables should be the very best possible quality, and the wiring and implementation of all equipment should be meticulous and professionally done. Practice! Listen to everything you can get your hands on in the environment where you'll be mastering. Anything you master should sound great in comparison to your favorite albums. It doesn't have to sound the same, but it still should sound very good.

## Monitoring Procedures

One of the essential factors in successful mastering is a finely tuned, finely designed listening environment. If your control room has inherent acoustical problems, everything you mix in it will have frequency problems. Acoustic problems are consistent, so they can usually be repaired during mastering. If your studio has a deficiency at 150Hz and 600Hz, you're probably putting too much or too little of these frequencies in every mix you complete. This typically makes the mixes sound bad in the car or in your friend's living room, for example. One of the primary values of a mastering engineer lies in the compensation for bad mixing rooms.

Most home recordists are set up in a room that probably wasn't designed for recording—it was probably designed for sleeping and storing clothes. Nevertheless, if you mix—on whatever system and in whatever room—in a way that sounds good to you, the mastering engineer should be able to quickly find any frequency discrepancies. Using global EQ, they can make the necessary repairs to insure your music's competitive viability in the world. If your mixes have too much data at 150Hz and too little at 600Hz, it's a simple matter to even things out during mastering by boosting and cutting the appropriate frequencies.

Even when the recordist learns to compensate for frequency anomalies and can produce mixes that sound good on other systems, a skilled engineer in a controlled mastering room is a valuable addition to any music produced for consumer consumption.

Monitors are fundamental to the mastering process. If you plan to master your own music, select high-quality monitors that are accurate and consistent. Good, highly respected, self-powered near-field monitors are usually the best choice. Self-powered monitors are most consistent over several hours of use. Since the amplifiers and crossovers are at the speaker, they receive a line level signal. Typically, the mixer's control room output plugs directly into each monitor. In this setup, the signal is then sent at line level to the crossover to be split into set frequency ranges. Once the signal is split, each frequency range is sent to its own amplifier—the amp sees the line level signal and efficiently sends it to the speaker. Self-powered monitors contain amplifiers designed and adjusted to work optimally with each component—and they sound good.

Non-powered monitors receive an amplified signal at the speaker input. The problem with this setup is that it becomes less accurate over long periods of use. Since the crossovers are getting a powered signal, they heat up. Once they heat to a certain point, they react differently, changing the monitor's sound. Though there are some excellent Non-powered monitors, self-powered monitors are conceptually superior.

## Assembling the Album

There is an art to assembling an album so that it draws the listener through all the songs. When all songs have been placed in an artful order:

- The album is easy to listen to as a complete work.
- Each song leads gracefully into the next.
- Contrasts in texture, tempo, and lyrical content hold the listener's interest.
- All material plays to the same audience, so your intended audience can relate to everything on the album—there aren't a couple tunes that seem out of place.

A good mastering engineer thinks of the flow of an album. Spacing between songs might be adjusted to hold interest or contrast textures. Throughout the course of an album, the level of the songs might increase to help hold attention, or the limiting might increase to make the songs seem progressively louder. In this way, the momentum of the songs seem to increase slightly, although the level of each song is still optimized.

Experiment with the order of songs. An album can have a totally different impact if you simply change the song order. Starting with a song that indicates power and quality to the listener is essential. Some albums start with the title song—the song the album is named after—and others start with a song that sets the mood for the rest of the album. There's no set standard for song order. Some albums reserve the third spot for the title song, using the first two songs to set the stage for what the album is all about. An album that has strong impact and powerful presentation is often thematic in its song content. This draws the listener through the progression of the album, both lyrically and musically.

Spacing is easily adjusted during mastering, but it's often best to listen to the entire album several times to determine if the spacing flows well with a natural momentum. Therefore, spacing between songs is often best determined prior to the actual mastering session.

# The CD Mastering Environment

There's more to preparing a CD master than simply digitally recording and spacing ten or so songs in the correct order. The format must be correct for the application. Codes need to be correct, verified, and confirmed. Protocol must be followed to insure proper duplication and replication.

In order to effectively operate in a CD mastering environment, make yourself familiar with its language. Absorb the specialized terminology that pertains to mastering alone. Be sure you know what the replication facility expects to insure the best possible outcome for your music.

## Write Modes

There are two basic modes used to write an audio CD:

• **Track-at-Once Mode** – This mode writes a track at a time. The laser is turned off and put to rest after each track, after the lead-in, and before the lead out. This system lets the user record song after song in different sessions and at different times. The material doesn't need to be recorded all at once in track-at-once mode. When the laser is turned off, small areas are left unrecorded on the CD media. These unrecorded sectors, called *runout* sectors, are perceived as corrupted by the player. While many CD players are able to skip over the corrupted areas, CD readers at the duplication facility are likely to view them as errors. Track-at-once offers the advantage of letting the user write more audio

data to the CD in separate sessions until the CD is full. This mode is best left for less-critical projects like quick references, compilations, or archiving mixes. Track-at-once CDs do not meet Red Book standard.

• **Disc-at-Once Mode** – This mode writes the entire disc, including the table of contents, lead-in, audio data, and lead-out, in one continuous pass. The laser is never turned off and there are no unwritten, or runout, sectors. This mode is the professional standard for the creation of a CD master. Disc-at-once mode conforms to Red Book standard.

## Red Book

Sony and Philips defined the Red Book standard (in the form of an actual red book) for playback of digital audio CDs (CD-DA). They also defined various formats for audio, video, image, and data storage. Each standard was released in a colored binder, hence the terms Red Book, Orange Book, and so on.

The Red Book standard defines the proper format for an audio CD to play back on a CD player, and it defines the format for a CD player to play back a CD. Any Red Book–compatible CD can play back on a commercial audio CD player.

The Red Book standard defines the number of digital audio tracks on the CD as well as the type of error correction used to guard against minor data loss. The standard calls for up to 74 minutes of digital audio, transferable at the rate of 150KB per second.

Red Book standard requires certain specifications be met:

• Each track must be at least four seconds in length.

• All track numbers and index times must be

unique and in ascending order.

- There must be a minimum Index 0 gap length of four seconds.
- The maximum number of tracks is 99.
- Index 0 must always be at zero seconds.
- Index 0 of the first track must be between two and three seconds in length. In other words, Index 1 must start between two and three seconds after Index 0.
- The disc must be finished. In Disc-at-once mode, the data is written from beginning to end without stopping; the laser isn't turned off during the write process. The table of contents, lead-in, audio data, and lead-out are written continuously and in order. This process conforms to Red Book standard.

Each CD track typically contains one song. Tracks are divided into 2,352 byte sectors that are 1/75 of a second long.

If a disc is scratched or dirty, Red Book standard specifies an error detection code and an error correction code (EDC and ECC), so the player can recreate the music according to code.

Most commercially produced CDs conform completely with the Red Book standard, which is also called the Compact Disc Digital Audio Standard. A disc conforming to the Red Book standard usually says "Audio CD" under the Disc logo.

## Yellow Book

The Yellow Book contains the standard for CD-ROM. When a disc conforms to Yellow Book standards, it typically says "Data Storage" under the Disc logo.

The Yellow Book standard emphasizes accuracy for data storage. Whereas an audio CD operates peacefully within an error correction scheme, errors in data storage easily render a file or application useless. Error–free schemes are essential for storage of computer data.

The Yellow Book augments Red Book protocol by adding two different types of tracks: CD-ROM mode 1, for computer data and CD-ROM mode 2, for compressed audio and video data.

## Green Book

The Green Book is the standard format for CD-I (CD-Interactive). This standard was designed for multimedia applications that play in real-time, combining sound, images, animation, and video. The CD-I format and the playback unit associated with it were designed to use an inexpensive computer and audio disc player along with an ordinary NTSC television as a monitor.

## Orange Book, Part I and II

The Orange Book standard defines the format for write-once CDs (CD-WO) of both audio and CD-ROM data. The Orange Book specifications are designed so that a Red Book compatible CD can be created on a write-once disc.

Part One of the Orange Book specifies the standards for magneto-optical systems that use rewriteable media (CD-MO).

Part Two of the Orange Book standard defines the CD-Write-Once specification (CD-WO). The standard divides the disc into discrete areas, each for a specific function. The Program Calibration area is used for a test run to calibrate the recording laser. The Program Memory area is used to record track numbers along with their stopping and starting points. The Lead-in area is left free to write the disc's table of contents after all data is completely recorded. The Program area is where the actual data is written, and the Lead-out area is placed at the end of the disc to let the player know when to stop reading.

## White Book

The White Book standard represents the fourth major extension of the Red Book standard. It is a medium-specific standard allowing for 74 minutes of video and audio on a compact disc in MPEG format. The Sony/Philips Video-CD is White Book compliant.

## Blue Book/CD-Extra

The Blue Book/CD-Extra standard stores Red Book audio in the first portion of the disc and Yellow Book data in the second, completely separate section. Since an audio CD player is a single session machine, it only recognizes the audio session, since it is first on the disc. CD-ROM drives are typically multisession devices, so they see both the audio and data sessions.

CD-Extra, originally known as CD-Plus, solves many of the problems originally encountered with enhanced CDs.

## Subcodes

### PQ Subcodes

All audio CDs have 8 channels of subcode information interleaved with the audio data. These subcodes serve various functions, depending on the actual digital information being stored. Some codes apply specifically to audio, some to video and graphics, and others to MIDI data. The subcode channels are identified with the letters P, Q, R, S, T, U, V, and W. Channels R–W are used to store video information on CD+G discs, or MIDI information in CD+MIDI discs.

Audio CDs use only the P and Q subcodes. The information on the P channel tells the CD player when the tracks are playing and when they aren't. The Q channel contains much more information, including copy protection and emphasis information, track and disc running times, disc catalog code, and track ISRC codes.

### IRSC Code

The International Standard Recording Code (ISRC) uniquely defines each specific track on the CD with information about the song's author, the country of origin, and the year of production. The ISRC can be written directly into the CD's Q subcode channel. Each track on the CD can have its own unique ISRC information.

### Emphasis

The emphasis flag in the Q subcode alerts the CD player to activate the de-emphasis circuitry in its analog output. Early CD players had poor quality digital-to-analog converters, so CDs were recorded with a pre-emphasis, high-frequency boost. Emphasized CDs must be played back through an analog de-emphasis circuit to insure accurate EQ.

Converters have improved dramatically over the years, and emphasis is no longer necessary; it's rarely, if ever, used. However, when source material is utilized that was originally emphasized, it must be de-emphasized in playback.

### SCMS

The Serial Copy Management System (SCMS) resides in the Q subcode. It allows the audio to be digitally recorded once but prevents second-generation digital copies. When the SCMS flag is present, it is encoded in the data stream when a digital copy is made. If the SCMS or Copy Prohibit codes are inactive, unlimited copies can be made from the source. Whenever distributing your material on CD for review, select SCMS or Copy Prohibit to help insure against piracy. However, these schemes don't offer much protection, since it's child's play for an adept tech-head to break the copy protection scheme.

## Track Number

Each song or contiguous audio segment on a CD is called a track. There can be up to 99 tracks on each CD, numbered from 1 to 99, always in consecutive, sequential order. A CD can start with any track number from 1 to 99, allowing for continuous numbering of tracks in multiple CD sets.

## Indexes

Each track on a CD can contain up to 100 marked locations, called indexes, within each track. The indexes, numbered from 0 to 99, are always in consecutive, sequential order. All tracks contain at least one index. Index 1 defines the start of the track. If there is a gap of silence after the previous audio ends and before the actual audio data begins, it's labeled as index number 0. All other index points are optional and user-definable.

There are two types of indexes: absolute and relative. Absolute indexes calculate and display all times relative to the beginning of the CD. Relative indexes calculate and display all times relative to the beginning of the individual track that they're indexing.

## Noise Shaping

Noise shaping is an option that is sometimes present in the dithering process. Previously in

this course, we discussed the value of dither when very low level signals are present. Noise shaping utilizes digital filters to remove noise that falls in the middle of the audible spectrum, typically around 4kHz—the human ear's most sensitive range. Since noise is actually important in the control of quantization error, it isn't completely removed through noise shaping but is, instead, shifted to a range which is harder to hear. Noise shaping lessens our perception of the noise essential to the dithering process.

# Equalizing

Equalization is an important part of the mastering process. Each song must sound compatible with the progression of the album. If one or two songs are deficient in low frequencies, or if a song or two lacks high end, they'll stand out over the course of album play. Each song has to sound like it belongs in the kettle with the rest of them.

Variations in EQ are common from song to song, especially when a project is completed of the course of several months. Equipment changes, tastes change, and skill levels change throughout the progression of any album. Try to mix all songs on the same monitors and in the same studio; it'll make life easier during mastering. Once a studio owner changed the weighting of the woofers without telling me, just before I mixed the final song of an album. When the low-frequency response changes dramatically, the resulting effect of the mix is very graphic. Once you get into the mastering studio, it's obvious that something went suddenly astray. The song I mixed on the woofer-altered speakers sounded like it had been mixed on a different planet compared to the other ten songs on the album. Fortunately, since the deficiency was global, the mastering engineer was able to pump a substantial amount of low-end into the song. In the final product, it flows very nicely with the other songs. You'd never know there was any problem with the mix.

Find a specific recording that you think sounds great. A group held in high esteem by the recording industry provides a strong example to compare your mixes to in each session. If you reference each mix to the same recording, you'll have a good chance of creating mixes that flow well together. When referencing mixes to confirm your mix integrity, listen to the low frequencies and very high frequencies especially. Listen to how transparent the mix sounds in the midrange.

## Real-time Analyzer (RTA)

Some engineers like to mix while referencing a real-time analyzer (RTA). This tool displays the level of specific frequencies across the audible spectrum. I've seen engineers that couldn't use the restroom without consulting their three-dimensional RTA. To top it off, their mixes didn't always sound that good. If you use a tool like the real-time analyzer, consider that it is just a simple tool designed to help. The true test is in the listening. A song can look mighty fine on the analyzer yet sound like garbage, or it might look bad on the analyzer and sound great. There's always the possibility it'll look good and sound good. I love it when that happens!

The RTA divides the audible frequency spectrum into regions—typically 31 regions, correlating with the 31 bands on a 1/3-octave graphic equalizer. Each region is represented by a series of LEDs, which indicate the region's en-

ergy level in the same manner as the audio level meter on your mixer or recorder. A good mix is typically flat across the spectrum, with a little roll-off at the very top and bottom of the frequency spectrum.

The RTA receives its signal in one of two ways:
• Through a calibrated microphone
• Through a direct line input

Use the microphone when checking the frequency integrity of your monitoring environment. If you set the microphone at the same position where you monitor the mix, then play pink noise through the system (all frequencies at an equal level) you should see each band on the RTA at the same level. If you see an abundance or a lack of certain frequency bands, you have a couple of options:

Make changes in the mixing environment, which will affect the acoustic character. Physical construction isn't always the easiest route to go, but, in the end, it's often the best solution. If you tune your studio so it's accurate, you'll be able to trust that your work will transfer favorably to the rest of the world. Hire an acoustics consultant. It could be the best money you spend on your facility

Run your monitor system through a graphic equalizer. This is the cheaper and easier way to solve frequency problems in a room. A 1/3-octave graphic EQ correlates directly with the bands on a real-time analyzer. If you have a predominance of energy at 500Hz, simply turn that frequency range down on the RTA until it registers flat. In this way, it's possible to get a room to register properly on the RTA, but it's not always preferable. Live systems must go through this process regularly, but in a mixing/mastering environment, try to adjust the room through acoustic design changes. The problem with running your entire monitor system through a stereo 31-band graphic equalizer is that it's difficult to see what's going on between the sliders. Simple equalization is accomplished through filters and phase-altering circuitry. These circuits have the potential of causing more problems in your listening environment than they're fixing.

# Levels

During the mastering process, mix levels are a primary concern. Optimizing levels is important during the mixdown process, but mastering is the place where the final adjustments are made in regard to the level, flow, and momentum of the entire album.

It's technically gratifying when each song on an album reaches maximum level at least once. However, some songs just sound louder when there are set to maximum levels than others. The ideal in the mastering process is to keep the levels maximized while at the same time creating a complete work that sounds great throughout its entirety.

## Normalize

We've previously discussed the normalizing process. It's kind of a last chance, easy way to move all the levels up to the point where the peak(s) hit maximum level. In concept, this helps insure that song levels are as hot as they possibly can be and that the full word is being used (the maximum number of bits). However, it should not be an automatic move to normalize every song on an album.

Young recordists, often without thinking, normalize each song. I don't see that happen

when I sit with some of the best mastering engineers in the business. What I do see is careful evaluation of the song, the sound, the style, the content, the character, and so on. Careful consideration must be given to the intent of the artist and to the music's audience. A plan should be developed for the impact of the album as a whole.

Normalizing isn't necessarily a bad thing to do, but it shouldn't be automatic. There are often other means that create the proper levels in a more pristine and musically desirable way.

## Real vs. Apparent Levels

A song's level seems blatant, right?. Either it's maximized or it's not. In reality, it's not that simple. Frequency content, instrumentation, and orchestration all play a part in how loud a song sounds. If your album contains a wide range of instrumentation, from full band with strings and horns to voice and guitar or even just voice, you'll need to evaluate the volume of each song in relation to the others. You won't be able to count on normalizing every track, that's for sure.

The fewer instruments involved in the mix, the louder it'll seem at maximum levels. Have you ever noticed how full and punchy basic tracks sound before all the synth and filler parts have been added? It seems that the song sounds softer and softer as you put more and more into it.

Tasteful limiting and compression can help even out the levels, but simply using your ears to find the levels that flow best from song to song is also a good plan. If you have level questions throughout the album, be sure to listen to the entire album on several different systems. What might seem like the perfect relationship between tracks in your studio might seem distracting and inconsistent in your car. It pays to check the level relationship in as many separate environments as is possible. One value of an experienced mastering engineer is the accuracy with which these adjustments are made.

## How Hot Is Hot Enough?

Throughout the course of each album, levels should reach the maximum several times. Some recordists like to leave a decibel or two of head-room in order to avoid overdriving the electron-ics of older CD players. That's not what I see happening in the real world. I see levels being pushed to the max, and then I see some peak limiting. Then I see levels pushed to the max again. It seems like everyone is trying to get the hottest mix on the planet. I've heard mastering engineers recommend pushing the digital levels over maximum.

This aggressive approach isn't appropri-ate to all styles, though. It's inappropriate for most jazz, classical, bluegrass, gospel, and coun-try western albums. Your understanding of the style you're working with should guide your de-cisions in mastering.

## Limiting/How to Sound Loud

The peak limiter can be your friend or your enemy. Most mastering engineers use some degree of peak limiting to help control sporadic peaks and to help keep the overall level of the album as high as possible within the con-straints of taste and style. Keep in mind that, if your peak limiter registers 6dB of limiting some time during the mix, you can boost the level of the entire mix by 6dB to reattain maximum levels. Therefore, your song will sound 6dB louder. That's an amazing difference in volume.

Best mastering results are accomplished using a multiband limiter. Dividing the frequency range into two or three separate ranges, which are limited separately, produces the most punchy and consistent sound. However, as the individual bands limit, they change in their relative levels to each other. When highs, mids, and lows are limited separately, there is potential for adverse impact on the sound you toiled over. It's a good idea to use limiting in moderation. The best plan is to mix with mastering in mind. If you create your mix so it maintains constant levels, and if you're very deliberate and precise in the devel-opment of your sound, there'll be little need for limiting. The mastering process might include slight peak limiting, which is used primarily to keep a lid on the level to insure against levels above digital maximum. This way, more integ-rity and control lie in your hands from the onset of the project through its completion and dupli-cation.

Overuse of limiting creates a sound that is thin and lacking in life. When the entire mix stays at maximum level throughout the song, there's no release. Transparency, contrast, and depth are lost. Even the best multiband limiters lose punch when they're pushed too hard.

## Image Files

If your project has been mastered in the com-puter domain and all files reside on the hard drive or drives in your system, you have the po-tential to create the cleanest and most accurate CD master possible. Since data transfers within your system have no error correction and should reflect a bit by bit transfer, this method is pref-erable. However, don't be afraid to go outside your system to utilize tools that will help your music sound better and more powerful.

When it's time to create your CD master, it's usually preferable to create an image file from which the actual CD master will be made. Any good CD mastering software provides a means of creating an image file. When an image file is created, all the songs and segments are copied to a contiguous section of one of your drives. When you create a CD from files that are scattered all over your drives, there's opportunity for inaccuracies and errors to creep into the data flow. However, an image file is an accurate and continuous copy of all data. When the CD master is created from an image file the data flows smoothly and freely on to the disc. The transfer can take place with greater accuracy and at faster speeds. When printing from an image file, it's better to print the master at faster speeds because the data will be backed up and bogged down at slower speeds.

The image file was originally used to facilitate the use of slower CD burners, but it offers a way to make smooth and accurate data transfers and provides a means for trustworthy archives of all audio data in a project.

## Mastering to Error Correcting Recorders

True random-access media, like hard disks, optical cartridges, WORM drives, etc., provide better and more accurate data transfer than sequential digital media, like DAT recorders. DAT recorders use an error correction scheme to fix occasional chunks of bad data. These corrections represent deviations from the actual data and, through multiple generations, accumulate in a destructive way. Though each correction might not be audible, it is inaccurate. It could manifest as a problem somewhere in the chain from your original master to the final product, espe-

cially if error correction is involved at several stages throughout production.

These errors explain the generation loss phenomenon of DAT recorders. In the early days of DAT, we were told that the digital copies were so exact they could be called clones. But error correction does not create exact clones! Listen to Audio Example 10-7. They demonstrates multiple generation DAT copies of a digital master. Listen to the sonic character of the music as the generations increase. Listen for definition changes, image shifts, EQ discrepancies, and general changes in impact.

---

*Audio Example 10-7 Comparison of First Through Sixth Generation DAT*
*CD-2: Track 82*

---

# 11 The Best of Both Worlds

Music in the third millennium holds many possibilities. New technologies provide a platform for creative freedom that is unprecedented. We can do things with audio and video now that weren't possible at any price just a handful of years ago. However, the trendy often gives way to the staple. The newest digital whizbang might take a while to catch on, but our industry is good at attempting to hold on to the brilliance of the past.

A classic tube microphone going through a great preamp is simply a great sound. Nothing will ever change that. The only event that will preclude the use of classic gear will be the development of digital simulations that are so authentic as to be undeniable.

Several companies are developing software that emulates vintage hardware. Earlier in this volume, we covered software plug-ins that provide amazing sounds. Many companies are developing software-based hardware to facilitate field use by the working musicians.

Always let the creative process dictate the use of technology. It's about making interesting and inspired communication of emotion and feeling. If that involves using only 48-bit samples at a rate of 192kHz, then great. If the sound that really gets the point across is an 8-bit 22kHz sample, that's what should be used. If it's analog gear that really says it all, use analog. Don't be limited by what somebody else has done. Too often, we decide that if Mr. Cool Producer used

a certain process, then we, too, must use the same process if we want to be taken seriously. Let the results speak for the process. Don't be intimidated by someone else's work. Hear your music; then make it happen. There's definitely more than one way to success.

## Acoustic Considerations

No matter what high-tech gear you've combined with classic vintage gear, if certain acoustic considerations haven't been addressed, you're going to have a rough time getting world class sounds. Vocals recorded in an empty bedroom are brutally damaged by standing waves and unwanted reflections. Once they're on tape or disc, they can't be made to sound as smooth and warm as they could have if they'd been recorded in a properly treated acoustic environment.

Somehow, your studio must be broken up acoustically. At home, most of us operate in a bedroom-sized recording room that acts as a studio, control room, machine room, storage room, maintenance room, office, and possibly bedroom. The disadvantage to this setup is that you can't spread out into areas that are optimized for a specific purpose. The advantage is that you probably have a lot of stuff in your studio—stuff that absorbs, reflects, and diffuses sound waves.

Though you might have a lot of furniture and gear in your studio, additional help should be considered. Shaping the space around your recording microphones is clearly advantageous, especially in a room that is acoustically live. Live acoustics are good when they're been designed to enhance the acoustic properties of a voice or an instrument. When acoustics are randomly active, they are potentially destructive and must be controlled.

Physical structures within the acoustic space provide the best confusion of otherwise detrimental waves. Though soft surfaces dampen high frequencies, the low-mids, which can be most damaging to sound, must be diffused or reflected in order to insure a smooth, even frequency response. Listen to Audio Examples 11-1 and 11-2. The first version demonstrates the intense room sound on a vocal mic in my family room. The second version demonstrates the same setup with the addition of a tool called a Studio Trap, from Acoustic Sciences Corporation. See Illustration 11-1 for a diagram of this setup.

---

*Audio Example 11-1*
*Voice Recorded With and Without Studio Traps*
*CD-2: Track 83*

---

When absorption panels are hung on the studio walls and tools like the Tube Trap or baffles are used to confuse standing waves, the sounds you record are easier to mix. All of a sudden, your recordings sound more like the hits you hear on professional recordings. To overlook these considerations is to create a troublesome situation for your recording and mixing sessions. Whether tracking or mixing, address these issues so your music can have the best possible chance of impacting the listener with the power and emotion you know it deserves.

Audio Examples 11-2 and 11-3 demonstrates more settings that benefit from acoustical treatment.

---

*Audio Example 11-2*
*Acoustic Guitar With and Without Studio Traps*
*CD-2: Track 84*

---

*Audio Example 11-3*
*Distant Voice and Guitar*
*With and Without Studio Traps*
*CD-2: Track 85*

---

## Chips or Tubes

Though solid-state technology was originally appealing because of its lightweight and efficient power delivery, it lacked the warmth and emotional appeal of tube technology.] The distortion sound created by an overdriven transistor is not appealing. It's harsh, brittle sounding, and grates on one's nerves. For this reason, the tube amplifier never died; in fact, it flourished as more and more guitarists, in particular, saw the light. Tubes sound better than transistors when they are overdriven—and what guitarist do you know who doesn't overdrive their setup?

The same thing happened in the microphone and mic preamp arena. Engineers all over started realizing that the vintage tube mics, preamps, and compressors built in the '50s and '60s sounded warmer and smoother than the newer technology of solid-state equipment.

Both tube and solid-state equipment have a viable place in recording and can peacefully coexist to the musician's benefit. I've found that whenever I need a pristine sound, I use a clean

## Illustration 11-1
### Molding the Recording Environment

Using a device like the Studio Trap from Acoustic Sciences Corp. (ASC) can make the difference between an amateur sound and a world class sound. Whether at home or in a commercial studio, we must always be aware of how the acoustical environment effects recorded sound quality.

In the example below, and in Audio Example 11-2, the vocalist and microphone are surrounded by the Studio Traps in a way that creates just the right acoustical feel. Using moveable devices provides the engineer the opportunity to customize each recording scenario by repositioning the Traps to support the sonic requirements of the music.

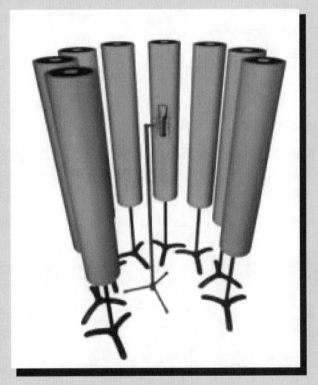

solid-state device that has lots of headroom. Some of the cleanest, clearest, and most accurate sounds come from solid-state condenser microphones through excellent solid-state preamps. These devices are amazingly clean and accurate up to the point where their circuitry is overdriven in even the slightest amount. Once they reach the point of distortion, everything quickly falls to pieces and the sound they produce is undesirable. Who knows, though? Maybe someday you'll use that sound in a way that revolutionizes the audio industry.

When you want a sound that is aggressive and even the slightest bit overdriven, try a tube mic through a tube preamp. As the tube circuitry begins to distort, it rounds off the peaks of the waveforms. In contrast, solid-state circuits clip the tops off the waveforms. The sound of the tube circuits distorting is much smoother and warmer than the sound of the solid-state circuitry distorting (Illustration 11-2).

Listen to Audio Example 11-4. Notice the difference in the sound of the vocal as the signal path switches from solid-state to tube.

---

**Audio Example 11-4**
**Vocal on a Tube then Solid-state Mic**
**CD-2: Track 86**

---

Now listen to Audio Examples 11-5. Notice the difference in the sound of the acoustic guitar as I switch from a tube setup to a solid-state setup.

---

**Audio Example 11-5**
**Acoustic Guitar on a**
**Tube then Solid-state Condenser Mic**
**CD-2: Track 87**

---

Each microphone manufacturer, each model, and each individual microphone have a unique personality. Variations between specific mics, even of the same model, are sometimes

# Illustration 11-2
## Solid-state Clipping versus Tube Distortion

Waveform A represents Waveforms B and C before they were electronically distorted.

Solid-state distortion (Waveform B) has a harsh and irritating sound. Signals that surpass maximum electronic amplitude limits are simply cut off (clipped).

Tube distortion reacts in a more gently attenuated, rounded off fashion (Waveform B). The waveforms aren't clipped. They're acted on more like an extreme limiting effect. Even though the waveform is still distorted, the resulting sound is warmer, smoother and less irritating than solid-state distortion.

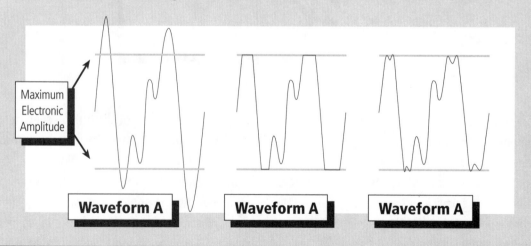

Maximum Electronic Amplitude

**Waveform A**    **Waveform A**    **Waveform A**

extreme. In a studio with ten U87s, it doesn't take long to find the one or two units that stand out as the best sounding of the bunch. With this is mind, it's not always fair to say one type of mic or preamp is any better than another. It all comes down to the specific mic choice, the specific instrument, and the specific piece of music. Listen to the differences in the recorded vocal sound from the tube microphones. They're all good mics, but each has a different sonic character and would be a great choice for some applications and a poor choice for others. Even identical models from one manufacturer might sound substantially different. Assess each mic on its own sonic merit.

## Combining Tubes and Chips

Many great sounds are achieved through the combined use of tube and solid-state technology. It's common to use a tube microphone in conjunction with a solid-state preamp or a solid-state mic along with a tube preamp. This technique takes advantage of the warmth and depth of the tube sound, yet keeps the amount of tube sound in check through the use of ultra clean solid-state circuitry throughout the remainder of the signal path. For this very reason, several devices are available that include both tube and solid-state signal paths.

With the continuing controversy over the merits of tube equipment compared to solid-state gear, its the engineer's responsibility to know the sonic character of each tool available. If you know the personality of the tools at hand, you'll be better equipped to augment your setup with additional gear. Your choices will be informed, educated, and respected.

## Digital Modeling

One of the exciting developments of the digital era is digital modeling. When I plug my Les Paul into my old Fender Deluxe amp, it produces a very characteristic and recognizable sound. That combination not only makes a characteristic sound that I could recognize a mile away, it also creates a unique and recognizable waveform that can be duplicated and repeated. It's a simple matter of mathematics to calculate the difference between the waveforms of the sound coming directly from the instrument and the sound after it has gone through the amplifier and out the speakers. Once we calculate the difference between the direct and amplified signal, that formula can be applied and added to any direct instrument sound. In this way, sonic character of nearly any amplification system can be cloned with incredible precision and accuracy.

The folks at Line 6 created an amplification system that uses this modeling principal in a very effective way. They have modeled the sounds of many different guitar amplifiers—the original Fenders, Marshalls, Rolands, Vox, and so on. They've also modeled the classic guitar effects, including specific types of compression pedals, delays, choruses, and reverbs. They've even modeled the sound difference between various speaker cabinet configurations, from a single 10-inch speaker to a cabinet with four 12-inch speakers. I've played through most guitar amplification setups and I'm amazed at how accurate these models are. They used a 24-bit waveform to recreate the sonic character of each setup. The beauty of this system is that the direct output of the amp sounds nearly identical to the miked amplifier sound.

Listen to the guitar sounds in Audio Example 11-6. I have a Gibson Les Paul plugged straight into the Line 6 amp, then running direct into the console. Those who've played guitar through these amps should recognize the sounds as very accurate and authentic. Since the modeling is so accurate, the amplification systems on these units must be clean and sonically transparent enough to faithfully reproduces the modeled sounds.

---

*Audio Example 11-6  Fender, Marshall, Roland
JC-120, and Vox Sounds
CD-2: Track 88*

---

This innovative company also offers The Pod, which has several different amps and effects available along with a software interface for storing effects and creating patches (Illustration 11-3).

Antares has developed several innovative products. Their microphone modeling systems lets the user dial up the vintage microphone of their choice. Simply plug any mic into the input, tell the processor what type of mic you've plugged in, and select the mic sound you'd like to hear from the device output. Microphones are popular tools, but they're very expensive—especially the classic vintage models. With a microphone modeler, more recordists have access to the warmth, beauty, and smoothness provided by the most sought-after microphones.

## Preamps

Microphone preamps are as different as microphones. To say that you love the sound of tube preamps is a bit dangerous. To say that solid-state preamps sound harsh and brittle isn't a secure platform on which to stand. There are some incredibly smooth and warm-sounding

tube preamps; and there are others that are not so smooth and warm. There are some harsh sounding solid-state preamps, but there are many wonderful sounding solid-state preamps. Many solid-state units exude purity, smoothness, and pristine clarity.

## Old Effects versus New

The audio industry is very driven by advertising. Once the new multi-effects processor hits the street, we lose respect for the old. But look at your effects as tools. Nothing sounds just like an old Yamaha Rev 7. It might not be the cleanest or the easiest to use by today's standards, but it has a personality that's unique and applicable to many situations. The Lexicon Prime Time digital delay was one of the first digital devices, and it still sounds good blended into the lead vocal track. If you're fortunate enough to have some real Master Room spring reverb cylinders around or an old AMS plate reverb, consider yourself blessed. These tools have amazing personality. Keep all your Quadraverbs, MIDIVerbs, Reflexes, etc.. If you're not using them a lot, at least wire them into a patch bay and remember they're available. Using these powerful tools combined with the new and amazing technological breakthroughs helps add individuality and character to your music.

## Mixers

In the upper echelon of audio recording, many engineers and producers prefer the sound of vintage large format consoles. Neve and Solid State Logic consoles dominate the upper-end studios. Neve is known for its smooth, clean sound. Solid State Logic is known for its aggressive edge. Having worked on both, I can attest to the fact that they are what they're assumed to be and

## Illustration 11-3
### MIDI Controlled Instrument Effects

Many effects provide MIDI controlled computer interface applications that let the user have easy access to all parameters. Packages like the one below from the Line 6 POD provide additional features and options within the software domain which aren't available on the actual hardware.

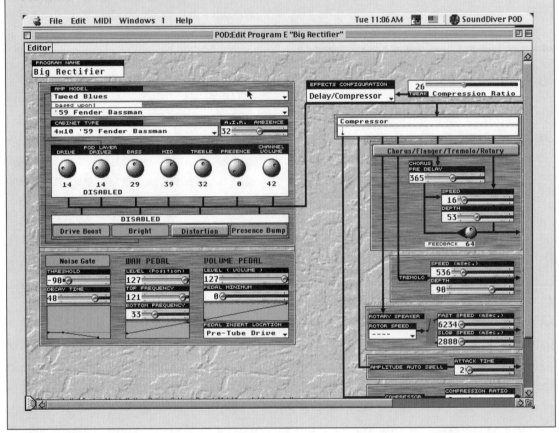

that they each have a personality that matches their reputation. The problem is that they're amazingly expensive. In addition, when I mix on a huge Neve VR series console with Flying Faders, I feel limited in what I can accomplish. The automation is archaic in comparison to the new digital consoles that serious home recordists can justify buying. The sound is very good, but the sound is also good on many of the new digital mixers. The Mackie D8B has amazing headroom in its preamps and includes Apogee converters. The sound quality is incredible. The Yamaha 02/R has been used for many very successful and wonderful sounding projects. Even the smaller and very affordable digital mixers offer good sound quality and tons of features.

Whereas the recording studio of the past centered around one huge console with an operator, the recording studio of the future will center more and more around a creative individual who can make incredible music. The affordability and flexibility of modern equipment is undeniable. It's exciting for all who participate. It's entirely possible to put together a setup in your spare bedroom that's capable of recording hit records, movie scores, sound tracks, video sweetening, or commercial music. In fact, it's done all the time.

# Cabling Considerations

## Some Cable Theory

An in-depth study of cable theory involves a lot of math, quantification of miniscule timing inconsistencies, and a pretty good grasp of quantum theory. However, basic understanding of a few concepts provides the foundation for good choices in cabling.

A cable recognizes a signal as voltage (electrical current). Small voltages travel down interconnecting cables (line level, instrument, data) and relatively large voltages (currents) travel down speaker cables. A magnetic field is created in and around a conductor as it passes electrical current. Any materials that optimize the accuracy of this conductance help the accuracy of the transfer process. Any design that takes into consideration the full-bandwidth of audio signal relative to frequency, time, and content, becomes complex—more complex than simply connecting a copper wire between the output and input.

Once a few manufacturers addressed the effect of cable on sound, it became apparent to those who truly cared about the quality of their audio work, that cable design makes a difference. Most inexpensive cables consist of a con-

ductor that's made of copper strands and a braided shield to help diffuse interference. Not much consideration is given to bandwidth, relative to frequency-specific capacitance, and potential frequency-specific delay considerations.

Two main considerations must be addressed in cable design: balance of amplitude across the full audio bandwidth and the time delays as different frequencies transmit throughout the cable length.

- **Balance of Amplitude** – Monster Cable addresses this with their Amplitude Balanced®Multiple Gauged Conductors. Since there are different depths of penetration into the conductor material by various frequency ranges, certain conductor sizes more accurately transmit specific frequencies. Therefore, it's implied that optimal conductance is accomplished by conductors that match the bandwidth penetration depth. With the frequency range divided among multiple types and sizes of wire, each frequency is carried in an optimized way.

- **Timing Considerations** – High frequencies travel at a higher rate than low frequencies throughout the length of a conductor (wire). Low frequencies can't be sped up, but high frequencies can be slowed down by winding the high-frequency conductors to create inductance at those frequencies. When the windings cause the correct inductance at the specified frequency bands, all frequencies arrive at their destination in accurate and precise timing and phase relation. This corrected phase relationship restores the soundstage dimensionality, imaging, and depth. When the frequencies arrive out-of-phase, they exhibit time-domain distortions of phase coherence and transient clarity.

All the major cable manufacturers vary slightly in their opinion as to how best to handle audio transmission through a cable. However, there is agreement that cabling is a major consideration. As end users, it's our responsibility to listen to what they to say. It's our job to listen to the difference cable makes and determine the most appropriate cabling choices for our own situation. Not everyone can afford to outfit their entire system with the most expensive cable on the market— I realize that some of us have trouble justifying even one expensive cable. But the more serious your intent in regard to excellent audio, the more you should consider upgrading. Upgrade the cabling in your main monitoring and mixing areas. Procuring a couple of very high-quality cables to connect your mixer to your powered monitors is an excellent place to start. If you use a power amplifier, get the best cables you can afford from your mixer to the power amp and from the power amp to the speakers. It'll make a difference in what you hear, and therefore on all your EQ, panning, effects, and levels.

## Do Cables Really Sound Different?

The difference between the sound of a poorly designed and a brilliantly designed cable is extreme in most cases. If a narrow bandwidth signal comprised of mid frequencies and few transients is compared on two vastly different cables, the audible differences might be minimal. However, when full-bandwidth audio, rich in transient content, dimensionality, and depth, is compared between a marginal and an excellent cable, there will typically be a dramatic and noticeable difference in sound quality.

Listen for yourself. Most pro audio dealers are happy to show off their higher-priced product. As a sound source, when comparing equipment, its usually best to use high-quality audio that receives industry praise for its excellence; if you compare it to your own music, keep in mind that if it was recorded using inferior cable at each stage, it's already lacking all that high-quality cable would have given it. The nuances just aren't there for an accurate comparison.

Young recordists are usually happy to get a system connected any way it'll work. To dwell on whether or not the cable is making any difference somehow falls near the bottom of the list of priorities. However, once the rest of the details fall into place and there's a little space for further optimizing, cable comparison might come to mind. In the meantime, we wonder why we can't quite get the acoustic guitar to sound full with smooth transients. We wonder why our mixes sound a little thick when we play them back on a better system, and we wonder why our vocal sound never seems as clear as our favorite recordings. We save a few dollars on cable while we make sure our mixer and effects are the newest and coolest on the block.

In reality, we'd be better off to build a system out of fewer components connected together with excellent cable. There are several very good cable manufacturers. Check with your local dealer to find out who's making great cable. It's not cheap, but it affects everything you do: how you mix, how you track, which effects you choose, and how you apply equalization—to mention a few. If the cables that connect your mixer to your powered monitors are marginal in quality, you'll base every decision concerning the sound of your music on a false premise.

If your microphone cables are of inferior quality, anything you record through them will be less full and contain less transient accuracy than if you used excellent mic cables. The same concerns apply to instrument cables, patch cables, and digital interconnect cables.

Listen to Audio Example 11-7. The acoustic guitar is first miked and recorded through some common quality cable. Then it's recorded through a microphone with some very high quality Monster Cable. Notice the difference in transient sounds, depth, and transparency.

---

*Audio Example 11-7*
**Mic on Acoustic Guitar Using Common Mic Cable
then Monster Studio Pro 1000 Cable**
*CD-2: Track 89*

---

Audio Example 11-8 demonstrates the difference in vocal sound using marginal mic cable first, then a high-quality mic cable from Monster Cable. Notice the difference in transient sounds, depth, and transparency.

---

*Audio Example 11-8*
**Vocal Using Common Mic Cable
then Monster Studio Pro 1000 Cable**
*CD-2: Track 90*

---

The following Audio Example is difficult to quantify because it involves my subjective opinion. However, I include it because I've experienced an extreme quality difference at this particular point in the signal path when cable changes were made. The comparisons in the previous two audio examples were performed with only one change in each example: the cable. In this example, I'll record an acoustic guitar while monitoring through powered monitors that are first connected to my mixer with inferior cables

and then connected with superior cables. My effort is focused on making the two examples sound the same when I monitor them. My EQ decisions are made based on the sound I hear. Listen to see if you can tell a difference between the guitar sounds in Audio Example 11-9.

---

*Audio Example 11-9*
**Guitar Sonically Shaped To Sound Good
Using Common Line Level Speaker Cables then
Sonically Shaped To Sound Good
Using Monster Line-level Speaker Cables**
*CD-2: Track 91*

---

Digital interconnect cables also have an effect on the sound quality of digital masters and clones. Listen to Audio Examples 11-10 through 11-14. In each example a different cable and format configuration is demonstrated. Listen specifically to all frequency ranges as well as transients. Also, consider the "feel" of the recording. Often, the factor that makes one setup sound better than another is difficult to explain, but it's easy to feel. The following examples use exactly the same program material as well as the identical transfer process to the included CD.

The differences you hear on your setup depend greatly on the quality and accuracy of your monitoring system as well as your insight and perception. Once you understand and experience subtle sonic differences you'll realize the powerful impact they hold for your musical expression. Constantly compare and analyze the details of your music. It will result in much more competitive quality. You'll realize more satisfaction and you'll probably get more work.

**Audio Example 11-10**
*AES/EBU to DAT Using Common Cable*
*then SP1000 AES Silver Digital Monster Cable*
*CD-2: Track 92*

**Audio Example 11-11**
*S/P DIF to DAT Using Common RCA Cables*
*then M1000 D Silver Digital Monster Cable*
*CD-2: Track 93*

# Illustration 11-4
## Waveform Differences Between Cable

In both of these sets of waves, the top wave was captured digitally through S/P DIF using M1000 D Silver Monster Cable and the bottom wave was captured using a common RCA cable. In case there's a doubt about whether the cable really matters in an audio environment, these comparisons speak very graphically that they do. If the transfers were identical in data, they'd look identical.

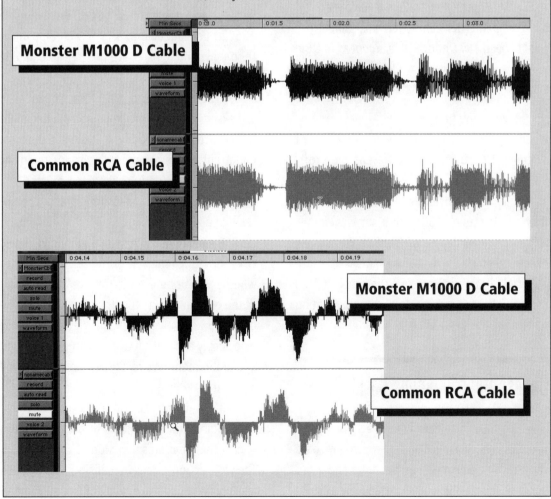

---

**Audio Example 11-12**
**Analog Out to DAT Using**
**Common XLR Cables then**
**Prolink Studio Pro 1000 XLR Monster Cables**
**CD-2: Track 94**

---

---

**Audio Example 11-13**
**ADAT Light Pipe into Digital Performer**
**Using Common Optical Cable, Bounced to Disk**
**CD-2: Track 95**

---

---

**Audio Example 11-14**
**ADAT Light Pipe into Digital Performer**
**Using Monster Cable's Interlink Digital**
**Light Speed 100 Optical Cable, Bounced to Disk**
**CD-2: Track 96**

---

If you can't hear much difference on some of these comparisons, try listening on different systems. Try auditioning different monitors, power amps, or mixers with your own system .

Cable differences are often so extreme that they can be seen in the onscreen waveforms. Illustration 11-4 shows two identical waveforms: one recorded through a common RCA cable into a digital S/P DIF input, while the other utilized an M1000 D Silver Monster Cable (Illustration 11-4).

# Choose Your Weapons Carefully

It's truly incredible where technology has taken us in the past years. Although many could see a revolution coming in the audio and video industry, few could really foresee how ingenu-

ity, technology, and art would combine to affect our working and creative options.

As you've progressed through this course, it's my hope that you've not only grown in your knowledge about recording and sound, but that you've grown in your desire to go even further with the knowledge you've gained. The recording world will never be cut-and-dried. Even as technology takes us to greater heights, music is art—that's unavoidable. Art is always progressing; true art is never stagnant.

One of the most exciting and exhilarating features of modern recording is the industry's willingness to embrace classic technology as well as current technology. Our industry is remaining open to the best of all worlds. We can use a 1950's mic plugged into a 1970's preamp and a third millennium mixer. We are free to combine the best of all eras.

When you record, select equipment with same care and consideration that a painter might take selecting and shading colors. Keep the most important thing, the most important thing. As long as technology is serving the music—not vice versa—the art will continue at a breathtaking pace.

If each of us strives to create the very best work possible, then stands back to evaluate whether it can be even better, we become part of the growth of our industry. I don't know anyone who is involved with the creative process who simply considers it a job to struggle through until retirement. We're blessed to be involved at any level.

It's really no less fun to do your very best in a home studio, than it is to do your best in one of the most amazing studios in the world. The satisfaction comes in realizing you've given it everything you have, and then a little more,

and then maybe a little more. Enjoy life. Enjoy
music. Enjoy the ride!

# Glossary

**A/D Converter**: The actual processor that samples analog amplitude at the specified sample rate and within the predetermined quantization limits, changing the analog waveform energy into binary data.

**Adaptive Transform Acoustic Coding (ATRAC)**: This compression architecture essentially eliminates the inaudible part of each word. It relies on the fact that any resultant artifacts or audio inconsistencies will probably be masked by the remaining sound, and that the compressed material might be below the hearing threshold of the human ear.

**aliasing frequencies**: When a digital recorder attempts to sample a frequency higher than half the sample rate, the sampling process produces inaccurate and randomly inconsistent waveform characteristics. These high frequencies, called aliasing frequencies, must be filtered out before they arrive at the A/D converter.

**authentic groove**: This describes the right groove for the job. Each style of music has it's own personality and character. Players entrenched in a particular idiom know just how to lock in to the stylistically correct musical attitude. A musician who doesn't know the mindset of any style usually sticks out like a sore thumb amidst the more stylistically savvy.

**binary**: A binary numeric system represents everything with two numbers: 1 and 0. This system is very convenient when it comes to data storage since a 1 is typically represented by a pit, a blip, a tick, or a pulse; a 0 is simply represented by a lack of those things.

**bit errors**: In the digital domain, two types of data errors occur frequently: bit errors and burst errors. Occasional noise impulses cause bit inaccuracies. These bit errors are more or less audible, depending on where the error occurs within the word. Errors in the least significant bit (LSB) will probably be masked, especially in louder passages. On the other hand, errors in the most significant bit (MSB) can cause a loud and irritating transient click or pop.

**bit**: (1. A single character of a language having just two characters, as either of the binary digits 0 or 1. (2. A unit of information equivalent to the choice of either of two equally likely alternatives. (3. A unit of information storage capacity, as of memory—a contraction of B(INARY) and (DIG)IT.

**burst errors**: These errors occur in groups and are usually caused by dirt or scratches on the surface of the storage media.

**byte**: An 8-bit word is called a byte. The term comes from the contraction of "by eight," which was derived from the concept of a bit multiplied by eight. When binary code is grouped into words, the power to accurately represent continuous data is greatly increased. Every time a bit is added to a word the computational power is doubled. Therefore, by increasing from an 8-bit word to a 9-bit word, our possible numeric combinations double—from 256 discrete binary combinations to 512—while the amount of data only increases by 12.5 percent. Doubling the amount of data, from an 8-

bit word to a 16-bit word, results in increased computational power of 25,600 percent.

**chord symbols**: On a lead sheet or lyric sheet, the letters above the words or notes are called chord symbols. These sometimes complex looking symbols tell the rhythm section players which chords to play or they tell other instrumentalists what the harmonic basis is.

**commercial Internet address**: Most businesses of any size, or serious intent, have an Internet website. If you're not familiar with the Internet, it's time to jump in with both feet. The best guess, when looking for a manufacturer, is to use the standard web address prefix (http://www.) followed by the business name, without any spaces (mixbooks) followed by .com (pronounced "dot com").

**comping**: Comping is the process of combining (**comp**iling) portions of several takes of the same musical part and segment, to create a strong and convincing version of a track.

**computer-based sequencer**: This type of MIDI sequencer utilizes the power and speed of a personal computer to perform all MIDI data storage, recording, processing, and manipulation. The onscreen graphic make this type of system the most convenient of all.

**controllers**: MIDI controllers alter MIDI param-eters. Standard MIDI controllers adjust volume, sustain, modulation, pitch bend, or even effects. However, most current MIDI devices allow for user-selection of any controller to adjust nearly any MIDI parameter.

**creative flow**: When musicians get together to write or produce songs, there's a synergy that results from the combined creative concentration. The flow of ideas from one participant feeds the flow of ideas from the others. The corporate

sensation is that of momentum and creativity greater than any individual, and often greater than the sum of the individuals.

**cylinder recorders**: Preceding the 78-rpm record, cylinder recorders were the original phonograph. The recording media was cylindrical, made from a hard wax material very similar to the 78, and a little larger than a toilet paper roll. Designed by Thomas Edison, this format offered better groove tracking than round disks but the cylinders were more cumbersome to deal with. Grooves etched on the outside of the cylinder contained the sound waves; music played back in a manner similar to the original Gramophone. Though the flat-disk record was a conceptually inferior design, it was eventually accepted over the cylinder recorded because of consumer convenience.

**D/A converter**: This is the actual processor that reconstructs the analog waveform from the stored digital data. The quality of the converter plays a large part in the final quality of the digital audio.

**data backup**: Part of our regular routine must be backing up data. To backup, simply make a copy of your audio or MIDI files to an additional location. An inexpensive, portable media like CD is ideal for data backup. This format is inexpensive enough that regular periodic backups are realistic. It's also a good idea to keep a current file copy on an auxiliary hard drive or removable storage medium like a Jaz or Zip disk.

**data dump**: This typically refers to a MIDI data transfer. Information regarding patches, songs, programs, and all other MIDI parameters are part of the MIDI data dump.

**data stream**: The flow of binary data. A data stream typically refers to the transfer of digital information rather than the flow of musical wave

**digital mixer**: A digital mixer typically receives a

combination of digital and analog inputs. Any analog inputs are immediately converted to digital data. Once in binary form, the audio signal remains in the digital domain throughout all changes (pan, EQ, effects, dynamics, etc.). A digital mixer can output an analog signal, if desired, but often the signal is recorded, stored, or transferred in it's binary data format. The data might not be converted to analog form until the consumer plays it back.

**DIN connector**: This multi-pin connector is common in the audio industry. A MIDI connection is made using a 5-pin DIN connector.

**dither**: Dither is simply white noise added to the program source at very low levels (typically half the least significant bit). Though it seems ironic to add noise to an otherwise noiseless system, the inaccuracies and waveform distortions of these low-level signals must be addressed. Dithering provides a means to more accurate recording at low levels.

**drum loops**: Traditionally a drum loop is a repeated portion of a percussion or drum groove taken from a prerecorded musical work. Loops taken from commercially released products have become popular, especially in rap oriented music. The main point of contention regarding drum loops is the legal aspect of profiting from someone else's work with no appropriate compensation.

**feel**: This refers to the emotional impact of the music. It's one thing to play the correct notes in the correct order at the right time. It's a completely different thing to perform music that conveys emotion.

**format conversion**: Digital audio that's stored in one format—a specific sample rate and word-length—often needs to integrate with digital audio of another type. Since digital audio is stored as binary data, any mathematical relationship can be easily calculated and set into motion at will.

Converting from 16-bit/44 kHz to 24-bit/48kHz is a simple matter of doing the math and waiting for the processor to complete the action. Although conversion algorithms are fairly accurate, critical assessment of the converted sound quality is usually disappointing.

**hardware control surfaces**: Digital devices have no need for a lot of controls. They can typically be operated with a few buttons, knobs, and sliders, along with a text window. However, operators need instant access to several parameter controls so manufacturers produce control surfaces that are typically very efficient for the user and often very similar in feel to the familiar analog console.

**house sync**: Video sync, also called house sync and blackburst, is a constant timing reference used in situations where multiple video tape recorders, switchers, edit controllers, and audio devices must interconnect accurately and reliably. The clock frequency of house sync is exactly 15,734.2657Hz.

**interleaving**: Commonly used to minimize the risk of losing large amounts of data. Interleaving data is similar in concept to diversifying investments. Interleaving spreads the digital word out over a noncontiguous section of storage media. That way, if a bit or burst error corrupts data it probably won't corrupt an entire word or group of words.

**interpolate**: When digital data is lost, the processor is programmed to calculate the probable status of the missing samples. To interpolate data is to take an educated guess, regarding its value prior to the error. Estimations are made in relation to the samples that come immediately before and after the lost data.

**jitter**: An audible digital timing inconsistency, similar in concept to tape flutter in the analog domain. It's eliminated by locking the playback clock to a stable source so that the pulse grid flows at a solid and controlled rate (44.1kHz for the standard audio CD). All data is forced to fall neatly into this solidly locked sync grid.

**Least Significant Bit (LSB)**: The digit on the right-hand side of the word is called the least significant bit (LSB). In theory, this is the least audible bit.

**linear recording**: Recording that involves tape as a storage media in real-time is linear. The audio is stored on the tape as it's created. Both analog and digital audio recorders can be linear. A reel-to-reel analog tape recorder, as well as a cassette, DAT, ADAT, and DA88 are all examples of linear recorders. A system where the user waits for tape to rewind for playback is linear.

**machine synchronizer**: References sets of time code from multiple machines, endeavoring to control the motion of each machine transport in a way that maintains a constant relationship between the time codes.

**master timing clock**: In a digital system, the master timing clock provides a means for constant data pacing. The master clock tells each connected device when to release each sample. With this system, all samples from all devices transmit in sample-accurate relationship. There's no fade or drift between transports.

**master transport**: Provides the transport commands and clock data for all connected devices.

**MIDI machine control**: This protocol allows MIDI connections to provide for machine control (record, play, stop, rewind, etc.) from within the computer-based software domain.

**mix controllers**: In the digital recording arena, although all options can be controlled onscreen within the computer or hardware, there's still a place for actually controlling the signal with a physical knob, fader, or button. Several companies offer hardware control surfaces for interfacing with some amazing software packages.

**Most Significant Bit (MSB)**: The digit on the left-hand side of the word is called the most significant bit (MSB). A problem with the MSB is a big and potentially fatal problem for its associated sample word.

**multimedia: A** combination of sound and picture. CD-ROM began the popularization of computer-based multimedia presentation. However, multimedia also consists of slide images along with music and often video, or any combined media presentation.. As technology has blossomed, so has the opportunity for multimedia productions and presentations.

**noise shaping**: Noise shaping is a part of the dithering process. It helps shift the dither noise into a less audible frequency range to provide the best results with the least audible noise. Digital filters move the dither noise out of the ear's most sensitive frequency range (about 4kHz) and into a less noticeable range. Noise shaping is not a necessary part of the dithering process, but it helps optimize the process through decreased audible noise.

**nonlinear recording**: Any recording system with instant access to any portion of audio. Hard-disk based systems are nonlinear because the user can skip from one part of the recording to any other instantly and at will. The nonlinear recording process is unrivaled in flexibility, speed, and creative freedom. In addition, all audio segments can be shifted, moved, cut, copied, pasted, and time-adjusted in small or large increments

**non-real-time digital effects**: Effects that can only be previewed in short segments. The user must guess how the effected track will sound throughout the song, then okay the computer to process the track or selected area. The result is an additional track that contains the effected sound with no means for real-time adjustment during playback. The only way to change a non-real-time effect is to go back to the original dry track and reprocess the audio at different settings. The positive factor regarding this type of effect is that, once the processing is complete, playback is less demanding on the computer's processing power than real-time effects. The downside of these effects is their lack of creatively spontaneous adjustment capability.

**oversampling**: The oversampling process is ingenious, requiring a processor capable of high sample rates. Typical oversample systems operate at between 2 and 128 times the regular sample rate. As an example, at eight times oversampling, seven artificial samples are created between the actual samples, all at zero level. Now there are eight samples in the place of the original one, increasing the sample rate by a factor of eight. A 44.1kHz sample rate would, therefore, be increased to 352.8kHz. The seven blank (zero level) samples are interpolated by the processor. In other words, it guesses what their values would be according to the status of the original samples. The purpose of oversampling is to increase the accuracy of the conversion system. The actual process creates a conversion that allows for a gently sloped and less intrusive anti-aliasing filter. Traditional sample recording and playback call for an extreme "brick wall" filter at the Nyquist Frequency (half the sample rate). A less extreme filter causes less phase error and results in a cleaner, smother digital conversion.

**parity**: Parity is the most basic form of error detection. The parity system simply adds one bit, called the "parity bit," to each word and attaches a meaning to its status. If there are an even number of 1s in a word, the parity bit status is set to 1. If there's an odd number of 1s in a word, the parity bit is set to 0. Once the parity bits have been set in the record process, they can be checked in the playback process. Parity is checked on each word

during conversion to analog. If a bit has been damaged, causing a discrepancy in the relationship between the odd-even status of the word and the parity bit, the word is identified to be in error. This is a simple system and introduces an important concept to error detection, though it begins to fail anytime more than one of the 1 bits have been damaged. In addition, it offers no means of identifying which bit has been damaged.

**plug-ins**: Additional program modules that integrate with existing software packages. To support digital audio software, for example, the software manufacturer, or a third-party manufacturer, often writes additional code to add features like delay effects, dynamics, special effects, et cetera.

**real-time digital effects**: Within digital audio software, an effect that can be adjusted anytime during the song, whether the transport is active or not. Real-time effects operate like any hardware effect in their constant availability for parameter adjustment. The downside of real-time effects is their continual need for processor power. When used on a small and slow computer, not many real-time effects can be implemented before the processor is overtaxed.

**sonic quality**: Sound quality. The term sonic is used in the industry as a respectful way to refer to how something sounds. Sonic quality, sonic character, sonic integrity, sonic personality, or sonic purity are all terms of endearment used by engineers and producers to describe the object of their toil, passion, and sweat. Like much industry terminology, the word "sonic" has become overused by those anxious to impress us all with their verbiage.

**soundcard**: Hardware that inserts into the computer's expansion port . This card often contains both analog and digital inputs and outputs. Sometimes the soundcard contains additional DSP power along with upgraded converters and interface capabilities for additional digital audio hardware.

**sync grid**: In a digital system, all connected devices should be locked to the same word clock while operating at the same wordlength. Plotting the word clock on the x-axis and the wordlength on the y-axis provides a grid, which contains all the possible time and amplitude values within a given digital audio structure.

**tech support**: Anyone who enters the sometimes painful, yet often exhilarating, world of cutting edge software and hardware soon must get to know about tech support. Technical support staff hangout at the other end of the phone, fax, or Internet and await your panicked call. They almost always know how to fix the problem you've just spent the better part of a day—or week— expressing your most inner feelings about. We often get frustrated at the wait on the telephone, or awaiting an email or fax, but these folks do a great job and we'd all be lost without them. Too many of us spend too much time venting and too little time praising, when it comes to support technicians.

**the groove**: Groove is the feel of a musical performance. It consists of such considerations as beat placement, accent placement, accent emphasis, note lengths, chord lengths, rhythmic interactions, emotional passion, and instrumentation.

**window dub**: A video work copy used in audio sweetening, ADR, Foley, scoring, or other audio-for-image applications. This copy has a window laid over the video image, typically at the bottom of the screen, which contains continuously scrolling time code reference taken from the master video or film.

**word clock**: The sample rate clock which controls to speed of sample playback and recording. Each digital device contains its own internal word clock. However, all devices connected to a digital recording system must be set to operate in exact sync

with the master word clock.

**word**: A word is simply a multidigit binary number made up of bits. The number of bits in a word represents the smallest unit of addressable memory in a microprocessor environment (a computer). The number of bits in a word is called its wordlength.

**zipper effect**: In the MIDI environment there are only 128 possible parameter values. In a MIDI controlled mix, these discrete values can sometimes be heard as stair steps in volume change. Instead of a long, slow, continuously varying level change, the audio steps can be heard in a manner that feels and sounds like an audio zipper. Some MIDI-based systems combine controllers in a staggered fashion to increase the zipper resolution to the point where it's not noticeable.

# Index